CREOLE ECONOMICS

Creole Economics

CARIBBEAN
CUNNING
UNDER THE
FRENCH FLAG

KATHERINE E. BROWNE

Line Drawings by Rod Salter

University of Texas Press ◆ Austin

Copyright © 2004 by the University of Texas Press
All rights reserved
Printed in the United States of America
First edition, 2004

Requests for permission to reproduce material from this work should be sent to Permissions, University of Texas Press, P.O. Box 7819, Austin, TX 78713–7819.

⊚ The paper used in this book meets the minimum requirements of ANSI/NISO Z39.48–1992 (R1997) (Permanence of Paper).

LIBRARY OF CONGRESS
CATALOGING-IN-PUBLICATION DATA
Browne, Katherine E.
Creole economics : Caribbean cunning under the French flag / by Katherine E. Browne.
        p.   cm.
Includes bibliographical references and index.
ISBN 0-292-70292-2 ((cl.) : alk. paper) —
ISBN 0-292-70581-6 ((pbk.) : alk. paper)
1. Informal sector (Economics)—Martinique. 2. Martinique—Economic conditions—1918- 3. Women—Martinique—Economic conditions. I. Title.
HD2346.M37B76   2005
330—dc22   2004000551

To Jane DeHart Albritton,
my partner in all things

And to the courageous and
beautiful people of Martinique
who helped me understand.

CONTENTS

My interest in Martinique began halfway around the world in the South Pacific, where indigenous Tahitian cultures had been colonized by the French. Following five months of graduate work in Tubuai, a tiny island on the Tropic of Capricorn in French Polynesia,[1] I was inspired to learn more about the particular style and legacies of French colonization. France began staking its claims on the five archipeligos that share Tahitian language and culture in 1842. About one hundred years later, in 1958, Tahitians were given the choice to fully incorporate into France as an overseas department, to maintain a more limited political relationship to France as an overseas territory, or to become altogether independent. The majority of islanders voted for the middle ground, thus becoming one of France's "overseas territories."[2] Today, French Polynesia's status as a *territoire d'outre mer* (or TOM) entitles islanders to French citizenship and certain benefits of association with France, though this status accommodates a high degree of Tahitian self-government and does not obligate France to deliver the same benefits as it does to its overseas "departments."

Native Tahitian culture has changed in many ways over time and in response to outside forces, but the effects of French involvement are readily apparent. For example, alongside Tahitian, standard French is spoken commonly and a majority of Tahitians observe Christian traditions. In addition, French systems of organization and management are evident in island schools, medical clinics, government offices, and agricultural development programs. In return for the use of French Polynesia for military and nuclear testing bases, the French government also subsidizes large government sectors and supports export crop prices and markets. Ritual holidays of France, such as Bastille Day, celebrating French independence, have been incorporated into national Tahitian holidays as well. But despite the extensive, 150-year sweep of French influences on economic life in Tahitian societies, native language and identities remain vital and a source of islander pride. Local currency, postage stamps, and an official flag that flies next to the French tricolor also attest to the symbolic continuity of Tahitian culture in these societies.

My experience in the Tahitian islands, where indigenous practices and values have not been overwhelmed by French systems of administration, language, and attitudes of superiority, stirred in me a desire to study an area where French colonization had penetrated even more deeply into the hearts and minds of a people. I found that place in the Americas, in the French Caribbean (also called the French West Indies or the French Antilles). In these societies of the Atlantic, the French colonized over a longer period of time than anywhere else in the sprawling reaches of the nation's several-hundred-year-old empire (hence the reference to France's *vieilles colonies*, or old colonies).

Colonization in the Americas was not only longer-running than other European colonizing missions, it was also more radical in nature: whole indigenous populations were wiped out, both from starvation and overwork imposed by European colonists and from their lack of immunity to the diseases these colonists brought from their home continent. Europeans in the New World thus turned to the forced migration and enslavement of Africans as lifelong laborers on plantations. For these reasons, the Afro-Caribbean populations of today bear the legacies of a unique chapter in European colonization.

In Martinique, I had the opportunity to study a "post" colonial people whose ancestors had been violently separated from their native cultures and all semblance of life as they knew it. The indigenous peoples of Tahiti or Indochina or Algeria also had had their sovereignty wrested from them by the imposition of French colonial control, but they had not been permanently dislocated from their native lands and natal families. Considering the particular harshness of colonization in the Americas, I was fascinated by the remarkable fact that in the French colonies of Martinique, Guadeloupe, and French Guiana, the descendants of slaves had actually pushed to become fully integrated into France as overseas "departments."[3]

How does one conjure up a context that could have led those colonized peoples who had been most egregiously abused and exploited to stand today as the most thoroughly assimilated overseas populations of France? In its overseas departments, the same French structures organize government, supply roads and infrastructure, and ensure legislative representation as any other department of the French state located inside the "hexagon" (a reference to the shape of the French state on the European continent). Symbolic testament to the fullness of DOM (département d'outre mer) incorporation is the ubiquitous presence of the flag of the French Republic that whips unchallenged in the tropical breeze of every island municipality and government institution.

A study in Martinique, with its unexpected degree of assimilation to

France, presented just the kind of detective work I had grown up fantasizing about. When a colony becomes politically integrated with its former colonizer, do cultural differences gradually dissolve? Do people's choices about how to make money come to follow predictably rational economic models and to conform to the incentive structures of the parent state? I had become interested in studying the informal economy as an anthropologist, since so few scholars outside the field of economics had investigated the phenomenon up close and from the perspective of the actors involved in a local setting. Knowing that the French system of labor protections and social welfare provisions require high taxes to finance, I expected that there would be many people in Martinique trying to avoid these taxes by not declaring the income they made. With Martinique society so deliberately tied to French systems and values, I would be able to ask: Is there a distinctively Martiniquais cultural pattern to the unreported activity of islanders? Or, is the economic logic operating in Martinique the same as that of continental France?

To learn more about how economists and other social scientists from the Caribbean region might regard my ideas for a research study in Martinique, I made a trip to Jamaica and to Martinique in the summer after my second year of graduate studies.[4] In Jamaica, I visited with faculty at the University of the West Indies, located in Kingston. At the university's Institute for Social and Economic Research (ISER), I met several social scientists, including economics professor Norman Girvan, who noted that Caribbean-based research on the informal economy could cast light on a well-recognized but little-studied pattern. Other meetings with ISER faculty were also encouraging and underscored the fact that the radically distinctive histories of Caribbean peoples would play a role in whatever else I might find here.

In Martinique, Professor Jean Crusol enthusiastically supported my interest in studying the informal economy locally. As a prominent author and professor of economics at the Université des Antilles et de la Guyane, Crusol argued compellingly that in Martinique, informal activity is rampant across all sectors of business and among people of all incomes. The most useful picture of Martinique's economy, he emphasized, would capture this reality. Crusol also made clear that the real breadth of "the problem" could only be seen in an urban area, where the widespread reliance on unreported income would be apparent in all its economic diversity. This conversation helped me realize the value of locating my study in greater

Fort-de-France, Martinique's capital, where nearly half of the island's population resides and where I could look at socioeconomically differentiated neighborhoods within a single metropolitan area. Other local economists concurred.[5] To pursue the idea of an urban study, I met with urban studies scholar Monsieur Serge Letchimy (then director of a local organization formed to study and improve urban sanitation and housing; now mayor of Fort-de-France). Letchimy agreed with Crusol's conviction that informal earning was commonplace across classes and added that these strategies are habits that have been nurtured over generations and adapted by rural migrants to their urban settings.[6]

The following summer, I met with more university researchers and government officials as well as a range of people operating in the informal economy. I sought out street vendors selling produce, spices, flowers, prepared foods, and a variety of small household goods. Street vendors were an easily observable part of the informal economy, but my professional contacts claimed that there were many less visible, and more affluent, people making undeclared money in Fort-de-France. To find the contours of a more complete local picture of informal earning was precisely what an anthropological approach could offer.

It appeared that Martinique presented me with the ideal setting in which to advance my inquiry into the Frenchness of a radically colonized people, and to channel this query in the service of an interesting economic question. Using anthropological methods, I could hope to document the fullest possible range of informal economic activity, both across class and by gender. Through personal interviews, I also hoped to learn whether the economic practices of Martiniquais were linked somehow to their creole histories and identities, or were instead indistinguishable from the economic behavior of metropolitan French. Either way, I would understand more about the relative grip of Frenchness in Martinique.

ORGANIZATION OF THE BOOK

The central argument of this book derives from my finding that creole values do indeed shape economic behavior in Martinique. This argument depends on an array of smaller arguments drawn from historic, cultural, economic, and literary material. Because these perspectives overlap and are not easily teased apart, I have tried to preserve their robust interconnectedness while following, to the extent possible, a chronological path. Nonetheless, the organization is more organic than linear, the arguments more interdependent than discrete.

The book is organized in three major sections that signal the three distinct types of material I want to present. Part One, "Groundings" (Chapters 1 and 2), maps out the terrain of interest for the book. In these chapters, I will introduce readers to the feel of Martinique and to the basic concepts, key terms, and overall goals I am concerned with. Here also, I provide an overview of French colonization in Martinique, one fitted to the task of this book. This abbreviated history will help make sense of everything else that follows, including why Martiniquais chose to assimilate to France and how this assimilation has created new struggles for islanders and a love/hate relationship with France.

Part Two, "Frameworks" (Chapters 3 and 4), brings readers into the heart of debates in economics and anthropology about how and whether economic behavior is patterned by cultural values. I will also develop in this section a context for the rise of creole cultures and languages in the Caribbean. I include ethnographic stories and many local voices expressing ideas about economic success. These forays into cultural attitudes will set the stage for understanding how a person's status in creole culture may be enhanced through the performance of illicit economic activity.

In Part Three, "Practices" (Chapters 5–7), I supply the bulk of my ethnographic material to demonstrate the variations, texture, and meaning of creole economics as understood and practiced by local actors. I begin with a view of slave-based patterns of economic cunning (*débrouillardism*) and then move forward in time to show how these patterns operate today. I point out that local versions of economic cunning are not universally appreciated and in fact generate contempt as immoral among certain groups in the society. Finally, I show how women have faced struggles distinct from those of men, and how their burdens have positioned them to embrace economic priorities that do not typically include creole economics.

The epilogue offers a final, brief note about the future of creole economics in light of recent changes brought by Martinique's membership in the European Union and the popular movement to embrace creoleness. Ultimately, I argue that if Martinique's informal economy is indeed a cultural economy, as this research suggests, then the irreducible complexities of local meaning and practice must be allowed to inform and recast development planning efforts.

ACKNOWLEDGMENTS

Long-term fieldwork in another society can demand a disorienting combination of skills—modesty but confidence, patience but initiative, conformity but an adventurous spirit. Because the work requires intimate engagement with the real lives and everyday dramas of strangers, the dizzying amount of information and the sometimes confusing instincts for how to manage life lead naturally to seeking help. A great many people in Martinique helped me unravel mysteries, understand my defeats, soften the edges of my hardships, and learn to inhale deeply the rewards and joys of local life. My enormous debt to these people is one I will acknowledge with a lifetime of love and gratitude.

For emotional support and concrete assistance *extraordinaire*, through each of my visits in Martinique, I thank the three remarkable women who started Transcript International: Ildiko Virag-Patocs, Yvonne Eadie, and Arlette Fadeau. I also thank my dear friends Louise and Geneviève Duféal for their good humor and many years of support and generosity. For unstinting help in generating valuable government data and explaining how the French system operates, I thank Frederic Vigée at the Chambre de Commerce and Jean-Claude Duville at the Chambre de Métiers. I also thank Justin Daniel at the Université des Antilles et de la Guyane for his warm, continued support of my efforts over many years. For his gracious gifts of time and knowledge, I thank Roland Suvélor. And for provocative insights and many wonderful conversations, I thank Marius Gottin. I also wish to thank all of my informants over the years, and the many artists, scholars, and government officials who shared with me their time and insights.

Encouragement is important at every turn and I am humbled by the sheer number of people in the US whose generous efforts on my behalf helped me undertake and complete this study. My advisor, Victoria Lockwood, took me to French Polynesia and exposed me to French colonization. She has continued to champion my work and offer me incisive feedback that sharpens its quality. Historian Dennis Cordell has nudged my understandings and inspired me to become a better-rounded scholar, more interested in the long view of culture. Richard Price and Sally Price have been for me models of the integrative power of deep scholarship, personal commitment, and shared joy in a part of the world that does not allow curious minds to rest. Their encouragement of my work is especially meaningful.

Reading chapters or drafts of manuscripts is a heroic act of kindness, and one for which I have many people to thank. A number of people read complete drafts of my manuscript, including Rhoda Halperin, Blane Harding, Victoria Lockwood, Richard Price, Estellie Smith, and Rick Wilk. I also wish to thank Dennis Cordell, Carla Freeman, Ellen Schnepel, and Jeff Snodgrass for reading portions of this manuscript. Their comments, and those of the outside reviewers for the University of Texas Press, have contributed substantively to the final book. In addition, I want to thank my outstanding student readers, Andy Read and Chris Weeber, who helped me clarify concepts and keep the language accessible. Two other exceptional students, Jill Lange and Nicole Mallette, proofread the manuscript. I am especially grateful to my parents, Donna and Leland Browne, who reviewed a draft of the manuscript as educated general readers. Their questions and insights helped me figure out how to better present certain parts of my argument.

I also wish to thank Theresa May and her tremendous team at the University of Texas Press, who made my first book publication a blessedly smooth experience. Allison Faust, Leslie Tingle, and Ellen Mackie all contributed impressive professionalism and welcome reassurances. Sue Carter is the most thorough and talented copyeditor any author could hope for. To her, I extend my warmest appreciation.

I owe very special thanks to my illustrator, Rod Salter, who is a gifted wildlife painter first, but who agreed to draw pencil sketches because they "help my painting." Mostly, I believe, he simply wanted to be nice. His work contributes substantially to the life of the book. I also wish to thank Dave Santillanes, the talented digital artist whose creative and technical expertise produced the beautiful Caribbean map. Thanks also to Michèle Nelson for her invaluable tutoring as I sought to comprehend the nuances of French law, institutions, and seven-course meals.

Without many sources of financial support, my research efforts would have been far more difficult, if possible at all. I wish to thank the National Science Foundation for grants supporting my dissertation and subsequent research in Martinique, the French Republic's Ministry of Culture for comprehensive funding of my dissertation research through a Bourse Chateaubriand, and Colorado State University for numerous small grants that made it possible to continue research and fieldwork in Martinique.

Of all my sources of aid and support, I have most of all to thank my partner, Jane DeHart Albritton, whose confidence in me and years of deference to my career is a gift beyond all measure. Willing, good humored, and fiercely intelligent, she has helped me at every turn through this project, in our countless conversations about the research and through her expertise as a professional editor. With her, I fully share this accomplishment and to her, I dedicate this book.

CREOLE ECONOMICS

PART ONE

Groundings

ONE

Elements

YOU COME FROM A PEOPLE WITHOUT MOTHER
TONGUE, WITH NEITHER PRIVATE VOICE NOR
PRIVATE DOMAIN; WITH NO PARTICULAR
GODS. THE ANTILLES: FIRES WITHOUT HEARTH
. . . YOU ARE BORN FROM A DEFIANT PEOPLE,
ACCUSTOMED TO GRASPING LEFT HANDED
NOCTURNAL FREEDOMS.

—Daniel Maximin, "Antillean Journey," 1998

My visits to Barbados, Jamaica, Puerto Rico, and a number of other non-French islands in the Caribbean did not prepare me for the visual or cultural environment of Martinique. One arrives at the island's magnificent airport, an overbuilt but proud testament to Martinique's membership in the First World. But Martinique's shiny, spacious airport is just the first indication of the island's place under the French flag. Outside, polished Mercedes taxis and well-heeled drivers with more French ennui than English language skills send another message to first-time visitors: here, we are part of the modern world, we are French and not some chummy, low-cost paradise for tourists.

More information pours in as the drive from the airport into Fort-de-France follows clean highways in good repair with familiar French signage and roundabouts. The fifteen-minute taxi drive in Mercedes comfort whizzes passengers past two giant hypermarkets, a chic retail mall, and a number of big box retail centers selling furniture, electronics, and home and garden products. Their enormous parking lots remain clogged with cars every day except Sunday, when they are closed. As you enter the capital city, the main boulevard, Charles de Gaulle, is flanked by both older, colonial structures which serve as government offices, and by recent, architecturally dazzling buildings housing the Central Bank, the cultural arts performing center, and the new city hall. The eclectic Frenchness of the boulevard attests to the longstanding and continuing presence of a world power. Unlike other areas of the Caribbean, Martinique projects affluence and modernity.

The relative prosperity of Martinique has many strings attached, however, as we will see. The complexities of islanders' relationship to France have fed many contradictions: living with affluence amidst dependency, benefiting from political assimilation in spite of cultural humiliations, desiring European respectability, but without sacrificing creole forms of status. These and other contradictions complicate the picture of prosperity and tell an important story about how multiple identities and the local sense of difference feed the practice of creole economics.

In this book, I show how in the economic realm it is possible to scrape away a little of that proud French identity expressed so well in the airport and find a deeper connection to creole values through the practice I call "creole economics," a culturally influenced form of undeclared economic activity. Martinique is an overseas state of France (just as the Hawaiian islands today comprise an overseas state of the US). Most islanders appear to embrace wholeheartedly their Frenchness today. In fact, quite unlike the case in Hawaii, the people of Martinique campaigned vigorously to become full citizens of France. Many political scholars marvel at this fact, considering islanders' long history of enslavement and exploitation by the French. As might be more predictable, islanders from most other Caribbean areas exploited by the British and Dutch sought independence and freedom from the yoke of their former colonizers. The flurry of postwar decolonization movements in Africa and Asia was the rule in the Caribbean as well; Martinique, along with Guadeloupe and French Guiana, were among the exceptions.[1]

Martinique is a tiny island, just 20 miles by 70 miles, a little smaller than Rhode Island. Only about 425,000 people live here, roughly the same population as Augusta, Georgia. It is not surprising that Martinique or the neighboring French department of Guadeloupe merit almost no attention in the world press. In fact, even social scientists long disregarded or denigrated research efforts in the smaller islands of the Caribbean since populations here are insignificant in number, are non-indigenous, and are a biological and cultural hodgepodge. But beginning in the 1990s, these same particularities of Caribbean societies invigorated a newly emerging scholarship concerned with border crossing, cultural fragmentation, ethnic dislocation, and plural identities.

The rapidly intensifying flows of people and goods, and the porous cultural boundaries that result, comprise a growing body of work known as "globalization" studies. But as the watershed for contemporary social science research, this concept is nothing new for the Caribbean. By the mid-sixteenth century, globalization was already becoming the life breath of Caribbean societies—conceived in colonial greed, sustained with transplanted African labor, and structured to serve transnational interests of colonizing nations.[2] As colonial fortune seekers thrust dislocated Africans into plantation labor, the elements of invented societies constituted new mixes of many cultures. The collision of cultures only intensified with nineteenth-century abolition, which brought new immigrations of East Indians, Chinese, Syrians, Lebanese, and others to the area. Caribbean societies today reflect a broad mix of cultural influences and colonial legacies more diverse than either North America (strongly European and Protestant) or South America (strongly Hispanic and Catholic).[3] Today, *Elements* the plural identities of islanders and the mixed political and economic systems embedded in Caribbean societies present one of the most compelling sites anywhere for the study of the predicaments of modern, postcolonial life.

European domination in these islands for three or more centuries left profound cultural imprints on Afro-Caribbean majorities, from language to sports to religious belief. Yet nowhere is the embrace of European identity so intimate and so enduring as in the French islands of Martinique and Guadeloupe. Compared to England, the Netherlands, Spain, Portugal, and the US, France knows no peer in keeping so many of its colonized areas inside its current orbit of influence.[4]

5

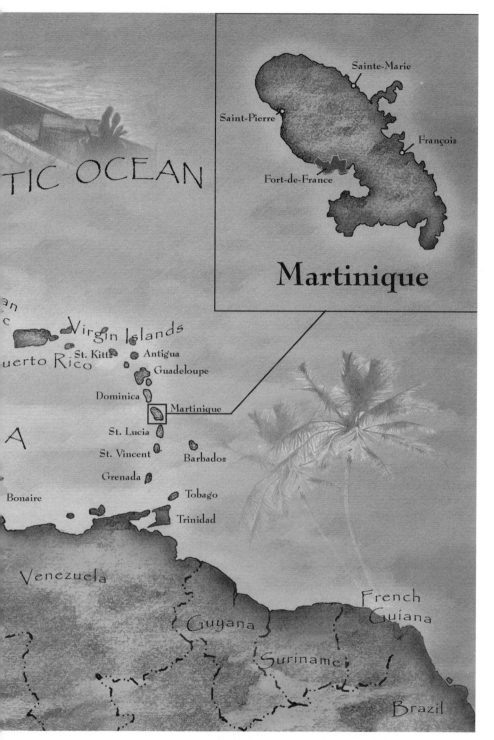

TIC OCEAN

Sainte-Marie

Saint-Pierre

François

Fort-de-France

Martinique

Virgin Islands

St. Kitts   Antigua

uerto Rico   Guadeloupe

Dominica

Martinique

St. Lucia

St. Vincent

Barbados

Grenada

Bonaire

Tobago

Trinidad

Venezuela

French Guiana

Guyana

Suriname

Brazil

Map by Dave Santillanes

For nearly twenty generations, representing close to 400 years, Martiniquais have experienced virtually uninterrupted French control and influence. Many would expect that after such a long time—and for the last half-century as full French citizens— the people of this Caribbean island could be considered as French as any family from the continent itself. Fort-de-France has in fact been French longer than current standard bearers of French culture such as Nice or Avignon. To an outsider who is familiar with French institutions, life in Martinique may appear altogether French. In and around Fort-de-France, one quickly observes that the island's infrastructure is definitively French—the Poste, the telephones, the Prefecture (like our state capitol), the French Police and Gendarmes, the excellent roads and signature roundabouts. Inside homes and hotel rooms, network TV channels are direct feeds from metropolitan France. The system of local school instruction follows the same doctrine of universally paced instruction, and Air France flies nonstop shuttles to Paris (4,000 miles away) several times a day.

French culture also permeates people's everyday lives and identities: standard French is ubiquitous; the overwhelmingly Catholic population fills cathedrals every Sunday; clothing styles are fashionably French; *confectionnaires*, *pâtisseries*, and *boulangeries* dot island towns and offer familiar French candies, pastries, and breads. In the homes of even moderately affluent residents of Fort-de-France, dinner parties are organized around traditional French decorum, beginning with aperitifs and advancing in sequence through numerous courses to a conclusion of cheeses, desserts, coffee, and liqueurs. Perhaps the most telling indicator of the degree to which urban islanders regard France as a natural part of their lives is that fully one-third of Martinique's native-born population now live in metropolitan France, and nearly every island family, poor or well-to-do, has relatives who live there. The influences are profound, cross-class, and constantly reproduced.

The lure of assimilation in Martinique and Guadeloupe was fed by French political elites, who had long imagined the Caribbean colonies both as a source of wealth and as vital cultural symbols of France's greatness. For various reasons that I will explore in this book, the descendants of slaves in the French West Indies wished to remain loyal subjects of

France. They rejected as folly the notion of independence and sought instead the rewards of assimilation to a great European nation. Ultimately, the kind of "benevolent" parental bond formalized in 1946 between France and her overseas Caribbean departments has led to vastly different outcomes in standards of living than those experienced by "independent" neighboring islanders. As full French citizens, the residents of Martinique, Guadeloupe, and French Guiana hold equal representation in France's national Congress and benefit from the same rights to social security and welfare entitlements as any other French citizen.

The contemporary moment of prosperity has, however, come at a steep cost. For despite the choice of most islanders to assimilate to France and to seek the promise of a European identity that political integration seemed to offer, the Afro-Caribbean people of Martinique continue to suffer two important indignities: they are utterly dependent on French citizenship for the abundant subsidies and transfer payments supplied to Martinique to finance an artificially high standard of living; and in metropolitan France (the heart of French culture), where many Martiniquais live and many more visit regularly, islanders of color are frequently treated as second-class citizens.

THE TUG OF PLURAL IDENTITIES

The very notion of islanders' willingness to assimilate and depend on France sets up the story I will tell: if Martiniquais have long been assimilating to France, then one might expect that creole culture and language, *Elements* here more than anywhere else in the Caribbean, would have nearly dissolved. Yet, my research reveals the enduring presence of much more than superficial and visible vestiges of creole expression, such as those found today in creole words, music, dance styles, and madras cloth. Instead, I have encountered deeply resilient creole belief systems and practices that transmit strong echoes of slave adaptations and that flourish invisibly, beneath the radar of the French state. For a people devoted to becoming fully French, what explains this continuing tug of creole identity?

In the will to assimilate its former colonies, France extended to Martinique and other overseas colonies an implicit promise of French identity and rights to the cherished founding principles of the Republic itself—

liberté, égalité, fraternité. Yet many in Martinique today view the fulfillment of that promise as flawed, even failed. In the chapters that follow, I argue that the tension produced by the problematic realities of Martinique's assimilation to France has provoked the reproduction of creole-based habits of survival. Considering that incomplete assimilation to France occurs in the context of the overwhelming dominance of French institutions in local life, the Martiniquais people have reached into their own creole identities to find the self-respect that continues to elude them. In a kind of infinite circularity, full cultural assimilation of Martinique to France can never be realized since creole identities remain insoluble; and creole identities remain insoluble because Martiniquais people are, biologically and culturally, only partly French.

One dimension of the complexity in Martinique's relationship to France is thus the fact that local values and practices strain assumptions of their assimilation; at the same time, however, these local values and practices help relieve the strains in the relationship. In Martinique, there are local indicators of creole culture, such as courtship and marriage patterns, gender relations, beliefs about supernatural power, folklore, music, and food—all of which are widely recognized as phenomena originally tied to creole innovations during slavery. This study investigates an aspect of being Martiniquais, of being creole, that is not commonly considered to carry cultural values: economics.

THE IDEA OF CREOLE ECONOMICS

"Creole economics" describes how the people in at least one island of the Caribbean are driven to make undeclared money in ways that earn them social status as well as income. That is, despite French economic and legal institutions that structure Martinique's formal economy, deeply rooted creole values channel people into the island's informal economy, where they can work for themselves to enhance their income, their personal autonomy, and their social prestige. The practice of creole economics suggests, first, striking continuities in the slave-born longings to be one's own boss and second, adaptive values of cleverness, intelligence, and opportunism. This flourishing system of exchanging undeclared goods and services operates among people at varying class levels, among young Martiniquais as well as their grandparents, and among many men and some women.

THE DÉBROUILLARD OF MARTINIQUE

Today in Martinique, people who improve their economic situation by finding unauthorized ways to profit are likely to regard themselves as gifted and intelligent and call themselves *débrouillards* (pronounced day-broo-yards), a French term sharpened in the local setting to carry an illicit edge. A *débrouillard* in Martinique is not merely resourceful (the French meaning), but also someone who is economically cunning and successful in unorthodox ways. In Martinique, creole-style *débrouillards* are local models for economic success, and while their behavior may extend beyond what is legal, it does not often transgress what is considered moral, at least by most. There are certain segments in Martiniquais society that passionately object to *débrouillardism* as it is practiced locally. For people in these groups, creole-style *débrouillardism* is an indefensible attempt to claim that even God can wink at behavior that is morally wrong. Among many more of my informants, however, "true" *débrouillards* are seen to push the limits of French law, but not to violate the culturally prescribed limits of what is morally defensible. I explore these variations in perceptions of the boundaries of moral behavior and *débrouillardism* in the chapters that follow.

THEORY AND PRACTICE: LOCATING CREOLE IDENTITIES IN POSTCOLONIAL STUDIES

The notion of fragmented identities that obtains in Martinique and in the wider Caribbean has attracted a wave of scholarly notice in recent *Elements* years. As one anthropologist noted, the Caribbean region has attained new status as a "master symbol" for the hybrid identities and cultural dislocations common to the postcolonial world today.[5] What gave birth to the modern Caribbean, a cross-continental circulation of goods and people, now seems to characterize much of the world, as the flows of people, languages, commodities, and ideas swirl in new circles and with new intensities. The collective impact of these heterogeneous influences is transforming local societies into polycultural worlds where new sources of knowledge and desire compete for space and where the practice of culture is no longer bounded to a particular place. These transformations in turn act to complicate individual identities among people who, through such flows of information, goods, and people, have come to value more than one cultural set of practices. The bewildering pace of change in the world's societies has inspired increasing numbers of scholars to look to the literature and research of Caribbean peoples, which can help make sense of newly fragmenting cultures and identities.[6]

In the energetic scholarship that is emerging to grapple with the problems of independence, modernity, and identity in postcolonial societies, the predicament of Martinique presents a special opportunity. Here, rather than choosing to become independent from the colonizing mother country, the colonized people became incorporated into their former colonizer's nation.[7] Many scholars of development view France's "benevolent" approach as far preferable to the promotion of a harsh, neoliberal basis of government. Yet the welfare-oriented style of development carries its own colonial baggage: material and identity-based problems resulting from complete dependency on France.

In contrast to the home-based dependency experienced by Martiniquais, independent states such as Barbados, Jamaica, and Suriname have become dependent on foreign investments, tourism, and aid in ways that undermine their own political independence. Indeed, economic studies of postcolonial societies have focused almost exclusively on the struggles of formerly colonized, now independent states. However, when a former colony becomes politically integrated with its colonizer, national assumptions of sameness can mask the significance of cultural difference. I will show in this book that the practice and meaning of creole economics in Martinique offers a good example of how cultural difference is reproduced below the French radar of sameness.

ASSIMILATION AND "DIFFERENCE"

The extent of assimilation and internalization of "French models of how to think and act" is reflected in Richard Price's anthropological diagnosis of the trend in Martinique toward a "folklorization of memory."[8] Price documents a spate of new local museums, restored plantation houses, and a bulging roster of government-sanctioned cultural events all oriented to scripting contemporary narratives about Martinique's past. Curiously, these public narratives share a similarly sanitized perspective on local history that avoids details from the most profound memories of all—slavery. The local initiatives behind these efforts and their popular local reception might suggest that at least some Martiniquais have so internalized the perspectives of colonial whites that they are able and willing to bury the ugliness of bondage, rape, and torture in return for being loved by France, in return for being France.

But as Price points out, and as other anthropologists like Paul Gilroy and Chris Bongie also argue,[9] internalizing European values is not the same thing as forgetting the past, nor is it the same thing as dissolving one's own history and identity into a European one. Despite the fact that Martinique has modernized drastically since departmentalization, exalting a "traditional" past as though it were frozen in time exaggerates the situation and falls prey to a grand narrative of loss.

Economic anthropologist Marshall Sahlins also warns against the facile assumption that "traditional" societies are "selling out" their cultural values as they scramble to participate in "modern" life.[10] For the Alaskan indigenous peoples he studied, snowmobiles, cell phones, and other capitalist trappings are put to use in ways that help sustain local values such as subsistence practice. Other anthropologists, like Jonathan Friedman and Ulf Hannerz, argue similar points from different perspectives: globalization may create many appearances of a single world culture, but changing technologies, commodity flows, migrating populations, and newly imagined lives do not flatten the field of cultural differences; rather, they alter their shape and scope.[11] Our task, then, is to engage with the reality of these abstract and concrete flows and their meanings in order to grasp how these influences reshape people's sense of difference and how these differences are lived and felt.

But how do colonized societies that have integrated into their colonizer nations fit into this task? In the context of exploring terms of differences, literary studies scholars Bill Ashcroft, Gareth Griffiths, and Helen Tiffin suggest a path that carries relevance for societies like Martinique. In the introduction to their thick reader on postcolonial studies, the editors call for greater attention to ways in which oppositional discourse and practice may be located within practices that appear to be "complicit with the imperial enterprise." To explore the predicament in which some postcolonial groups are required to express their difference by resorting to "opposition within complicity," these authors suggest focusing on settler colonies, such as Australia, Canada, and South Africa. In these societies, they argue, the "problem of complicity" is "more obvious" because the opportunities for oppositional discourse and practice are more limited.[12]

Compared to the large land masses and populations comprising these British settler colonies, the French DOMS seem almost insignificant. Yet when it comes to exploring how opposition to dominant European values gets expressed in spite of the appearance of strong assimilation to these values, the French overseas departments are exquisitely positioned. As Price says of Martinique, "With expressive resources reduced by overwhelming external controls, Caribbean people have always asserted their individuality, and resistance, as best they could through verbal play, pilferage, satirical song, deception, and small acts of defiance."[13]

Feeding this continued need to express one's individuality and sense of difference is a callaloo of structural and psychological contradictions that reminds Martiniquais that they are not autonomous and they are not fully French. Together, material dependency on France and psychological rejection as true French reproduce the tensions of assimilation and reinforce an irreducible "twoness" of identity. Without full legitimacy as French, Afro-Caribbean islanders find refuge in creole culture, including the practice of creole economics.

FIELDWORK AND METHODS

Following two preliminary research visits, I conducted fieldwork interviews for this study beginning in 1990 and continuing over many visits to Martinique through summer 2001. My long-term fieldwork involved an uninterrupted research stay of twelve months followed by successive research visits in summers of 1996, 1998, and 1999, and a six-month research stay during spring and summer of 2001. These subsequent visits were prompted by various goals of investigation, but each included informal interviews and conversations with new as well as renewed contacts about the widespread practice of work "off the books." Considering that my research on this topic has spanned a period of eleven years, I can attest that the phenomenon I am calling "creole economics" is as vital today as it appeared to me during my initial investigation.

In addition to many dozens of informal interviews over the years, I conducted more than 300 formal interviews for this study in targeted residential areas of Fort-de-France. With the help of local officials from INSEE (the French government bureau that tracks economic and demographic trends), I located three socioeconomically distinct neighborhoods from which to draw my sample. The research included data for 200 households, 700 individuals, and more than 500 undeclared economic activities. In Chapter 6, as preface to my findings by socioeconomic class, I provide an ethnographic view of each of the three neighborhoods where I conducted the formal portion of my research.

All people I interviewed, excepting scholars, authors, and artists, are identified by pseudonyms. In fact, since one of the granting organizations for my research was the French government, I purposely decided not to collect names even at the point of interview. Instead, I coded all materials by household number and assigned each individual within a household a different number. Many people, especially those in lower- and moderate-income households, expressed no hesitation to name themselves when I explained my techniques for ensuring anonymity. Nevertheless, I have used no one's real name, and where necessary to ensure their anonymity, have altered details about their households. The illustrations included in this book are composites, drawn loosely from my photographs of local people and intended only to evoke images of the varying "looks" of Martiniquais.

Finally, I have included almost no discussion of the relationship of *békés* (the tiny, powerful minority of white Creoles who are descendants of slaveowners) to creole economics. I leave them out for the simple reason that, almost without exception, they were not willing to be interviewed for this research. Moreover, because my argument depends on historical perspectives from slavery, I do not consider the economic lives of other small minorities on the island. Afro-Creole people, the focus of my study, represent 90 percent of Martinique's population today.   *Elements*

KEY ARGUMENTS OF THE BOOK

My overall goal is to present a case that creole culture shapes local economic practice. I want to show that creole culture and history matter to the way people work off the books in Martinique. Because most people, including scholars, do not associate economic behavior with cultural patterns, the creole contours of such behavior have gone largely unnoticed. Likewise, scholars of creolization and creole identities have only begun to mine the economic dimensions of these identities. This study investigates how people of Martinique generate undeclared income, how they explain why they do it, and how these values connect to cultural patterns that resonate across Caribbean societies.

To show how culture shapes economic behavior, I will distinguish the types of forces (non-economic and economic) that spur the practice of creole economics. For example, economic motivations to work off the books relate often to high taxes on labor, high levels of unemployment, and weak systems of law enforcement. Earning undeclared income also flows from Martinique's intensely "gaze-oriented" social environment, where personal "style" as reflected in one's public appearance and material possessions is the subject of constant scrutiny. Whether a person is unemployed or well employed, strong pressures to look successful prod many to earn income on the side in order to consume more and look better. But non-economic factors, like the cultural value of being a good *débrouillard*, also contribute to the practice of creole economics. Men especially strive to be seen as *débrouillards* in the local sense because it affirms their personal autonomy and intelligence and mitigates the stigma of being a person "of color."

A second, less ambitious but more practical, goal of this book is to offer anthropological insights about the meaning of a cultural informal economy to development planners. The patterns I found contradict many commonly held assumptions among economists and development planners about how informal economies work. In brief, I argue that no informal economic system can be fully understood as the product of high taxes or restrictive labor laws, nor are these economies universally dominated by poor people whose low-end products and services primarily serve other poor people. An argument for recognizing the cultural form of an informal economy—in this case, creole economics—calls into question generalized development strategies targeted at informal economic actors. The implications of culturally shaped informal economies are important since they suggest that development planners must understand the local context in order to devise effective intervention strategies.

TWO

Social Histories

THE WEIGHT OF FRANCE
IN MARTINIQUE

FRENCH POLICY AIMED . . . TO MAKE COLONIES
LITTLE OVERSEAS FRANCES AND PERHAPS, IN
THE FULLNESS OF TIME, TO TURN AFRICANS,
ASIANS, AND ISLANDERS INTO FRENCH MEN
AND WOMEN OF A DIFFERENT COLOUR.

—Robert Aldrich, *Greater France*, 1996

Five giant grocery stores, known as *les hypermarchés*, squat in retail centers sprinkled in and around Fort-de-France. Like Walmart or Target, these big box stores offer vast supplies of imported durables and food, highlighting the lack of locally grown food and other products in Martinique. In familiar French fashion, one finds the lineup of *les chariots* (grocery carts) in the parking lot and places a token in the slot, which releases one from the others nested in a row. These *chariots* are larger than US-sized grocery carts, an early clue that the items one might want to purchase can take up a good deal of space. Inside, the wide shopping aisles are flanked by shelves brimming with well-organized and deeply stacked items. Uniformed checkers, produce weighers, and fish, meat, cheese, and traiteur packagers, all there to serve, remind shoppers that consumption is normal. To an outsider from the US accustomed to ordinary-scale grocery stores, the glamorous interiors and array of specialty offerings here offer testament to the everyday affluence of Martiniquais and to the expectations of very high levels of local consumption.

The stock is overwhelmingly metropolitan as opposed to local, another indication of the extent to which assimilation has occurred in the area of food. Cheeses are very popular, and most of these stores feature dozens of French varieties. Yogurts, custards, and creams originating in the metropole also occupy a high proportion of floor space. In the produce section there are local offerings of squashes, eggplant, okra, mangoes, bananas, pineapples, and melons. Equally extensive are displays of continental-grown tomatoes, peaches, apples, grapes, oranges, broccoli, and cauliflower. Imported cereals and rice concede almost no shelf space to locally grown rice. French-imported patio furniture, cookware, lotions, shampoos, and perfumes further attest to the non-local supplier, just as the vast selection of imported wines and champagnes upstages the selection of local rums and juices. Even some of the elaborately displayed fish is fresh frozen from the metropole. What someone in Martinique cannot find at one of these dazzlingly modern grocery stores is hard to imagine. And while the greatest proportion of items for sale comes from metropolitan France, local production and exports do not begin to finance the cost of these imports.

A different projection of Frenchness greets the visitor to Fort-de-France's waterfront Parc Savane, a great expanse of manicured green lawns, palm trees, wooden benches, and bandstand. The park remains elegant, despite its reputation for nighttime danger. Fronting the park on its commercial end, the busy Rue Lamartine houses French icons of belonging, including the Poste and the city library, Bibliothèque Schoelcher. Daily, a pod of languid Mercedes taxis collects in the parking spaces that face the street, with drivers draped coolly over their doors or chatting in animated exchanges with each other, seemingly uninterested in would-be passengers. Opposite this bay-end of the park stands a once-proud statue of Empress Josephine, a *béké* woman Napoleon took for his wife.[1] Unsuspecting passersby are startled to realize that atop her gracious form, which is draped in a lovely gown, there is no head. Not only has Josephine's head been severed, but the concrete wound has been painted with blood-red streaks that drip onto her gown in dramatic fashion.[2] The blood is refreshed regularly, I was told by informants, to reinforce the point: "Yes, we are France, but we are in pain, we are in pain." The juxtaposition of these two images—grocery stores that evoke the great City of Oz and the headless statue of Josephine—captures a vital complexity about Martiniquais' simultaneous embrace of and disdain toward France.

In this chapter, I will discuss how the island of Martinique (like Guadeloupe and French Guiana) became French, and thus more affluent and less autonomous than other areas of the Caribbean, and how these qualities provide the stimulus today for the practice of creole economics.

Martinique's current situation is grounded largely in the particular strategies of French colonization, which differed in important ways from those of the Spanish, British, or Dutch. Because each New World colony developed around a colonizer's own home language, religion, philosophy of colonization, and ideas about race, the legacies are also distinct. These colonizing differences help explain many distinctions across islands today, from the languages spoken to the variations of skin color, and from the political role of ex-colonizers to the standards of living today. Most Caribbean islands did not achieve independence until the 1960s; thus, the tenure of colonization and its related influences were long running. To provide a context for the patterns that distinguished the French colonies from others, it is useful to review first how Caribbean plantation economies emerged and evolved.

THE 300-YEAR BASIS OF ISLAND SOCIETY:
THE PLANTATION ECONOMY   *Social Histories*

As cultural geographer David Lowenthal said of the Caribbean, "Here, the deepest wrong was done. These are the most colonized of all colonized societies."[3] From the late fifteenth century to the mid-1600s, Spanish invaders dominated the colonization of the New World. Their quest for treasure began on the large islands of the northern Caribbean, but after discovering that vast stores of gold and silver lay buried in mainland areas of Mexico and Peru, they abandoned their focus on the islands until late in the eighteenth century. During the sixteenth century, before northern Europeans had identified their own source of wealth in the form of sugarcane, merchant groups from rival European nations fed off the Spanish by sponsoring pirate attacks to pillage treasure-laden Spanish ships headed back to Spain. Their profits helped finance the establishment of settler colonies on the smaller islands, controlled respectively by England, France, and the Netherlands. Colonists from these home countries thrived by growing tobacco and other export crops, using forced indigenous labor. However, native groups proved unsuited to the strenuous agricultural labor imposed on them and many perished from overwork and starvation. Others died from European diseases they became exposed to and had no immunities to fight. Virtually all native peoples were exterminated in the Caribbean, and in the Americas generally, scholars estimate that only about 6 percent of the native population survived European colonization.[4]

By the mid-seventeenth century, colonizers from England, France, and the Netherlands had found an alternate source of labor in Africa and a far more profitable crop for export: sugar. While the Spanish remained focused on exploiting indigenous labor to mine gold and silver from mainland areas, the British, French, and Dutch colonies imported massive number of slaves to the Caribbean area to work the sugar plantations. This second wave of Europeans thus found their own source of "gold" in the cultivation of sugarcane.[5]

The monocrop plantation system that developed over the next 300 years represents one of the world's earliest engagements with a global economic system, one propelled by the infamous "trade triangle."[6] The trade triangle brought European goods to tribal chiefs in Africa in exchange for slaves, who were shipped across the Atlantic to the New World in the notorious "middle passage." In the West Indies, the slaves were sold to plantation owners, who kept them in bondage in order to produce sugar, rum, and molasses that were sold in North America and Europe. Martiniquais society is thus rooted in a set of social and economic factors that also conditioned the growth of British and Dutch island colonies in the New World: slavery and a monocrop plantation economy.[7]

RACE-BASED SOCIAL HIERARCHIES
DURING SLAVERY

The sugar and slavery formula for building fortunes depended on colonists' ability to maintain rigidly stratified societies. Mutual distrust and fear characterized relations between groups, especially once African-descended populations became the overwhelming majorities on islands where sugar dominated local cultivation. At the top of this hierarchy in Martinique (and the other French-controlled islands, including Guadeloupe and Haiti) were the European colonists from France, known in Martinique as *békés*. These white settlers had come to the West Indies, less often as sons of noblemen than as ordinary Frenchmen. A few were second or third sons of noble families—families that had left their fortunes to the firstborn as tradition dictated. These colonists either brought along or later recruited laborers, *engagés*, to work for them until those *engagés* could earn enough to purchase some land for themselves. Once the laborers had become landowners, they sometimes purchased or borrowed the name of a noble family whose last known relative had died. These two original groups of Frenchmen came to represent the more-affluent and less-affluent ends of the *béké* continuum; they were united by their common desire to keep their offspring white and their fortunes intact.[8] Although today the *grands békés* still distinguish their ancestry from that of the *petits békés*, the important distinction remains whether you are white or a person of color. *Békés* still prefer to marry other *békés*, or at least other whites, and most continue to segregate their social lives from those of other islanders.

At the bottom of the plantation colony hierarchy were the slaves: Africans and their plantation-born descendants. After being captured in Africa, a slave would be loaded into the dark and dirty hold of a slave ship and packed shoulder to shoulder for the several-week "middle passage" across the Atlantic. Many perished on the journey from disease or hunger; many others were separated from their kin and from those who spoke their same language.[9]

Dehumanizing treatment continued in life on the plantation, which involved a grueling day of twelve or more hours of work, six days a week, with very little time to rest.[10] But even more severe than the physical hardships were the social and psychological difficulties of life without family or, often, a common native language. In order to communicate with each other, slaves forged new, creole languages which combined elements of their native languages with the language of their European masters. Music, dance, storytelling, and religion became the expressive anchors of their humanity and affirmed a group identity in the midst of individual misery and alienation.[11]

On the plantation, slaveowners put male and female slaves to equally demanding physical labor. In fact, because colonists regarded women as less intelligent than men, female slaves were more often relegated to the lowest status and thus to the most strenuous jobs on the plantation—work in the cane fields. In field tasks such as digging holes, weeding, and reaping, women slaves generally outnumbered men.[12] The "ablest and strongest" male slaves, by contrast, were chosen to fill more skilled positions such as drivers, foremen, blacksmiths, and carpenters.[13]

The forming of two-parent slave families was effectively discouraged or prevented. As Bernard Moitt, historian of slavery in the French Caribbean, noted, "The institution of slavery itself was antithetical to the promotion and development of strong family units on a broad scale."[14] The impediments to forming slave families resulted in part from planters' casual practice of selling off slaves without regard to their interpersonal relationships. The ill health resulting from harsh treatment of slaves—including the routine rape of women by both masters and fellow slaves, malnutrition, lack of medical care, and grueling labor—posed another obstacle to stable family life. Planters generally found it too costly to maintain healthy slaves who could breed and reproduce a labor force; they could more cheaply purchase fresh slaves.[15] By the late 1700s, however, when the source of cheap new slaves was being threatened by the specter of abolition, European planters began to offer rewards and mete out punishments to goad their female slaves into having more children.[16] These incentives had little effect on the low birthrates among slave women: not only were they often badly nourished, overworked, and in poor health, but they may also have actively resisted bringing children into slavery.[17]

In addition to the European masters and African or African-descended slaves, there was another, in-between group that emerged in New World plantation societies: the *gens de couleur libres* (free people of color). This small but important group represented a third tier of plantation society that included primarily mulattos (those born of one white and one black parent) but also a small number of freed blacks.[18] As children of colonial masters and slave women, mulattos were frequently able to inherit their father's wealth, receive good educations in Paris, and own slaves themselves.[19] They also enjoyed the advantage of having lighter skin, which elevated their status among darker-skinned blacks.[20]

By the mid-1700s, as many as 60,000 African slaves were arriving in the New World each year. Island demographics in the French and British sugar colonies shifted to overwhelmingly black populations, averaging eight to nine slaves for every ten residents.[21] Martinique was typical: by 1789, 85 percent of the nearly 100,000 population was composed of slaves.[22] In the colonial period between 1518 and 1870, estimates of the total number of Africans forcibly removed from their native societies to work as slaves in the Americas range from 10 to 15 million.[23]

After France decreed abolition in its colonies in 1848, the racial basis of hierarchy became more complicated with the import of East Indians as indentured servants to meet the labor needs of planters who had lost their workforce of slaves. Between 1850 and 1914, more than 25,000 East Indians were imported to Martinique alone. Meanwhile, the mulattos, who frequently benefited from metropolitan educations, were in a position to leverage their advantages into a class of homegrown professional elites.[24]

EXPLOITING OPPORTUNITY AND MAKING FORTUNES

What could have driven one group to enslave another, generation after generation, for more than 200 years? The staggering fortunes that became possible through sugar cultivation. Planters were able to earn fantastic profits because only modest capital investments were needed to produce and market sugar. More importantly, land was free and labor, for a labor-intensive crop, was cheap. Eager consumers in Europe and North America craved the sweet taste, and as its consumption increased, monocrop production in the islands increased.[25]

By the mid-1600s the French, as well as British and Dutch colonists, had turned the cultivation of sugar into their primary profit-making venture and smallholder farms had become absorbed by great estates.[26] By the late *Social Histories* 1600s, the smaller islands of the eastern Caribbean,[27] as well as Haiti and Jamaica, were controlled by England, France, and Holland, each competing in a "perpetual war" for the control of the islands.[28] The sugar and slave trades stimulated vital economic growth in the metropolitan centers, particularly in industries such as shipbuilding and copper production. In fact, the revenues generated from this transnational commerce helped finance Britain's industrial revolution.[29] The flourishing trade also developed numerous seaport towns such as Nantes and Bordeaux in France,[30] and Liverpool and Bristol in Britain.[31] Put simply, slavery was good for business.

By 1674, the French-controlled colonies of Martinique, Guadeloupe, and Saint Domingue (later renamed Haiti) were producing 5,400 tons of sugar annually. Just ten years later, the same areas would produce 9,300

tons. Nearly 175 years later, on the eve of French abolition in 1847, the number of sugar refineries in Martinique alone had increased to nearly 500, while the count of slaves, who had numbered 16,731 in 1701, had increased to 72,859.[32] By the mid-nineteenth century, some estimates suggest that the French islands were supplying 40 percent of the sugar consumed around the world.[33]

FRENCH AND BRITISH COLONIZING STRATEGIES

Several factors distinguished French attitudes and practices from those of other colonizer nations in the New World. For one thing, because neighboring islands were controlled by colonists from different European countries, "the islands were kept unnaturally apart for three centuries."[34] French and Spanish colonizers brought Latin cultural histories and philosophical orientations that contrasted with those brought by Anglo Saxon colonists from England and the Netherlands. Both the French and Spanish, for example, brought Catholicism (though the Islam-laced version of Spanish Catholicism was stricter, especially in matters related to gender).[35] In addition, the constitutional basis of colonization for the French and Spanish involved much stronger forms of political centrality and authority than existed in the British system.[36] Spain built massive baroque structures in centers of their control, such as Havana and Santo Domingo, and both French and Spanish men frequently regarded their children by slave (or native) women as legitimate offspring and heirs. This recognition commonly allowed for the children's freedom and provided them with access to education, wealth, and status.[37]

But as suggested earlier, the timing and experience of Spanish colonization was different in kind from that of the British, French, and Dutch. These differences distinguished the Spanish colonial legacies in the New World.[38] By the time the Spanish settlers turned to their island possessions as large-scale producers of sugarcane, the number of slaves they brought to Puerto Rico and to the Dominican Republic had much less demographic impact on the established Hispanicized mix of people.[39]

The shared interests of England, France, and the Netherlands in New World sugar plantations did not translate into identical colonizing practices, however.[40] In fact, it is clear that each European nation developed its New World colonies "in its own image" as colonists brought distinct sets of home country values, religious doctrines, and philosophical traditions into their relationship with the slaves in their particular overseas island possessions.[41] Contrasts between the French and British legacies are especially striking. Lowenthal noted that, as a result, "The British West Indies are less Anglicized than the French West Indies are Gallicized."[42]

In general, the attitudes of French colonists toward slaves, such as their status as human beings, their worthiness for religious education, and even their desirability as sexual partners revealed a more paternalistic involvement than that shown by British colonists. Many historians indicate that the British maintained a greater distance from their slaves, in part a reflection of the conviction that slaves were not worth Christianizing.[43] These realities cannot be interpreted to suggest that Caribbean slavery was less severe in French than it was in British areas, however, for slavery in the Americas was everywhere a horrific institution.[44] Certainly, the French were interested in the profits their colonies could return to them. But, alongside the material gains, the French promoted the ideal of fulfilling a *mission civilisatrice* (civilizing mission), viewed as a noble colonial mandate to teach the primitives how to recognize and emulate the superior culture and religion of Catholic France. To Christianize the slaves was to justify one's rightful superiority over them. Ultimately, by converting and civilizing the "heathens," so as to make them good Frenchmen, the French could demonstrate their nation's enduring strength and international power.[45]

The paternalistic approach of the colonial French government is also apparent in the Code Noir, a series of legal provisions put into effect by King Louis XIV in 1685 to protect the property rights of slaveowners but also the rights of slaves. The Code conferred a legal status on slaves, detailed how they should be governed, and outlined the minimum provisions they should be supplied in the areas of food, clothing, and shelter.[46] Ostensibly, the Code also ensured the humane treatment of slaves, though in practice these articles of the Code were rarely observed.[47] Still, compared to the British colonial system, which lacked a comprehensive code and permitted colonists autonomy to decide their own regulations, the Code Noir made significantly more allowances for granting free status to mulattos.[48] In addition, unlike the effectively "bipolar" racial system of the English colonies, the French and Dutch Caribbean included almost as many free people of color as whites.[49] By 1789, at the time of the French Revolution, mulattos in the French Caribbean numbered 40,000, a number significant enough to allow them to press for equal status with whites in Paris after the Revolution.[50]

The high numbers of free people of color in French areas of the Caribbean can be linked in part to the institution of concubinage in seventeenth-century France. The custom of concubinage was adopted in the tropical environment of Caribbean islands with French masters taking slave women as mistresses. The practice of concubinage was much less common in Britain and, likewise, in the British-controlled Caribbean. As one scholar of Caribbean history noted, "The French colonists never displayed the British icy racism and didn't have Puritan scruples, so became father to countless half-caste children."[51]

This seemingly small detail of French colonial values created large-scale consequences. Not only were the mulatto offspring of master/slave liaisons generally freed in the French areas, but over a 200-year period of slavery, these offspring and their offspring ultimately contributed to a "whitening" of the population and the present-day fluid spectrum of skin colors one encounters in Martinique.[52]

That French colonists were relatively more involved with their slaves and their island colonies than the British is also apparent in their greater tendency to reside locally and to keep somewhat smaller scale plantations with lower ratios of slaves to whites.[53] One important implication of these differences involves the lack of British infrastructure in the islands they controlled,[54] an outcome some attribute to the high incidence of nonresident British plantation owners.[55]

The particularities of French colonization strategies in the Caribbean are further distinguished after 1789. Over the 150 years following the Revolution, the Republican ideals of "fraternity, liberty, and equality" gradually became recognized as ideals that should extend to France's colonial subjects.[56] The choice to assimilate to France in 1946 reflects the conviction of French Caribbean islanders that being French is their rightful identity. In contrast, even the settler colonies of Britain, such as Canada, Australia, New Zealand, and South Africa "never envisaged the complete integration of colonies with the metropole."[57] After World War II, Britain promoted self-government among its colonies, leading ultimately to full independence, a political status also sought by the vast majority of the colonized peoples that Britain considered "the white man's burden."

EVOLVING COLONIAL IDEAS ABOUT RACE

Slavery has existed in many societies, over several thousands of years.[58] But as anthropologist Audrey Smedley argues in her examination of comparative systems of slavery, prior to the eighteenth century there was "no society that categorically denied the humanity of slaves in law and social beliefs."[59] Unlike the type of slavery that emerged in the New World, the many varieties of slavery practiced in the Old World demonstrated recognition of a slave's humanity. This recognition appeared in slave op-   *Social Histories*
portunities for manumission (the granting of freedom), the right to marry, the right to own property, rights to training and education, and rights of protection for women and children. Moreover, justifications for slavery in Old World societies did not rest on assumptions about inferior races.[60]

European rationalizations for enslavement in the New World were multiple and evolving. As discussed earlier, the strong economic interests of colonists in the institution of slavery coincided with religious and, later, scientific convictions about natural hierarchies of life. The Christian church did not interfere with the European practice of slavery, arguing, to the contrary, that it followed a clear hierarchy intended by God. Despite differences inherent in Catholicism and Protestantism, European Christendom was "itself contained within a model of territorial expansion" in

which shared understandings included a "superior, white European region and an inferior, black African one."[61] In short, slavery was seen to reflect a "natural law."[62] As historian Seymour Drescher notes,

> Christian institutions, liturgy and theology were established along-side the institution of slavery . . . [and] its clergy made no attempt to mobilize the slave population as a whole for conversion nor were they pressed to do so by their metropolitan superiors . . . Most planters, like the slave traders, never pretended that the massive conversion of slaves was either the norm of the islands or their particular aim.[63]

In contrast to the British Anglican practices, which did not stress the conversion of slaves to Christianity, the Catholic orders of France did promote salvation among slaves. Still, they themselves owned slaves and did not support abolition, even on the eve of its enactment in France.[64]

Despite the church's unspoken assumption that blacks were naturally inferior to whites, not all scholars agree that it was racial differences that led colonists to seek Africans as appropriate subjects of slavery.[65] Instead, some authors contend that Africa simply offered the closest source of cheap labor for planters. This view holds that not until the ratio of Africans to Europeans increased did race become the dominant justification for slavery. Thus, with rapidly shrinking ratios to black slaves, colonists reacted to their fear of "going native" and of "degeneration" by casting plantation hierarchies as natural reflections of inherent differences in the races.[66] Yet as sociologist Chris Smaje points out, whether or not the choice of African slave labor was motivated by assumptions of racial inferiority, it is clear that race-based justifications came to dominate colonial explanations of New World slavery.[67]

The Catholic assumption of African racial inferiority came early. An example from the historical archives in Martinique indicates that in 1671, Père Du Tertre, a local priest, suggested that the enslavement of Africans had perhaps been ordained by God. Even earlier, a Jesuit priest, Père Pelleprat, had called slaves in the French West Indies the "designated creatures of Satan." Du Tertre provided an explicit rationale for African inferiority by referencing the biblical account of one of Ham's four sons, Canaan, who had been cursed for his rebellion. God's response to Caanan's revolt explained that some of the descendants of Ham "had been blackened and degraded to the status of natural slaves as punishment for their ancestor's sin."[68]

On the basis of such biblical references, black skin became associated with evil and sin. Moitt explains that "color symbolism, linked as it was to this biblical curse, provided justification for enslavement."[69] Another local priest in Martinique, Père Labat, equated slaves' blackness with their unworthiness. Labat told those slaves who weren't working hard enough that he had once been black himself, and that through devotion and goodwill toward the master, they too could turn white.[70]

Race-based depictions of slaves on plantations in the Americas had become commonplace by the late seventeenth century. Historians and sociologists reveal that British planter diaries and archives "depicted blacks as violent, primitive, untrustworthy, and troublesome"[71] and spoke of slaves as "the internal or intestinal enemy."[72] Early in the colonial period, it was clear that French planters, like their Dutch and English counterparts, considered slaves to be "inferior, lacking in intelligence, lazy, and 'happy-go-lucky.'"[73] They regarded black and mixed-race women as oversexed pleasure seekers. In contrast, white women were seen as standard bearers of respectability. Gradually, a "pigmentocracy" emerged to anchor these stereotypes to race-based principles of "natural" inferiority. The darker the skin, the closer the bloodline to pure African, and the more degenerate the outcome. Because mulattos showed the closest approximations to white skin, their character was correspondingly more salvageable.

By the nineteenth century, European and American scientists were lending credence to the popular stereotypes about blacks and mixed-race individuals. Using cranial measures and other anatomical techniques to offer evidence that blacks were an inferior race, Georges Cuvier, for example, asserted that blacks were "the most degraded of human races, whose form approaches that of the beast." Louis Agassiz, a naturalist and Harvard professor, suggested that blacks were a different species altogether.[74] Josiah Nott, a British doctor, used cranial research to argue that Negroes were a degenerate race not made for freedom; that instead, they were like children who thrived best in the structure and direction given them under slavery.[75]

Race thus came to be seen as a direct measure of human capacity. Because of the inherent inferiority of non-white "races," the mixing, or "métissage," of whites with such inferior stock would lead to racial degeneracy and unless stopped, would ensure the rapid decline of European nations.[76] These folk views of blacks were framed as science at a time when science was coming into its own as a prestigious and authoritative source of knowledge, holding a strong grip on the public imagination.[77]

After Darwin's mid-nineteenth-century ideas about natural selection became extended into the ideas of social Darwinism, colonial planters and other colonialist sympathizers in metropolitan centers came to understand race less as an innate basis for superiority or inferiority than as a reflection of a society's "stage" in the evolution of its potential.[78] Black populations were seen as "unevolved" and, therefore, well suited to the direction and control of "evolved" Europeans.

Not all scientific discourse found its way into the service of rationalizing slavery. In eighteenth-century Europe, for example, numerous travel accounts and scientific papers portrayed a more complex picture of New World slavery. In France, two of the most widely circulated publications included the abbé Raynal's *Histoire des Deux Indes* and the comte de Buffon's many-volumed *Natural History*. Raynal attacked the harshness of West Indian slavery and encouraged slaves to rise up and overtake their owners. Buffon believed in the theory of "monogenesis," the idea that all humans have descended from one original human population. His idea that "if subjected to the temperate climate of Europe and introduced to French foods and culture, Black men could become white,"[79] say some historians, "predisposed Frenchmen to look sympathetically on the long-term possibility of assimilating Blacks into French culture."[80]

THE DECLINE OF SUGAR AND PRESSURES FOR ABOLITION

For roughly 200 years, the Caribbean islands represented the uncontested "sugar bowl" of Europe. But by the early 1800s, even before slaves were freed, the economic basis of the profitable formula of slaves and sugar had begun to erode. When Great Britain's blockades of Europe cut off supplies of sugar from the islands, domestic sugar beet industries emerged in both France and England to meet demands. Moreover, slaves and mulattos in Saint Domingue rose up against French colonists and after many years of struggle, eventually became independent in 1804.[81] Once the flagship producer of French sugar and the single largest sugar producer in the world, independent Haiti withdrew from the world market. This sudden and drastic loss of profits leveled a serious blow to French colonial power and had the effect of spurring the development of rival sugar producers in Cuba, India, Africa, and Asia. By 1850, the lucrative sugar-producing islands had declined in prosperity because of competition from these European as well as non-European industries.[82]

Competition from cheaper sugar producers was one of the forces that led to the ultimate abolition of the institution of slavery. The decline of profits for sugar exports created economic pressures not easily resolved when all the resources of an island had been channeled into sugar production. Slaves themselves had contributed to these pressures even before the French and American Revolutions. After realizing that freedom could be won, and especially after the successful slave revolution in Haiti, slaves on other islands staged riots and rebellions and, increasingly, interfered with the smooth flow of production. Political economists in metropolitan centers added their own weight to the discourse, claiming publicly that slavery was not an economically rational system. Adam Smith, for example, argued in 1830 that freeing laborers to choose their own economic livelihood would create a much more efficient system than slavery.[83] Moreover, new laws prohibiting the transatlantic trade in slaves in 1807 forced up the cost of buying slaves since they had to be clandestinely imported. Together, these realities exposed the economic costs of maintaining the system of slavery.

This new assessment of the economic costs of slavery was buttressed by moral arguments waged by humanitarians and religious groups in the metropolitan centers. It was thus the combined effect of local and metropolitan pressures that brought about abolition. By the 1830s, European planters seemed to be the only group determined to continue slavery. But by then, since metropolitan companies were able to purchase lower-cost sugar from India or even their own beet sugar industries, the clout of the once powerful West Indian planter lobby had weakened.[84] The double-barreled ammunition against slavery positioned metropolitan governments to claim moral objections to an indefensible system of labor exploitation while also realizing the economic benefits of abolition. With the subsequent French Revolution of 1848, France abolished slavery. Between 1833 and 1888, each of the colonizing European countries freed its slaves. Planters in all European colonies were compensated for the "loss of slaves."[85]

HOPES FOR SOCIAL MOBILITY AFTER ABOLITION

After the French decreed abolition in 1848, all former slaves in Martinique were made citizens of France and males were given the vote in French national elections.[86] Economically, however, there was little change. Though former slaves could now earn a small wage, many were forced to continue work on *béké* plantations. Some were able to become full-time peasants, working a small piece of their own land. If they wanted to advance their economic and social status, however, both the mixed-race and black-skinned populations could only move in one direction: *francisation*. This term referred to cultural assimilation of French values that resulted in "the adoption of French language and learning, [and] Christian practices and patterns of behaviour that resembled those of the Europeans."[87]

The male mulatto offspring of planter/slave unions (many of whom had been granted their freedom and made financially independent) were of course those best positioned to perfect their language skills and to emulate most convincingly the coveted Frenchness. Throughout the French colonies of Martinique, Guadeloupe, French Guiana, and Réunion, this third tier of society with mixed parentage were, by the nineteenth century, already completing their educations in Paris. Mulattos returned home to

GROUNDINGS

32

Martinique with their French education, language, and material trappings, becoming doctors, lawyers, colonial administrators, and teachers. They wore European clothing, bought European furniture, practiced orthodox Catholicism, and entertained in styles consistent with European decorum. Because status in the eyes of the French required cultivated, European language and manners (not to mention whiteness), the light-skinned métis from the island colonies came to disdain the creole culture and language associated with black skin.[88] In turn, the mass of blacks, also seeking the status of respectability, emulated the mulatto model.

The impact of differing models of Frenchness is depicted in complex hierarchies by Patrick Chamoiseau, a Martiniquais writer. In his award-winning historical novel, *Texaco*, the author tells a story that spans several generations in Martinique, beginning in the final years of slavery and continuing forward 150 years, into the twentieth century.[89] His early characters are slaves, and the story continues through several generations of their descendants. Through the experiences of Esternome, born into slavery in Martinique, the reader learns that field slaves imitated the dress and behavior of freedmen in town, and that each rung of the rigid hierarchy involved one group's imitating another. Thus, the reader observes "the mulattoes imitating the *békes*, the free blacks imitating the mulattoes, and the slaves imitating the free blacks."[90]

HOW MARTINIQUE BECAME FRANCE

THE REVOLUTION OF 1789 AND THE LIMITS OF LIBERTÉ, EGALITÉ, FRATERNITÉ

When revolutionaries stormed the Bastille in 1789, the French Empire was still more than 100 years away from reaching the full extension of its muscle around the world.[91] But it was this Jacobin revolution and its egalitarian ideals of *liberté, egalité, fraternité* that would eventually shape the promises to and expectations of France's oldest colonies in the West Indies. How these ideals were understood by whites, free people of color, and the slaves varied significantly and fed the conflicts between these groups for years to come.[92] On that July 14, 1789, revolutionary victories laid the groundwork for modern France—overthrowing the absolutist monarchy, replacing aristocratic rule with that of bourgeois capitalists, drafting a constitution that recognized the unity of France, and developing laws that reined in local and regional power and asserted in its place new authority vested in a strong, centralized state. The new authorities partitioned France into *départements* (like states in the US), each run by a *préfet* (like a governor) representing the central government in Paris.[93]

The Revolution of 1789 promised equality for all, but it became quickly evident that these promises were not intended to apply to the colonized subjects of France, much less to slaves.[94] The radical Jacobin government voted to abolish slavery in 1794, but because the French sugar colonies were at their peak of prosperity, the planters' lobby was formidable.[95] Thus, in response to pressures from planters, combined with the chaos of Saint Domingue's slave revolution and the resulting French losses, the government acted to reassert metropolitan control in the colonies and to make up ground lost to Britain's superior strength at sea. The reaction took the form of intense new protectionist policies toward the colonies. As part of this general plan to compensate for the loss of Saint Domingue and the implication of this loss in commercial trade, Napoleon reestablished slavery (after eight years of official if not actual abolition), and sugar production in the colonies was intensified.[96]

Ultimately, the egalitarian rhetoric of the Revolution provided mulattos and slaves in the Caribbean a political tool they would use in their fight for equality under the French flag. Another tool for mulatto and slaves' political leverage was the French state's own professed goals toward its overseas colonies. As a sense of nationhood and French national identity began to coalesce in the late nineteenth century,[97] an assimilationist agenda toward France's colonies also emerged, an agenda consistent with the French mission to colonize for national glory, and not merely for riches. French colonial subjects were taught to understand the natural superiority of French culture and take it as their own. This attitude constituted what Martiniquais poet and politician Aimé Césaire rejected as the "universalizing" assumptions of assimilation—that French colonized peoples could and should strive to become good Frenchmen.[98]

CONTESTED METROPOLITAN VIEWS OF ASSIMILATION

Among metropolitan French, the only commonly held view on the topic of colonialism and expansion of the empire was the notion that France carried a moral responsibility to "civilize the uncivilized."[99] That French society represented the most advanced civilization appeared self-evident to leaders and citizens alike: its Greek and Roman heritage, its Christian religion, its role in advancing the Enlightenment, its modern science, its capitalist economy, and its white "race."[100] By the nineteenth century, with the sustained propaganda efforts of varied parties loosely cohering as the "colonial lobby," the French public gradually came to view colonial expansion and protection of France's colonies as a good, moral cause that also offered advantages to the French economy.[101]

By ensuring that the colonies had the same institutions, courts, schools, and administrative systems as France, and that colonists enjoyed the same rights and obligations of any French citizen, French policy aimed to "make colonies little overseas Frances and perhaps, in the fullness of time, to turn Africans, Asians, and islanders into French men and women of a different colour."[102] The geographic distance from France of the Caribbean and Indian Ocean colonies—regarded by some observers as France's "love children"—did not diminish hopes among French politicians for the colonies' eventual assimilation.[103]

While French policy toward its colonies might be satisfactorily explained as a combination of French pride and enlightened self-interest, that the majority of Martiniquais were in favor of assimilation to France strikes many outsiders as curious.[104] In the US, where plantation slavery followed many of the same patterns as in the Caribbean, American blacks had no choice: they were a demographic minority in a society controlled by whites. For them, assimilation was inevitable. By contrast, in most Caribbean societies with populations dominated by Afro-Caribbean peoples, islanders chose to end their relationships with former colonizers and map the political and economic road ahead on their own terms. So why were blacks in Martinique not compelled to seek independence, like their British-colonized neighbors in Trinidad or Jamaica or Barbados?

It seems that the revolutionary ideals of 1789, declaring liberty, equality, and fraternity "planted the seeds of a peculiar devotion to France in the hearts of the mulattos and blacks of the islands."[105] Thus, in a rare twist on the usual rally for independence among colonized peoples, in Martinique the colonized found the ballast provided by the weight of France appealing. The powerful minority of creole whites (*békés*) opposed this goal and instead promoted local autonomy and independence for the island.

BÉKÉ RESISTANCE MEETS MULATTO INSISTENCE

As island-born descendants of the French slaveholding families, *békés* never were interested in invoking the liberty, equality, and fraternity for the benefit of slaves. As mentioned earlier, although the radical postrevolution government did abolish slavery in 1794, more than thirty years before any other European country, Napoleon reinstated it in 1803, largely in deference to the white *béké* planters among whose population he had found his Empress Josephine. The *békés* realized that their fortunes depended on the continuity of cheap sugarcane workers, so they fiercely opposed any prospect for increasing the rights of slaves. Abolition posed a nightmare, and the strong *béké* lobby effectively postponed it until 1848.

Locally racialized attitudes persist to this day. As one *béké* reported to ethnographer Kovats-Beaudoux in her study of Martinique's *békés*, "It is we who have created this country, who have made it what it is."[106] By the mid-twentieth century, 100 years after abolition, this tiny white minority of powerful *békés* still owned most of the island's land and still controlled the population's workforce. The disparities in income and lifestyle between them and the majority slave-descended population were nearly as vast as before abolition. As local elites, 4,000 miles from any other authority, *békés* were thus predictably opposed to any change that would extend rights to the majority blacks and threaten to unravel the control over local labor that they had so long enjoyed. Elevating the status of France's overseas colonies to full overseas departments (*départements d'outre mer*, known commonly as DOMs) was just such a plan. If ordinary blacks could make claims of the French state, if they could migrate legally to the metropole for work, then they would no longer need the low-paying jobs on *béké* plantations. Ensuring that France's overseas possessions would be French through and through simply did not interest the *békés*: there were no real benefits to their own autonomous clan.

Despite their biological relationship to the all-powerful *békés*, the emerging mulatto class, educated in Paris, lobbied hard for DOM status. Because their light-skinned existence testified to the success of integrating former slave populations into French life, their voices carried unique credibility in demanding that the moral platform of *liberté, égalité, fraternité* be applied to France's overseas colonies by fully incorporating them into France. Moreover, their European sophistication and success helped translate the allure of French values to the majority black population and reinforced to them the economic potential of becoming "respectable" by becoming French.[107] Demonstrating their commitment to status based on the "respectability" of the elite European system, mulattos denigrated all visible manifestations of creole culture in favor of French attitudes, French products, and French language. As a result, increasing numbers of dark-skinned islanders learned to imitate European behavior and French language in public and to hide creole culture—and its association with crudeness—at home.[108] In his piercing 1952 study of Martinique and the connections between race, nationalism, and psychological health (translated in 1967 as *Black Skin, White Masks*), Frantz Fanon notes that Creole language was then so stigmatized in Martinique that the only time it was spoken in middle-class homes was to address servants, not to converse with family members.

AIMÉ CÉSAIRE: EARLY PROMOTER OF POLITICAL (NOT CULTURAL) ASSIMILATION

The idea of Martinique's political assimilation to France held such power that Aimé Césaire, who helped develop the concept of Negritude,[109] campaigned for it. To Césaire, arguing for political integration did not imply a desire for cultural integration. It was less a contradiction than a pragmatic recognition of the arrangement that promised the most to his fellow Martiniquais.[110]

This pragmatic concern for the material benefits of becoming part of France was fresh in the minds of local residents following a period of severe austerity during World War II. Because the Allied forces opposed the Vichy regime in France and had blockaded access to its Caribbean colonies, all French imports were halted for four years. For the first time in their history, Martiniquais were cut off from their French lifeline and forced to rely on themselves to invent the staples of life, from soap to glasses. The economic insecurities fostered by this experience of isolation helped Césaire convince local people that his native island could realize the security of becoming part of France politically without having to subsume its history and local cultural identity under a totalizing French one.

One year after the end of the war, in 1946, widespread popular support among islanders led four French island colonies—Martinique, Guadeloupe, French Guiana, and Réunion (an island in the Indian Ocean, off the coast of east Africa)—to become officially integrated to France. Political integration meant that the former Caribbean and Indian Ocean colonies became DOMs. The new elevated status of DOM accorded Martiniquais full rights and privileges as French men and women, like citizens of the Loire or Côte-d'Or or any other department in France. That the island was separated from the metropole by more than 4,000 miles of water made no difference. A departmental "prefect" from the Ministry of the Interior replaced the "governor" from the Ministry of Colonies, and

Martiniquais were granted representation in both the French National Assembly and Senate. Literary observer V. S. Naipaul noted the significance of Martinique's DOM status from his perspective as a native of British-colonized Trinidad. Although Martiniquais people had already signaled their Frenchness by adopting Catholicism, the French language, and French manners and values, said Naipaul, with departmentalization, they officially *were* French and Martinique *was* France.[111]

In the 1950s, when Martinique-produced sugar could no longer compete with cheaper African or Indian sugar on the world market, the French state was obliged to act. Perhaps driven by guilt, as many of my scholar-informants contend, France chose to invest monies in the economic development of an island that had, for nearly 300 years, enriched France because of a single crop, sugar. In addition, France's investment in Martinique may have also reflected ulterior motives to undermine any move toward independence. Some scholars assert that by ensuring Martinique's dependency on France, the metropolitan elite could continue to bask in the prestige and tropical sun of their own island in the New World. Metropolitan companies could also be assured of overseas markets.[112]

Originally, the economic effort was regarded as "assistance" required to build up the infrastructure and to stimulate the industries of agriculture, tourism, and fishing.[113] But, despite these efforts, the primary agricultural sector continued to contract, and the resulting loss in productivity was never offset by real economic development. Not so gradually, social transfers, subsidies, and public aid became the controlling force of the economy. Between 1950 and 1980, the rise in total public transfers multiplied more than eighty times, averaging an annual growth of 16 percent. In the same time frame, the number of public sector jobs increased from 5,516 to 26,440.[114] The metropolitan infusion of investment into the local economy brought new infrastructure, better schools, higher salaries, comprehensive social security protections, and vastly improved overall standards of living.[115]

Because Martinique is politically incorporated into France, it has "profited" from subsidies and social benefits pegged to approximate the levels of living attained in continental France. Yet, because the island's rapid growth and modernization since the 1970s has been the product of a welfare-based system of transfers rather than the product of locally expand-

GROUNDINGS

38

ing business or industry, the shrinking productivity and stagnant job base led to extremely high unemployment rates.[116] Dominated still today by its nonproductive service sector, Martinique's economy has continued to stagnate. The population faces an intractable 30 percent level of unemployment and growing numbers of households in personal debt.[117]

LIVING WITH PARADOX AND A SENSE OF ENTITLEMENT

The welfare state that France has created in Martinique has introduced a paradox in the local economy: at the same time that productivity has fallen dramatically and unemployment has risen sharply, people's incomes and standards of living have soared.[118] Even the unemployed are able to access a guaranteed minimum income subsidy and claim many health benefits from the French state. Certainly today, most Martiniquais are quick to hail the benefits of being "French." They point to the independent nation of Barbados, which ranks nearly as high as Martinique in per capita income but which does not benefit from Martinique's French-supported roadways, schools, hospitals, or from its overseas tax relief and subsidies for imported products. And Martinique is not only far more prosperous than its independent neighbors St. Lucia and Dominica, it is also European. Haiti, independent since its successful revolution ending French control in 1804, offers an especially grim reminder of the advantages Martinique reaps from its unbroken connection to France. Still, the paradox of simultaneous affluence and dependency puts a newer kind of pressure on the lived quality of Martinique's assimilation to France.

Social Histories

CONCLUSION

For nearly 400 years, the weight of France in Martinique has exerted unabated and undeniable force on the structure of the island's economy and on the nature of relations between colonists and slaves, *békés* and mulattos and, today, metropolitans and Martiniquais. Resembling few other areas of the postcolonial world, Martinique's integration into its colonizing nation bears testimony to the distinctive strategies of French colonization, and to the promises and hopes of assimilation these strategies offered to slave-descended island populations.

Prior to departmentalization, Martinique had produced more earnings through exports of sugar than the costs of imports from France. But in the decades following departmentalization, this balance of credit shifted dramatically. The island that had once specialized in production for export became transformed into an island importing and consuming eight times more than it produced.

As the unpredictable and uneven process of assimilation to France increased the island's standard of living, it introduced new tensions. Most Martiniquais readily proclaim that the greatest asset of being French is the prestige of being European and economically advanced. Politically, this loyalty is reinforced at every election, and the small number of votes for independence rarely cause concern among the majority of citizens. Local intellectuals, however, respond to this argument of island prosperity by asserting that, in fact, being French is a great economic liability. This contradiction stems from the economic prosperity ensured by France on the one hand, and the utter dependency generated by an affluence that is not tied to local productivity on the other.

Relative affluence in Martinique, then, has come at the cost of dependency. Many local scholars and intellectuals complain that Martiniquais are developing a dangerous mentality of entitlement and that an entire generation of residents now depends more on French handouts than on its own initiative. They argue that this dependency is so broad and deep that it virtually precludes the possibility that islanders will ever consider becoming an independent people. The effect of these psychological burdens, they argue, defines the insidious character of neo-colonization—to render a people apathetic in the face of their own inferiority and impotence.

In the realm of the economy, economic dependency, which here occurs as a wide safety net coupled with artificially high standards of living, creates an unearned base income that may encourage the notion that it is possible to earn more without accepting the "cost" (i.e., in taxes) of getting it. Furthermore, with improved standards of living amidst sliding economic productivity, it is not surprising that some of my informants expressed a sense of detachment from the rules of economic legitimacy. Perhaps this paradox holds the key to understanding how, indirectly, economic dependency has produced an exaggerated need for informal economic activity. For not only do the unemployed have to find a way to earn income, but those who have jobs are often not satisfied with this income alone.

PART TWO

Frameworks

THREE

Cultural Economies

RELATING SOCIAL VALUES
TO ECONOMIC THEORY
IN MARTINIQUE

> ANY [ECONOMIC] MODEL . . . WHETHER
> LOCAL OR UNIVERSAL, IS A CONSTRUCTION
> OF THE WORLD AND NOT AN INDISPUTABLE,
> OBJECTIVE TRUTH ABOUT IT. THIS IS THE
> BASIC INSIGHT GUIDING THE ANALYSIS OF
> ECONOMICS AS CULTURE.
>
> —Arturo Escobar, *Encountering Development*, 1995

My first day in Martinique, a charming young man helped me navigate the French public phones. I laughed at my ignorance, he laughed at my laughing, and before I knew it, we were off on an unexpected journey that involved the next several hours. The story of my encounter with Patrick is relevant for understanding the cultural dimension of Martinique's informal economy. But before I tell this story, and before we zoom in to see what has cultural meaning in the fascinating and complex world of Martinique, I want to show how many anthropologists have come to view economies as cultural in nature. The first part of this chapter is thus laid out like a series of stepping stones, designed to help unacquainted readers manage academic waters that go much deeper. The relationship between anthropological studies and economic theory has long been troubled, and remains so today. But it is my hope that the case of Martinique's cultural economy will contribute to a more unifying perspective of the value of both anthropology and economics in understanding human behavior. As we will see, cultural motivations to work off the books in Martinique interact with a host of economic realities compelling people to do so.

What difference does it make how local people think about their undeclared activities? To most development planners and economists, the "ideology" of noncompliance is not important: the point is that people respond to the incentives created by too much regulation or too few legitimate opportunities. Because in their view these "structural" realities spawn informal economies, it is logical to assume that the way to manage these economies is through structural-level inputs.

For anthropologists, however, the question concerns not *that* people earn off the books, but rather *how* they do it: what kinds of cultural factors channel their choices, how people explain what they are doing, and what these activities might mean besides income. If the *way* people earn undeclared income relates to a system of local values, then any attempts to alter behavior or "harness" informal operators without consideration of such values are unlikely to succeed. In our society, local values do not provide validation for people's undeclared income schemes or tax avoidance. Except for the small jobs that people do for cash, like babysitting, yard work, or house cleaning, most cheating on taxes takes place quietly and alone.[1] Here, there is no widespread pattern of work off the books and there is no status derived from one's ability to act outside the law to earn

more money.[2] In Martinique, the game is different.

ECONOMICS AND ANTHROPOLOGY—
FINDING CULTURE IN ECONOMY

When North Americans think about the "economy," they are likely to think about the cost of things they want to do or buy, whether their jobs are secure, how their investments are doing, and what the future holds for their children. These individual concerns are important to US economists as well, for modern economic theory, known today as "neoclassical economics," is strongly tied to western ideas about the importance of individual desires and actions to fulfill them.[3] The central assumption in neoclassical economics is that individuals make "rational" (calculating) choices in order to maximize their own self-interest. Until recently, most economists also assumed that an individual's self-interest concerned material gain. Individuals were seen to make choices that would best satisfy their own material wants for the least effort.[4]

By the 1960s, problems with neoclassical assumptions about human nature had emerged as anthropologists tried to apply the logic of western economic systems to non-western societies. Where neoclassical theory assumed that choices are individual, that "wants" are material, and that economies can be analyzed as a separate domain from other domains of life, anthropologists like George Dalton and Marshall Sahlins claimed otherwise. Positioning themselves in contrast to the dominant "formalist" logic of economic theory, these "substantivist" economic anthropologists asserted alternate logics to neoclassical theory.[5] Substantivists were inspired by their own research findings as well as those of earlier anthropologists like Bronislav Malinowski, who had conducted fieldwork with the Trobriand Islanders off the east coast of New Guinea. Malinowski claimed that Trobrianders were rational, but motivated more by social concerns of prestige than by material interests.[6]

The ideas of Hungarian economic historian Karl Polanyi were especially important to substantivists. Polanyi argued in the 1950s that economic behavior in non-capitalist societies followed a different logic, not a logic oriented to maximizing an individual's self-interest.[7] Economic anthropologists in the substantivist camp built on Polanyi's ideas and eventually concluded that even in capitalist societies, economic behavior was socially embedded in institutions and social relations.[8]

Cultural
Economies

Substantivists challenged the assumptions of formalist economics in several ways. First, if a person's status in a given society depends on his or her ability to fulfill kinship obligations or other social expectations, for example, then the economic choices these individuals make are not really independent at all; rather, they are choices that are channeled or constrained by others. Second, people do not necessarily strive to satisfy their own material wants, particularly if social status is tied to prescribed behaviors, not material assets. How status is achieved in a given society, said these economic anthropologists, carries implications for how people produce and consume goods and services. In fact, in the strongest version of this substantivist view, economic actions are guided entirely by social ties and social values, making the economy itself a product of social life.

45

The recognition that social values influence economic activities has contributed to shifts in the claims of western economic theory. Most economists now acknowledge that when people make economic choices to "maximize self-interest," they are referring to any number of desired outcomes—material gain, prestige, respect, autonomy, whatever interest an individual chooses to satisfy at a given moment. Yet despite such revisions to neoclassical economics, central tenets remain and insist that economies are discrete domains and that individuals make economic choices as "autonomous decisionmakers."[9] Anthropologist Richard Wilk describes the position of orthodox economists in the following way.

> Many economists have no trouble accepting the general proposition that culture shapes human values [but] although values may be culturally relative, . . . logic and rationality are not; no matter what culture people belong to, they use the same logical tools to translate their values into ordered preferences and then seek to maximize them in a predictably rational way.[10]

The grip of neoclassical economics and its universalist assumptions about individuals and rationality remains firm in the academy, in international development circles, and in public life generally.[11] And, while the formalist-substantivist debate fizzled out without a "winner" in the 1970s,[12] some ideas stuck. Today, most anthropologists (and a small group of institutionally oriented economists) have absorbed the more moderate position of the substantivist argument. For them, economies are not discrete domains of society that can be analyzed apart from the local context or social environment of actors. Economic anthropologists like Marshall Sahlins, Stephen Gudeman, Rhoda Halperin, and Arturo Escobar argue that actors in a given system act economically in ways that are consistent with locally meaningful values.[13] As Escobar states, "The economy is not only, or even principally, a material entity. It is above all a cultural production, a way of producing human subjects and social orders of a certain kind."[14]

The idea that economies are patterned on cultural values is apparent in Sahlins' simple demonstration of food preferences in American society. We eat beef, he says, "not because beef is cheaper to produce or more suited to the ecology of the United States Great Plains, but because of the way American culture symbolically orders and organizes the animal world, making dogs and horses taxonomically closer to inedible humans than to edible cows."[15]

CULTURAL WAYS TO CHEAT THE STATE
IN CENTRALIZED ECONOMIES

To recognize that people make economic choices in ways that serve cultural values is not to say that social values determine economies. Rather, the point is that in the context of particular economic structures, people find ways to honor those social values that may enhance their status or prevent social stigma. A person's social concerns may coincide with material self-interest, as we will see is often the case in Martinique. Sometimes, however, when economic obligations to social relations constitute a central ethic of exchange, the normative system may place limits on the ability of individuals to accumulate resources.[16] Understanding how cultural values may channel economic behavior and affect the opportunities for upward mobility requires a close-up view.

Recent close-up investigations of post-Soviet states and China demonstrate that within similarly oppressive economic structures (modeled on central planning rather than free markets), people must typically cope with product shortages, the high cost of basic supplies, and long lines to purchase ordinary goods. These structural problems compel people to invest energy in securing resources outside the official circuits of state control. What form these energies take, however, draws on culturally meaningful patterns. In other words, economic behavior is governed by more than the laws of supply and demand: how people illicitly tap into the state's distribution system to siphon off goods and services for their private use tends to occur within the constraints of local norms and values. In many of these cases, the role of social relations is of primary economic importance.

On-the-ground studies in these societies reveal how people use culturally familiar resources to survive in places where "nothing is legal but everything is possible."[17] The Russian tradition of *blat*, for example, engages people in securing goods and resources illicitly by soliciting favors from people who are kin, friends, or acquaintances.[18] Although bribery exists and, like *blat*, circumvents formal procedures for acquiring things, it is distinct from *blat* because it involves immediate payoff to someone unknown and is seen as morally unacceptable and dangerous. Also, whereas bribery can be analyzed according to equivalencies of favors in return for cash, *blat* is not easily translated into such equivalencies.

A cultural variation on this pattern has been documented among Kazakstanis, who similarly distinguish impersonal bribes from socially mandated gifts that function to redistribute goods. Unlike bribes, which are viewed as immoral, systematic gift-giving to those in one's social network is regarded as both traditional and necessary in order to avoid public shame.[19] A study of Romanian responses to Soviet controls demonstrated how people took supplies from collective farms in order to increase output on their own. They also avoided the cultural shame of being regarded as stingy when they were short of resources. When they had nothing to offer their friends as gifts, they adapted by not inviting them to their homes. At the same time, it was culturally appropriate to leverage one's ethnic affiliation in order to access political and economic gains, despite attempts by Soviets to suppress these distinctions.[20] Other studies have shown that Chinese populations, both in China and overseas, practice *guanxi*, a system of reciprocity which obligates people to distribute personal economic gains to others in their network.[21]

Each of these examples demonstrates the legacies of substantivist logic: that cultural expectations and social relations shape economic meaning, decisions, and practice. Moreover, they may place limits on an individual's ability to accumulate resources. In the context of centralized economies (and as formal economic logic would argue), the cheating people often engage in is a "rational" response to state controls on the supply of goods. However, economic ideas that narrowly tie rationality to individuals who act alone to optimize their self-interests fall short in explaining the social values that constrain these choices. For this reason, a majority of anthropologists today believe that the local role of cultural values and social institutions cannot be ignored in any robust analysis of economic behavior.

FRAMEWORKS   It is not *that* people cheat, but *how* they cheat that intersects with local values and institutions. In Martinique, onerous French taxes and extensive labor legislation provoke people to keep their side activities off the books. Avoiding compliance is a predictable, rational reaction in overly regulated environments. My argument, therefore, attempts to recognize both universally meaningful structural factors and locally meaningful models of behavior. "Creole economics" refers to the family of local economic strategies that sidestep the legal claims of the French state. Yet, because status in Martinique can derive from being one's own boss and being clever at the expense of the state (attributes of *débrouillardism*), local patterns for avoiding compliance are not only rational, they are also culturally specific.

In short, no matter how oppressive the tax code or labor laws, the factors that move people to cheat the state are not the same factors that drive them to certain forms of cheating over other forms. Like the American choice to eat beef rather than horsemeat, the key is not the biological need to eat but rather, how Americans define food. People in Martinique may be driven to cheat because of the high cost of doing work legally. But there are many options for getting around the system to make money. An ethnographic approach deepens the analysis of economic behavior by helping identify how people define value and choose appropriate strategies. That culture shapes and limits economic action is, therefore, apparent in the specific ideas about what makes sense in a given setting.

INFORMAL ECONOMIES (OR HOW THE POOR BECAME THE SOLUTION)

There is a bewildering array of labels used to identify economic activity that operates outside state regulation. Terms like "informal," "parallel," "underground," "black," or "second" economy are all the more confusing because they mean different things to different speakers.[22] Today, most anthropologists and sociologists, as well as geographers, historians, political scientists, and economists, employ the term "informal economy" to refer to activity that is unregulated and undeclared in a social context in which there are legal requirements for such.[23] But not all illegal income belongs to the informal economy. For example, economic activities such as prostitution or drug dealing are criminal because the productive act itself violates the law. These activities are generally excluded from the designation of "informal" and called by other terms, such as "criminal" or "underground."[24] By contrast, the informal economy is generally understood to involve economic activity that is otherwise legal but not reported.[25] Unlike criminal activities which violate the law at the point of production, informal activities violate the law at the point of exchange, where taxes are not paid. Thus, such obviously legal activities as shoe repair, massage therapy, or private tutoring become illegal (and a part of the informal economy) when the income earned from the exchange of such production is not reported.

The legal systems in many countries like the US and France distinguish between those activities that are inherently illegal (e.g., prostitution, smuggling), and thus prosecuted in the courts, and those that involve an IRS violation (unreported income), which are resolved by negotiations

Cultural
Economies

49

with the federal bureaucracy. Distinctions between these types of activities are widely accepted among social scientists,[26] and also among development planners.[27]

What I am calling "creole economics" in Martinique is usually consistent with activity I have defined as "informal" rather than "criminal." I will demonstrate in later chapters using specific case studies how, on occasion, even criminal activity may occur within a morally defensible realm, so long as there is no "victim" who is deemed hurt by one's activity. I will also show how local views about what is moral and what is immoral contribute to the cultural shape of Martinique's informal economy.

The idea of informal economies grew out of Keith Hart's on-the-ground anthropological research in Africa, published in 1973. Hart's study of urban dwellers in Ghana demonstrated that the urban poor, assumed to be "unemployed" by the state, were in fact busy generating income to live on. They simply were not declaring it.

Hart's work helped to reverse an assumption of modernization theory

and alter the course of development policy in the Third World.[28] What had been called the "modern" sector (where people were employed) and the "traditional" sector (where they were not) became, for Hart, the "formal" sector of employment and the "informal" sector of employment, respectively. Today, international development planners recognize that informal economies exist in every society with codified law and systems of taxation. Anywhere the state imposes regulations or demands part of the income generated by individuals, there will be some who attempt to evade the costs of compliance, if only to survive.

Invigorated by Hart's findings, economists and planners quickly seized what they saw to be a promising new avenue for solving the trenchant problems of poverty in developing countries. The poor could no longer be seen as marginal, unemployed, and unassimilated members of urban society who posed obstacles to modernization efforts. Almost overnight, these same people were reframed as productive and creative economic actors who might provide sorely needed solutions to economic stagnation.[29] Through proper interventions and nurturing (and sometimes by legalizing these actors' economic activity), informal operators in a developing country would be empowered to unleash their latent economic potential. In so doing, they would relieve their own poverty and fire the "engine" of national growth and productivity. By the late 1970s, policy initiatives were springing into place to "harness" the energy of informal operators—street traders, dressmakers, and cobblers—turning them into legitimate entrepreneurs.[30] The excitement created in development circles about reorienting intervention efforts to a micro level helped stimulate more research on the informal economy.

In the three decades since Hart's work was published, studies have shown that for cities in Africa, Asia, and Latin America, as much as 60 to 80 percent of total economic activity can be attributed to the informal economy.[31] According to a 2002 document by the International Labour Organization, "In the world today, a majority of people work in the informal economy—because most of them are unable to find other jobs or start businesses in the formal economy."[32] Even development agencies now acknowledge that the impacts of neoliberal policies have led to "flexible" work arrangements such as outsourcing and subcontracting, an important factor propelling the growth of the world's informal economies.[33] The practical as well as theoretical implications of such a global phenomenon have attracted the attention of economists, development planners, and social scientists from every field of study. Many of these scholars have focused their work on attempting to relate the extent of informal economic activity in a given society to government policies toward the regulation of labor and capital.[34] Another strongly researched phenomenon shows how informal economies are dynamically linked to formal economies and often, to the larger capitalist world system.[35]

Most studies of informal economies, however, have focused entirely on low-income populations of developing societies. This methodological bias has effectively obstructed from view the interconnections of informal operators across class and the cultural meanings that may encourage informal operators to remain outside government regulation. Variations of informal employment by gender are also limited by their focus on the poor alone.

Through "on-the-ground" research, anthropologists and sociologists have helped put a face on informal economic actors and their strategies and struggles, as well as the nature of their activities. Most have focused their research on informal operators who share a particular occupational niche, like street trading, or who comprise an ethnic enclave.[36] These efforts have led to many insights about the diversity of small-scale producers, how they produce and market informal goods, how they depend on formal sector inputs and sales, and how their products may subsidize the middle class and the formal economy by lowering both the costs of labor and the costs of goods.[37] Some anthropological research has specifically focused on explaining how informal operators are adaptive and resilient despite government harassment and local ordinances.[38] Among those whose lives depend completely on informal income, researchers have shown that women, youth, elderly, and minorities are most likely to be poor undeclared workers. As marginalized members of society who frequently lack adequate education, skills, or social networks, these groups are least able to compete for the jobs that are socially valued.[39] Rarely, however, research has shown how informal economic activity operates across class or how it functions as a springboard to upward social mobility.[40]

Nonetheless, the commitment to "developing" the potential of informal economic actors has penetrated development planning circles so thoroughly that today, virtually all major international development agencies are devoting some portion of their resources to targeting poor informal operators. In part, these efforts reflect the goals of poverty reduction, but they also recognize the needs of states to regulate economic activity in order to collect taxes and control labor practices. Underlying these initiatives, therefore, is a pair of related assumptions: (1) those who operate informally, off the books, are overwhelmingly poor, low-skilled people who are unable to find formal employment;[41] and (2) informal operators are often incipient entrepreneurs who can "graduate" to the formal economy given proper inputs.[42]

With few exceptions, the focus on the urban poor in both scholarly studies and development planning has had the effect of emphasizing that it is the poor who pursue informal income because they have no choice. Although the bias that causes planners to tie informal activity to the poor is understandable and even justifiable considering the urgent needs of the world's poor, the assumption limits the understanding of the phenomenon. Compounding the view of informal activities as survival strategies is a related assumption that poor people produce informal goods and services for other poor people. By this logic, if more affluent members of society consume an undeclared good or service, if they act as the patron in a patron/client relationship, the vertical linkages binding them to lower-income people would remain undetected. Basic economic sense holds that monetary exchanges require at least two parties—a buyer and a seller. So it is with the informal economy: to create income, every undeclared activity requires a market, a buyer of the service or good for sale. Without knowing who buys as well as who sells informally, the picture of informal economies is incomplete.

In Martinique, the hidden patron/client relationships connecting informal buyers and sellers across classes build strategic economic bonds and loyalties. Missing this piece of a local picture can complicate universal understandings and jeopardize targeted interventions. Poor, full-time informal operators are well aware that the affluent participate actively and often in the informal economy. Moreover, the regular involvement of middle- and upper-income people in undeclared activities helps reinforce the perception that there is no particular benefit to earning an income through strictly legitimate means. Yet for whatever insights such locally sited research may provide, anthropological studies of economic behavior are not generally read by development planners, who are guided by their own economic models and policies.[43]

Cultural
Economies

The value of looking at academic research about local economic contexts is apparent in what planners identify as "sustainable" projects, those that continue to work without degrading the long-term viability of resources. The need for sustainability is increasingly urgent for, as anthropologist Arturo Escobar notes, "instead of the kingdom of abundance promised by theorists and politicians in the 1950s, the discourse and strategy of development produced its opposite: massive underdevelopment and impoverishment."[44] Sustainable development projects share a key factor: they are compatible with local values, grounded in everyday understandings of what life is about. Michael Cernea, a senior-level sociologist at the World Bank, published a World Bank discussion paper entitled "Using Knowledge from Social Science in Development Projects." In this paper, Cernea shares a candid analysis of the relatively few project successes by the Bank.[45] What did these projects have in common? Unlike the failed projects, he asserts, this small number of successful projects each involved a consideration of social and cultural factors on the front end of project design. Others inside the development establishment are beginning to agree with Cernea that the dominant development paradigm, which applies western technology and western goals without consideration of local context, must change.[46]

Successful, homegrown lending projects targeted to informal operators, like the Grameen Bank in Bangladesh[47] and the Self-Employed Women's Association (SEWA)[48] in India, have inspired development planners to target interventions at the local level. However, the successes of both these local development efforts are built on economic attitudes and practices that correspond to a particular cultural context. In these cases, local factors are not only accommodated: they are the very basis for the way in which the micro-level loans are conceived and made available. Thus, the secret to their success is not merely offering low-cost loans to single individuals, but realizing the way in which the economic behavior of local people is wedded to the social fabric of their particular society.

Yet, as anthropologist Daniel Miller elaborates in his study of the volatile and culturally embedded forms of capitalism in Trinidad, "the World Bank is notoriously insensitive to the particularities of any given region. Since the solution is always going to be the same, they need almost no knowledge about the particular local problem".[49] Considering the important differences in cultural contexts across developing societies, it is unlikely that what makes a successful entrepreneur in one society will also make a successful entrepreneur in another.

CARIBBEAN HISTORIES AT WORK
IN ECONOMIC BEHAVIOR

There are not yet cross-class studies of informal economies in other Caribbean societies,[50] but key cultural features of Martinique's informal economy echo patterns observed in other ex-slave societies of the Caribbean. These patterns include (1) seeking autonomy and being one's own boss, and (2) pursuing mixed economic strategies, or "multiple livelihoods."

Caribbean studies focused on economic behavior demonstrate that the historical particularity of slavery and sugar plantations has manifested in widespread concerns for personal autonomy. In his cultural geography of West Indian societies, David Lowenthal argues that the severe nature of colonization in the Caribbean left an "overriding sense of individuality" and a desperate need for "psychological autonomy."[51] In a related vein, Bonham Richardson explains that because Caribbean peoples were forced to work the plantations of colonists, it is not surprising that the key economic goal for many today is "personal control" over their own resources.[52] Several contemporary ethnographic studies also demonstrate the value that many Caribbean people attach to being one's own boss.[53] These themes appear in the work of Caribbean literary artists as well. In Patrick Chamoiseau's historical novel *Texaco*, for example, what slaves wanted most after emancipation was personal autonomy, the freedom to work for themselves.[54]

Research in other island societies also indicates that among low- and moderate-income wage earners, there is a common emphasis on maintaining "occupational multiplicity."[55] In a classic work based on 1958 fieldwork, Lambros Comitas observed that the fishermen he came to know in rural Jamaica were engaged in multiple occupations. His findings challenged the conventional wisdom that there were only three types of economic actors in Caribbean settings: plantation workers, farmers, and peasants.[56] And Peter Wilson's seminal economic study of Caribbean life shows how men's reputations on the island of Providencia often depend on their prowess at generating income from multiple sources, which is a way to

Cultural
Economies

55

prove their masculinity in the domain of work.[57] This pursuit of "side" income from an undeclared activity is a documented pattern in Barbados, where Carla Freeman has studied women employed as data entry workers in the offshore infomatics service sector. She says, "Most of the women operators simultaneously engaged in one or more forms of informal income generating activity 'on the side,' including baking and decorating cakes for special occasions, hair styling in their kitchen 'salons,' and buying and selling clothing and accessories to networks of kin, friends and workmates."[58]

As Freeman points out, this work on the side is not necessarily just about money. Some of these pink-collar women share an ambition to open a business in order to "be my own boss."[59] Others, such as long-distance "higglers," who travel abroad to buy and bring back clothing for sale, reported that even if they didn't make money, the pleasure of "getting out there" was worth it.[60] According to another study, West Indians who migrate to the US also demonstrate their orientation to keeping multiple jobs.[61]

The patterns associated with being one's own boss and holding multiple occupations have largely been drawn from studies of poor- and moderate-income groups in Caribbean societies. Very little social science research has considered the economic values and practices of Afro-Caribbean peoples who are situated in the middle and upper classes.[62] The findings I discuss in this book suggest that creole-derived "cognitive orientations"[63] toward economic autonomy also ring true among people in more affluent class positions in Martinique.[64]

MEETING PATRICK AND DISCOVERING
THE CREOLE DÉBROUILLARD

Anyone who presumes to knock on someone's door to ask them to please detail the ways they earn illegal money is, well, ambitious. But on a prefieldwork site visit to Martinique, something happened that convinced me that my research topic was not only timely, but possible. I had arrived late one evening, so the following morning offered the first opportunity for me to look at the place I had chosen for my fieldwork. I ventured out from the modest, park-front hotel that I had found through a guidebook. Not knowing a soul in Fort-de-France, or anywhere else on the island, I knew it would be up to me to strike up conversations and get myself around during this quick ten-day visit. I set out to explore the area around the hotel: the famous Parc Savane, the waterfront and dock for small boats, clothing boutiques, gift shops and cafes clustered around the grand old post office and town library, French banks and moviehouses. But the streets were still; the shops, offices, and newsstands were all closed. Downtown Fort-de-France on a Sunday morning was all but empty.

I decided not to worry about what a deserted-looking town meant to my first day and to focus instead on making a call home. I had come equipped with French coins, but the public street phones had no slots to receive them. The longer I poked the odd-looking machine for hidden slots, the more anxious I grew. Frustrated by my annoying ignorance of how to use a French public phone, I began to worry about bigger issues: where would I eat, how would I meet people, what I was doing here? I fought self-doubt as I poked at the contraption again and again, hoping for a revelation to strike me.

Suddenly, a man sped up in a four-door blue Peugeot, exited and strode with confidence to the trio of French phone booths. He smiled, instantly grasping my state of need. "Je peux vous aidé? Vous voulez faire un appel?" (Can I help you? Do you want to make a call?) He had his calling card ready, slid it into the only mouth the machine offered, and handed me the receiver. "Tell the operator the number you want and it will go through." Thank god, I thought. Things aren't so bad. If a complete stranger is willing to lend me his card for an international call, this place must be OK.

But the encounter wasn't over. The young man made his call and wandered off. After I hung up, I looked around. There he was, strolling down a side street coming toward me. I noticed this time his golden-brown skin, his designer jeans, and smart leather jacket; he was the very model of the style-conscious, urban Martiniquais. He was in his early thirties I guessed. He asked if everything worked out all right with my call. Yes, yes, I answered gratefully. "So, what will you do today?" he asked, perhaps sensing my indirection. Of course, the deserted streets made me wonder what was possible to do today. "Would you like to come to lunch at my house? I know my mother would be pleased to meet an American girl. I can show you a bit of the countryside. We live in Carbet, near St. Pierre. There's not much to do on Sundays in town. It's dead."

I was aware that he might have more than lunch on his mind, but having no other prospects for the day, I decided to take my chances. What

other options did I have, I rationalized.
As it turned out, the adventure was exactly
what I needed to convince myself that the study I was contemplating
doing—how the informal economy works across classes—was a very

good idea.

Patrick preferred to drive fast, testing his control on each winding curve as we hurtled our way up the dramatic northern coastline to Carbet. When we arrived in the small fishing town, he announced that there would be a few quick stops before we got to his house. Uh-oh, I thought, I should have known. But the stops had nothing to do with me.

"Come," he said, after parking on a hill clustered with brightly painted and carefully tended wood frame homes. He popped the trunk lid and pulled out three large suitcases. I was mystified. What was he up to? He rang the doorbell. A young woman with a lovely amber face answered. She went to call the others. We were invited to sit in the upright chairs of the foyer as Patrick lay each suitcase on the floor. He unzipped each of them before folding back the cover on any. After the ritual presentation to the three teenage daughters of the household, I was eager to see the contents. He pulled things out on hangers, a few at a time: sexy two-piece bathing suits, very much à la mode.

He later explained to me that he had just returned from a trip to Brazil, where he had loaded up his suitcases with bathing suits. Now he would visit as many of his contacts as he needed to in order to sell the 200 or more suits he had returned with. The girls in this household sighed quietly as the father sat in judgment over each set they tried on and modeled. With his blessing, the three girls decided on five suits between them. I didn't ask how much they paid, but Patrick said they were less than half the cost that they would have to pay to buy such fashionable suits here. "We all win this way," he said, noting that the profits to him were also substantial. "I can pay for the trip and make good money, too, by selling to my friends." I asked him if he always gets bathing suits. "No, sometimes jeans or other clothes. And sometimes I go to Venezuela."

The other stops were not as lucky for Patrick. One household was empty; one said he would have to come back next month when there was more money. But he was undeterred. "I have friends everywhere—Fort-de-France, St. Pierre, in the south."

Patrick earns his "regular" income from a formal sector job as a wholesaler of fish to local fish retailers, but he has been clandestinely importing and selling clothes for many years. "I'm a *débrouillard*" (a cunning economic achiever), he said, with a knowing smile.

The experience with Patrick reassured me that I was on the right track with my research plans. Clearly, in Martinique the poor were not alone in working off the books, as the economic literature had suggested. And if Patrick was any indication of how others felt, work on the side was a source of pride, perhaps even a source of prestige. I could see, for example, how Patrick's house calls were helping to build and reinforce his social networks. At the same time, this side work positioned him as an autonomous operator, someone smart enough to pull off a clever idea. Yet, for as much as I could see that Patrick enjoyed his solo earning scheme immensely, it was surely not the easiest path for earning extra money. Traveling to Brazil took money. Locating the bathing suits took time and planning, and selling them locally took contacts and more time. Only much later would I realize that this chance encounter on a Sunday morning had laid before me many of the clues it would take months of future fieldwork to piece together.

I returned to Martinique the following summer to begin my research. As I will elaborate in later chapters, my long-term fieldwork helped reveal how the creole usage of the French term *débrouillard* both carries a powerful meaning for islanders and is commonly associated with people who earn undeclared income. Some of these people, like Patrick, self-identify with the crafty creole *débrouillard*; some clearly do not. Others believe they sometimes act with *débrouillardism* by displaying qualities of economic cunning, but do not consider themselves true *débrouillards*.

In later chapters, I elaborate on the variations in local understandings of *débrouillardism* and show how these understandings correspond to the practice of creole economics across class (Chapter 6) and gender (Chapter 7). In the rest of this chapter, I will outline the many ways in which an economic actor like Patrick reveals his commitment to certain cultural values.

MARTINIQUE'S INFORMAL ECONOMY: NOT JUST SURVIVAL

Martinique's informal economy is interesting because it is not primarily a phenomenon of survival, as most development economists and lending agencies assume. Nor does it more than superficially resemble the informal economy of continental France, despite identical economic loopholes and political structures. In metropolitan France, as in most western industrialized states, including the US, informal economies involve mainly underreporting income and tax fraud.[65] In Martinique, creole identities emphasize the display of autonomy and cleverness (as I will elaborate in the next two chapters). Because these values compel many people in Martinique to perform undeclared work on the side, the contours of the informal economy here are discernibly creole.

Patrick's entrepreneurial instincts are not only about taking initiative and making money—he also works to bolster his reputation for worldliness and for cleverness. By displaying transnational connections, economic cunning, and personable charm to a wide circle of people, Patrick builds loyalty among his buyers, whether he is selling clandestinely imported swimsuits or Levis or sneakers. Patrick has no interest in transforming his import activity into a legitimate storefront business, for the very sources of status he seeks depend on operating illicitly.

Suppose, then, that the informal economy in Martinique involves people who are not only concerned with earning income but, like Patrick, are also concerned with demonstrating economic cleverness and *débrouillardism*. How can we recognize the cultural values that give rise to Patrick's concerns? What is it about *débrouillardism* that works to enhance a person's social ties and local reputation?[66] I will explore these ideas more fully in later chapters, but there are three points I want to make here.

First, in Martinique, individual profit-making schemes have grown up alongside the oppressive and controlling institution of slavery as forms of resistance: escape channels for exercising personal autonomy and freedom. Indeed, the positive value placed on undeclared side work expresses a longstanding orientation to *débrouillard* behavior that is undeclared, profit oriented, autonomous, within moral limits, and, generally, productive. What people do to generate informal income tends to reflect these values. The pride alone that Martiniquais express in their undeclared work provides a telling contrast with how people in "western" societies generally hope to avoid exposure for theirs.[67]

Second, the view of informal economies as dominated by people simply trying to survive has led some development agencies to conclude that the undeclared activities of affluent populations are different in kind and, thus, effectively unrelated. This assumption is misleading.[68] What I found was that middle- and upper-income people in Martinique are not operating in some "other" informal economy. The more affluent not only sell professional services and high-end merchandise to each other off the books, they also frequently operate as the buyers of undeclared work and goods provided by lower-income members of the society. Just as the regular, formal economy is built on a market of buyers and sellers, the informal economy also represents a market of buyers and sellers. Extensive vertical linkages connect affluent buyers to lower-income sellers (see Figure 2 in Chapter 6). Thus, in Martinique, and probably in many other societies, it is inappropriate to treat rich and poor activities in the informal economy as unlinked phenomena, even if the scale of their earnings differentiates them.

Figure 1 shows how undeclared earnings vary by the socioeconomic status of households. Total informal earnings are calculated on the basis of both the income generated by households from selling undeclared goods and services and the savings generated by a household's purchase of lower-priced informal labor and goods. And while this graph makes clear that the proportion of undeclared earnings to total household income is

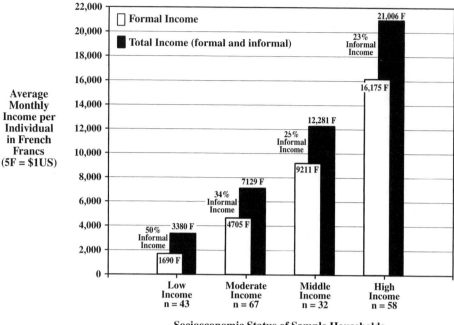

Relationship of Official, Formal Income to Actual Income Earned

Average Monthly Income per Individual in French Francs (5F = $1US)

- □ Formal Income
- ■ Total Income (formal and informal)

Low Income n = 43: 50% Informal Income, 3380 F, 1690 F

Moderate Income n = 67: 34% Informal Income, 7129 F, 4705 F

Middle Income n = 32: 25% Informal Income, 12,281 F, 9211 F

High Income n = 58: 23% Informal Income, 21,006 F, 16,175 F

Socioeconomic Status of Sample Households According to Cluster Analysis

FIGURE 1 *Relationship of official formal income to actual total income earned as a monthly average for individuals in my sample. For an explanation of the basis for deriving socioeconomic status of households, see Chapter 6, note 2. Discrepancies in the two bars reveal the proportion of income earned from undeclared activity.*

FRAMEWORKS highest in low-income households, the actual amounts of money involved in informal earning are much greater at the highest income level of households (4,831F per month compared to 3,070F in middle income households, 2,424F in moderate-income households, and 1,690F in low-income households).

Finally, as the case in Martinique suggests, low-income informal producers are not necessarily good candidates for the kind of development intervention that would turn them into law-abiding taxpayers. Many value the patron/client networks that connect them to more affluent members of their society. Meanwhile, many who have more economic cushion purposely locate part or all of their economic activity in the informal economy in order to escape state regulation and taxes. This practice allows them to earn not only economic capital, but also social and cultural capital.[69] Generating social capital involves strengthening personal networks, including those that lower-income clients are able to form with more affluent patrons. This social capital is enhanced with the cultural capital earned by the successful *débrouillard*, who works as his own boss, off the books. In Martinique, a person's "reputation" can develop from exhibiting autonomy and cleverness in making undeclared money. Because earning social and cultural capital through *débrouillardism* follows from earning undeclared money, creole cultural values act to validate work outside the law and limit the appeal of strictly legal work.

THE MANY SEDUCTIONS OF INFORMAL EARNING

Cultural motivations to work off the books in Martinique feed easily on the larger French political and economic structures that encourage it. The strong appeal of doing things off the books in the first place can be understood in part as a product of legal incentives and disincentives related to the French system. In Martinique, as in metropolitan France, the economic logic of the French welfare state "pushes" many to seek more income without regard to the tax owed to the state. For one thing, the high cost of legally declaring one's employees (about 50 percent more than the wage itself) leads many employers to make under-the-table arrangements with workers. Often, low-income workers (e.g., single mothers, youth in training, and the working poor) are content with such arrangements since their "invisible" earnings allow them to continue to receive state aid (*les allocations*).

Another set of economic pressures favoring a flourishing informal economy in Martinique relates to the dramatic rise in income and standard of living since the mid-1970s. With the influx of capital from the French state, islanders' sudden prosperity and the modernization of Martinique's infrastructure have been apparent in significant increases in the minimum wage, premium salaries for city and state functionaries (civil servants),[70] and public investment in electrical and water utilities for households in both urban and rural areas of the island. Meanwhile, the high salaries earned by functionaries put pressure on other sectors of employment to increase salaries, especially in quasi-public organizations, banks, and private firms.[71] By the late 1970s and early 1980s, boutiques in Martinique had multiplied, elite new shopping centers had emerged, and luxury car dealerships had found lucrative markets. The BMW dealer told me that his dealership regularly sells more BMWs per capita in Martinique than in continental France.

Encouraged by the availability of public money (if not the availability of formal employment), Martiniquais at all income levels in Fort-de-France have become voracious consumers. Anthropologist Daniel Miller reported similar outcomes following Trinidad's oil boom in the 1970s and 80s. The unprecedented prosperity of Trinidadians became rapidly translated into consumer displays that empowered people to assert their global as well as local identity. According to Miller, Trinidadians "took to affluence like ducks to water."[72] In Martinique, the explosion of consumerism in the last two decades has also led people to deploy consumer goods to signal their modernity in both locally and globally meaningful ways.

Today, for example, people of moderate income levels attempt to secure late-model cars and display chic clothing to project themselves as thoroughly "modern." At middle income levels, consumption patterns reveal that consumer "needs" are ratcheted up to include the latest home appliances, computer gadgetry, and high-end, late-model cars. Even low-income people, who depend on public transport and who rarely have secure employment, manage to purchase their own cell phones. The new expectations set by new levels of living can only be met by having more money. For this reason, a lot of Martiniquais pursue strategies to earn more than their regular wage, whether through undeclared income or through a state-supplied allocation such as the guaranteed minimum income.[73]

CARIBBEAN STYLE AND CONSUMPTION IN MARTINIQUE

Newfound prosperity may translate predictably into new consumer desires and buying patterns. But, what people buy and what it means locally cannot be generalized under the umbrella of any universal patterns. In Afro-Caribbean societies, it is easy to recognize the value placed on clothing, jewelry, hair, and cars.[74] What people buy often reflects an intense pressure exerted by the need to look successful. In Martinique, how people consume reflects a concern for stylish clothing and cars and much less concern for fashionable home furnishings and decor. Few people socialize with friends and acquaintances in each other's homes; it is primarily the affluent who host home-based gatherings. My own impressions, gleaned from visits with people in several hundred homes in and around Fort-de-France, were echoed in the words of a moderate-income man who explained to me in a bemused way:

> Nothing is more important for a Martiniquais than to look good, to look successful. We see each other out, and so what you are wearing, how you look, tells others if you are succeeding in life. People also notice your car. First, it's how you look, then it's what you drive. Do you have a new car? A 4 x 4? We hardly ever see each other's homes. We see each other out—shopping, at the movies, in town, in our cars.

There are good reasons for Caribbean people to invest in their "look." Small island societies of the eastern Caribbean are like fishbowls: they are populated by people whose movements cross each other frequently and produce a kind of "gaze-oriented" environment in which people make note of those around them in public places. In addition, many scholars consider the legacies from slavery to remain a potent "mental map" about signaling individuality. Because slaves were treated as a mass of undifferentiated bodies, forced to work in identical clothes and forbidden to wear hats or shoes, the struggle of a slave to define herself/himself as human took the form of physical adornment.[75] For this reason, some anthropologists reject any inference that the emphasis on fashion and "style" among many Caribbean peoples is a superficial and trivial aspect of social identity.[76] Expressions of identity that are "performed" through personal style are also of growing interest to anthropologists outside the Caribbean, as both *Cultural* Jonathan Friedman and James Ferguson document in their studies of the *Economies* postcolonial Congolese and Zambians, respectively.[77]

Patrick's look signaled his success by reflecting one version of the local emphasis on smart dressing. He wore a leather jacket over a crisply ironed white Oxford shirt, a pair of ironed Levis made to look casually chic with a silver-buckled leather belt, and leather shoes with tassles. He accessorized with gold jewelry (two gold necklaces, one with a cross) and drove a late-model car (a snappy two-door blue Peugoet).

Patrick's "cool" western style is casual but upscale, a look that translates easily in his circles of South American friends and business contacts. More typically, though, in urban Martinique, style-conscious men emphasize a warmer and more masculine appearance. Their look involves softer fabrics made of lush silk or linen in bold, earthtone colors like mustard, olive, burnt orange, and caramel. With pants that drape elegantly from the waist, and deeply open-necked, silky shirts that ripple freely with the breezes, this urban look of success is unmistakably sexualized.

Apart from both of these self-conscious performances of identity, white men in Martinique—including creole *békés* and French metropolitans—dress in a comparatively bland manner, neither crisply professional nor colorfully sexualized. A forty-year-old Afro-Creole mother and airline clerk noted in passing that the dress of white men is "nothing that inspires a second look." Her casual comment reinforced what became patently evident to me in my first few months of life on the island—that Martiniquais dress to be seen, to make an impression.

Women of color in Martinique also set high standards for successful dress. In urban areas especially, professional women's everyday attire tends to involve fabrics of silk, linen, or rayon in vibrant colors. Women wear dresses and skirts that are belted or gathered at the waist. Deep, feminine necklines and styles tailored to fit their curves accentuate their femininity. When they wear pants, it is usually a complete "ensemble" with matching top and slacks. Fitted jeans are increasingly common, especially with snug-fitting feminine tops and high-heeled shoes. The labels and quality of fabric and "fit" vary by class, but the concern with style and sexuality is apparent at all income levels.

To an extent, local patterns of dress may thus reflect the urge toward seeking what Peter Wilson has called "reputation," status tied to creole, rather than European, values.[78] Both men and women of color in Martinique use bold colors and sexualized dress to communicate to each other about what matters. These patterns create notable contrasts with the dress patterns of whites in the society.

Yet the stakes of successful dressing cannot neatly be reduced to a dichotomous quest for local-style reputation or European-style respectability. For as islander income levels rise, colors and styles do not "switch" to some European model; instead they simply reflect more muted shades and more expensive materials. Thus, a person's relative affluence appears to shape the extent to which European standards of respectability may coexist seamlessly within styles that carry local status.

Irrespective of income, people routinely buy on credit. Many informants told me they enjoy buying on credit because, at the time, they per-

ceive it to cost them nothing. Even those who resell merchandise off the
books and without a declared storefront sometimes offer credit purchases
to their clients. One such example is Justin, a successful, undeclared entrepreneur who imports high-end shirts, trousers, blouses, and belts from
Italy, France, and Spain. He sells the goods he finds in Europe out of a van
that he bought with his earnings.

> My clients are middle-income professionals. They want a look that
> other people don't have. They want to avoid showing up to work or to
> a performance with the same outfit as someone else. I find things that
> make them feel special. I have to offer them the chance to pay it out
> over a couple of months. It makes paying for my inventory hard, but I
> have to do it.

Justin's undeclared business illustrates many useful points. First, the fact that I was led to him early on in my research by a senior-level government official amused at my research topic suggests the casualness of local attitudes toward informal work. Second, Justin's van-based operation reflects the invisibility of people who have the financial resources to keep their undeclared activity out of sight from work inspectors or police. And finally, knowing that his clientele is already relatively affluent and in search of new ways to signal this affluence without having to pay retail prices for it suggests both the obsessive local concern to project an identity that translates as stylish and successful and the willing participation in illicit economic activity to achieve just that.

Considering the desire to model high standards of consumption, it is not surprising that outings to malls and retail stores are an event for many Martiniquais. As Emma, one of my middle-income, female informants candidly said,

> If I don't look good or feel good, I don't go shopping or to the movies. If I want to see a movie and I don't want to see people I know, I have to go to the early-afternoon showing on a weekday. Otherwise, it takes me an hour to dress and do my hair. It's a small world here and everyone watches everyone. Word gets around fast.

Over time, I came to realize that I, too, would see people I knew at the large grocery store in Cluny where I usually shopped. Routinely, I encountered people who remembered me from an interview or even a party. Gradually, I fell in step, making the trip to the store less and less often, even for a stick of butter, if I wasn't properly dressed.

The analyst at the Central Bank's distinguished chrome-and-glass building on Boulevard Charles de Gaulle offered a telling perspective on recent consumer patterns. Standing outside the iron gates that surround the building, I indicated to the security guard that I had an appointment. He allowed me entry, but once inside, I was asked again to produce documentation of my identity. The interior space of this government bureau was one of the most elegant I have seen in Martinique. A wide, polished wooden staircase spirals up to the second story offices. Inside the office of the French metropolitan economist with whom I met, there were custom, serpentine wood desks, floor-to-ceiling windows, rich carpeting, and handsomely upholstered chairs.

In responding to my questions about his view of local consumption, Marius Bellance[79] had little to offer since neither he nor most of his metropolitan staff, he said, knew local people; they simply prepared economic reports for France. However, he did share with me an interesting detail he had recently become aware of in researching the context for the high rates of local indebtedness: so many people buy things they cannot really afford that there is a huge repossession market in Martinique, especially for cars. This information confirmed what I had learned from my interviews, in which some people referenced a deliberate, short-term car-buying strategy they attributed to reputation-driven men. In fact, three different moderate-income men (all under age forty) reported to me that their new cars had been repossessed because they could not finish paying for them. I asked each whether he had thought at the time of purchase that he might not be able to make all the payments. The men had different answers, but the point they all agreed on was that whether or not you could keep up the payments, it was worth it to have had a nice car even for a little while. It is no coincidence that, as credit companies have multiplied since the late 1980s, personal debt has reached crisis proportions.[80]

THE LAW WITHOUT JAWS

The local emphasis on certain forms of consumption combines with the local status of displaying economic savvy and independence from a boss. People build status in locally meaningful ways both by earning extra money through work off the books and by modeling the goods this income finances. Enforcement authorities themselves point out that the widespread pursuit of undeclared economic activity in Martinique seems to result from cultural attitudes. Moreover, very few disincentives to operate informally hinder people like Patrick. On the contrary, the weak local enforcement of laws, combined with high French taxes, only encourages people to participate in the informal economy.

In numerous informal conversations, I asked outright why someone would take the risk of violating the law. As a sixty-three-year-old man who works at a local packing company said, "Everybody does it!" His strategy to earn extra income involves a planned system of absences at the plant.

Regularly, he has someone cover for him so he can leave for a half day and pursue other income. He clearly felt no reluctance about his illegal activity; he shrugged, "The people who are supposed to enforce this are just like us, so they close their eyes."

To get a better look at the informal economy in Martinique from the perspective of law enforcement, I conducted interviews with more than a dozen local authorities whose job it is to track down and punish those who violate the law by hiring laborers they do not declare, or by otherwise avoiding taxes through economic practices that the state considers illegal. The primary loophole they exploit is the poor enforcement against such activity.

STATE INSPECTION AGAINST EMPLOYER FRAUD

IN MARTINIQUE,
THERE IS RESPECT FOR
CRAFTINESS . . .

—M. Arnaud, Martiniquais
work inspector

The first level of attempts by the state to control illegal economic activity is situated at the Work Inspection Bureau, known as Direction du Travail under the Ministry of the Interior. When I visited this government bureau, it was housed in an old neighborhood clinic, easily the most modest accommodations of any government office I have seen on the island. The cluster of single-story, bland buildings was filled with people, mostly those looking for work or appealing a penalty. Monsieur Arnaud was the Martiniquais work inspector whose job is to control employers' use of clandestine labor. Before meeting with him, I waited nearly a half hour along with a dozen troubled looking others. We were kept in an outer room, just inside the front door, but away from the sounds of clerks and phones. The room was furnished with nothing but two once-painted wood benches facing each other. I realized as I waited that the sheer scope of this man's job must be overwhelming.

Indeed, in the course of our conversation, M. Arnaud's face filled with the stress and anxiety that, after subsequent visits, I came to recognize as his usual look. He seemed to be an idealistic man, someone who had been beaten down by years of overwork and distress at the impossibility of his task. The problem, said M. Arnaud, is that "in Martinique, there is respect for craftiness and resourcefulness, versus any strong respect for doing what is lawful." For example, he continued,

FRAMEWORKS

70

In the building industry, I don't know of a single clean, legal enterprise. At the very least, they do not declare all their workers. With unemployment so high, employers can find skilled laborers that they can pay less than minimum wage and not declare. This is how they make a lot more profit for their companies.[81]

Another sector dominated by informal labor which has boomed in the last few years is the car repair industry. The scale of abuse leaves M. Arnaud's office grossly underequipped to handle the cases.

> What makes the problem so insidious to control is that so many violations occur in small-scale, decentralized operations. With a staff of only five inspectors to cover all work-related fraud on the island, our team of inspectors presents a very minimal threat to employers who use illegal strategies. Considering the inadequate state resources to confront these problems, all we can really hope to do is track down abuses by larger firms, whose violations are easier to find and monitor.

M. Arnaud went on to discuss other ways in which the deck is stacked against him and his colleagues. Whatever violations they do find, he said, are rarely prosecuted, since the violators make a big show of coming into compliance with the law. He said they simply learn how to hide their illegal strategies better, to better anticipate visits by inspectors. Even if he catches the firm still in violation after they promised to correct the situation, the chance of their suffering a penalty is minimal. He noted that of the seventy-eight cases his office brought to the tribunal level for prosecution that year, only two were prosecuted. In this same time period, nearly 7,000 violations were cited.

With an enforcement system as feeble as this, and punishment sentences so light (fines range from 2,000 to 20,000F, or about $400 to $4,000US; prison terms, two months to two years), the risks do little to discourage those inclined to escape the law. If a company is fined for violations, the cost to them is usually less than the taxes they avoided paying by using undeclared labor. Logic says it does not pay to do things the straight and legal way.

Another factor which contributes to the market for clandestine labor is the willingness on the part of the worker to remain undeclared. With so many people out of work, most laborers are glad to have a job at all and do not wish to press their luck by asking to be declared. Moreover, as of 1995, when comprehensive medical coverage was extended to unemployed citizens, the "costs" of not being declared have been lower. And, as indicated earlier, those who are working at lower-income jobs are inclined to avoid declaring at least some of what they earn so they will qualify for *les allocations* on the basis of their lack of income. Such practices are abetted by a conspiracy of silence, which people mentioned again and again and which works similarly in other sectors of the economy and makes the attempt to control illegal work relations especially difficult.

M. Arnaud showed little sympathy for employers who claim that without resorting to illegal practices that reduce costs, they could not survive. In fact, he is a crusader about trying to correct the perverse economic system he sees in Martinique.[82] Having spent five years doing the same work in metropolitan France, he has a unique perspective from which to evaluate the cultural differences with regard to the respect for economic legitimacy. Speaking as a proud Martiniquais, M. Arnaud still indicated that his job in the metropole had been completely different because the metropolitan French have the habit of being more law-abiding.

STATE TAX COLLECTION AND CONTROL

IT'S A QUESTION OF THE
MENTALITY HERE . . .

—M. Monrose, metropolitan
senior tax official

FRAMEWORKS

Another person with a useful view of fraud Martiniquais-style is Monsieur Monrose, a senior tax official charged with overseeing income tax collection in Martinique. His office is part of the Service des Impots (Tax Bureau), located in a modern government complex in a light commercial area of the middle-income neighborhood called Cluny. M. Monrose is a small, trim, metropolitan man. He wears round glasses and has a tousled head of wavy, graying hair. Fortunately for me, he found my questions intriguing, and indicated more than once that he was pleased to know that an anthropologist was actually trying to understand the widespread phenomenon of unreported income here. We spoke on several occasions. Each visit I dug more deeply into the nature of fraud, the types of penalties that were possible, and the way in which cultural issues played into local patterns. As someone who had spent most of his life in Paris, M. Monrose stressed that the patterns he had seen in his four years in Martinique were unique: "It's a question of the mentality here. It spans all income sectors, and people—individuals as well as businesses—willingly commit fraud."

72

One of the first examples he gave was of functionaries (civil servants) who manage retail concerns on the side. Although the law permits them to be stockholders, they are not legally permitted to run the business or have anything to do with its operation. He said, echoing what I had heard many times from informants, that the way they get around this prohibition is to put the business management in someone else's name, keeping their own names out of all official documents submitted to the state. Generally, the person named as manager knows nothing about running the company and has no actual power. He emphasized that this was not an exceptional situation but, rather, commonplace.

This example points up the difficulty his tax office has in chasing down fraud. He said unless someone reports this kind of offense, his office was simply not staffed to investigate every potential case. Moreover, since Martinique is a "small world" where people know each other, no one is willing to report someone else for fear of retaliation. So, for the most part, he said, the abuses go unchecked. As one middle-income woman reported to me on this topic, "In Martinique, we will lie to save someone, but never to hang him."

M. Monrose did say that since the mid-1980s, the government had computerized its record-keeping systems, so that agencies expected to control fraud—including his tax office, the Direction du Travail (Arnaud's group), and the social security office—can at least have up-to-date, accessible files to work with. One benefit this new system has produced is a lowering of fraudulent applications for state aid. Now people wishing to apply for Revenue Minimum d'Insertion (RMI), a guaranteed minimum wage, for example, have to file a declaration of income, even though they do not make enough to be taxed. It is still possible for them to lie, he said, but it is less likely that they will sign their name and risk a serious penalty to do it.

Cultural Economies

Further questioning, however, revealed the limited scope of this new effort. Monrose noted that despite the new technological management of information, there is a French law forbidding the sharing of computer files across bureaus of control. Called La Commission National Informatique et Liberté (CNIL), the law sets severe restrictions on how computer files can be accessed by agencies which do not originate the files. This makes it entirely possible for someone to be declared with social security, but pay no income taxes, since the two offices of control are separate and do not have efficient ways to share information. M. Monrose continued, "We still do not have a complete picture of a taxpayer—his income and his property."

He also said that unless the abuse was very large scale, his office would not have the resources to investigate. It is simply not empowered as an agency to show up at someone's home and check whether the family lives too well to merit a poverty pension. M. Monrose said that French law, in general, is designed to protect *les droits d'homme* (rights of the individual). Unfortunately, he said, these rights effectively disable the control of fraud.

THE JUDICIAL LEVEL OF PROSECUTION

THE PARALLEL ECONOMY
IS VERY IMPORTANT
HERE . . .

—M. Guillaume, metropolitan
state prosecutor

A third government bureau devoted to controlling illegal economic activity in Martinique is the District Attorney's office. This bureau is located inside the Palais de Justice (Justice Building), which was originally the city hall, a lovely colonial structure in the middle of downtown Fort-de-France. The charm of the building is less apparent inside, where a maze of hallways and stairs leave first-time visitors wandering for clues. Two dreary flights of stairs up, I found the office of the state *procureur* (prosecutor), with whom I had arranged an interview. Monsieur Guillaume tries most of the defendants whose cases involve fraud related to taxes, undeclared income, and undeclared labor. Inside his office, the charm of the building seemed to reemerge—the space was air-conditioned and well appointed, with a massive mahogany desk, lateral file cabinets, and a large shuttered window overlooking the bustle of street traffic below. M. Guillaume is a slight man physically, but his polite and concise manner carried an edge that suggested power and no time to spare. After about forty minutes, it became clear that our meeting was concluding. "*Voilà!*" he then said, punctuating the fact that there was nothing more to say. Indeed, he had explained a great deal about the judicial perspective of undeclared work and other forms of tax evasion.

M. Guillaume is metropolitan and, like M. Monrose, is shocked by the degree of undeclared economic activity in Martinique. And, like both M. Monrose and M. Arnaud, he is overwhelmed by the prospect of trying to control it. He said near the beginning of the interview, "L'économie parallèle est très important ici" (the parallel economy is very important here).[83] How do you know, I asked? He replied,

> Martinique covers about 16 percent of the cost of its imports with exports. Yet this economy is based almost entirely on consumption. With 30 percent of people unemployed, how do people survive? How do they consume so much? You can do the math and realize that all *les allocations* and transfers are not enough to finance this consumption. It's financed through the "underground" economy.

The primary abusers M. Guillaume tries are employers who do not declare their employees. He said that now there are many *syndicats* (unions) to help employees understand their rights under the law. One of these *syndicats* comprises domestic workers, who are traditionally undeclared and very poorly paid. M. Guillaume said that their organizing efforts have helped bring pressure on their employers to declare their housekeepers so that they can have a retirement pension. But among my middle- and upper-income informants who use domestic servants, many complained that they cannot afford to declare them, since the cost to do so would nearly double the price they pay for their services. Moreover, many domestic workers understand that their job may be contingent on their willingness not to be declared.[84]

Penalties for those who produce undeclared goods and services are technically the same as for those who buy undeclared goods or labor. But, M. Guillaume said, it is the employer, not the undeclared employee, who is most at fault in the eyes of his prosecuting team. Like M. Monrose, M. Guillaume emphasized that the philosophical foundation of French law protects the rights of workers. He also believes that many of these clandestine activities are required for local people to survive: "If one tried to eliminate the underground economy here, there would be a revolution."

M. Guillaume agreed that the enforcement system was too weak to act as a deterrent to anyone wishing to earn extra money illegally. It is extremely rare for anyone to go to prison here for evading taxes, no matter how great the offense. Most people get off with a fine, which makes it worth the risk to violate the law.

In sum, the weak enforcement structure against undeclared income relates largely to the institutional approach of the state. In Martinique, discovering and sanctioning economic activity that occurs "off the books" is

Cultural Economies

focused primarily on large-scale abuses of tax law by employers. Yet as this research documents, the scope of tax violations that occur between individuals on a small scale is a significant phenomenon at all class levels. What drives this behavior is only partly about economic and structural factors.

BEYOND ECONOMIC MOTIVATIONS: THE ROLE OF CREOLE VALUES IN CREOLE ECONOMICS

Considering the high taxes on labor, the weak enforcement system against undeclared activity, and the rapid rise in incomes and consumerism in Martinique, it seems that economic motivations alone might well explain the thriving informal economy in Martinique. Because personal indebtedness is higher among well-paid government functionaries than it is among low- and moderate-income earners, it is not surprising that for those with good, formal sector jobs, making extra income on the side is desirable, even necessary. Do middle- and upper-income people thus earn undeclared income because from their perspective they "need" to, and because there is little "cost" to doing so? Let's look more closely at these ideas.

If it were only about money, how could we explain why a certified public accountant chooses to work evenings and weekends for his own clients rather than simply cheat on his income taxes? By fudging his expenses or underreporting rental property income, it would be simple enough to effectively "earn" more. Instead, however, this CPA chooses to perform side work, a strategy that resembles that of a retail plumbing clerk with a high school education who works weekends as his own independent plumber. These two men are situated differently in the local economy, but each uses the resources available to him for social as well as financial gain. Like Patrick, and many of Martinique's informal operators, these men are motivated by goals of becoming their own boss and displaying economic cunning. Being seen as an autonomous and successful economic actor can enhance a person's social networks and translate into cultural capital that men and women recognize and admire, as we will see in the following chapters.

For scholars and policy planners interested in targeting informal economic actors to help stimulate entrepreneurship and power an economy, these kinds of locally based realities carry important implications. With-

FRAMEWORKS

out understanding the non-economic motivations that shape the logic of informal economic behavior in a given setting, attempts to intervene in order to channel or "formalize" the informals will be fraught with problems. Patrick will never be an on-the-books swimsuit salesman because what is meaningful economically in Martinique leads him to make other choices. Because local forms of status place value on certain types of undeclared economic activity, we can identify the ways in which social factors influence informal earning. To review, these factors include the following:

1. *It's good to be your own boss.* In my sample, significant numbers of people in middle- and upper-middle-income groups participate in strategies to earn income off the books, a fact that seems curious for people who might more easily put needed money into their pockets by cheating on income taxes. For many practitioners, the extra income from entrepreneurial moonlighting or working elsewhere during secret work absences offers the satisfaction of "being your own boss," feeling a sense of autonomy in organizing a side activity and maintaining a clientele built through personal networks.

The contemporary male obsession for autonomy from a boss may be traceable to certain forms of repression and resistance that developed on slave plantations, as I discuss more fully in Chapter 5. In brief, the plantation environment that slaves endured created longings for reversing boss/slave roles with the master. These longings forged a set of adaptive values that rewarded prestige to those demonstrating cleverness, intelligence, opportunism, and the pursuit of dignity in the context of one's own "social death."[85] Since abolition, islanders have faced numerous historic upheavals that have continued to challenge their personal autonomy. For this reason, the commonly stated desire for autonomy among informal operators in Martinique today reflects the continuing relevance of values cherished by their ancestors.

Shaping one's informal activity to correspond to local systems of meaning makes sense for people at all class levels. Today, even upwardly mobile, lighter-skinned Martiniquais must confront the intractable obstacle their skin color presents to their claim of Frenchness in the metropole. Whether conscious or unconscious, the exercise of autonomy stands up to history and blunts the cut of continuing racism.

2. *Being your own boss usually involves productive activity.* The search for personal autonomy is consistent with the early ethnographic work in

Caribbean societies in which the phenomenon of "occupational multiplicity" was identified as a primary strategy of survival. More recent studies indicate that these multiple sources of income remain vital for Caribbean residents.[86] In Martinique, the informal economy operates as an economic cushion, one that provides a crucial source of autonomy and income for people across classes.

People who earn undeclared income typically do so by engaging in productive work. People who lay brick, install satellite TVs, upholster furniture, inoculate patients, or breed livestock are all doing work that is inherently legitimate and made illegal only by the fact that they are not declaring to the state their earnings from such activity. Borrowing tools, resources, or company time may be a form of theft, but these resources are used to invest in a productive activity, hardly the conceptual equivalent of criminal activity such as drug dealing or contraband smuggling.

The specific choices people make to realize their desire for more income are a product of the opportunities available to them. For example, a functionary has the time to manage a cultivation business outside of the city and the high-placed local contacts to sell the harvest to a local hospital; a high-end shoe merchant has the supplier contacts in Brazil to import clothes, cell phones, even computers without declaring them at customs; a city's kitchen director is positioned to divert surplus meals and food supplies to family and friends and informal customers; a Peugeot car mechanic easily finds clients to support his private "garage" service on evenings and weekends. The specificity of opportunity helps explain the immense variety in economic activities that operate off the books.

3. Clever economic actors gain status. To work *à côté* (on the side) offers people like Patrick a site for the exercise of authority, cleverness, and autonomy from a boss. Such qualities characterize creole-style *débrouillardism* and confer status on those who demonstrate competence in these areas. As will become clear in later chapters, creole economics is also an entrée into the social world of men. Consistent with other Caribbean scholars who link the exercise of personal freedom and autonomy to an Afro-Creole system of status known as "reputation,"[87] Niels Sampath's research in Trinidad showed how "a strong reputation which emphasizes personal 'freedom' is deemed important in the post-slavery, post-plantation, post-colonial environment.[88] In Martinique, this "reputation-oriented" status in the economic realm depends on illicit, but productive, activity because here one is required to take illegal risks and to demonstrate intelligence and cunning. In these material and symbolic ways, the practice of creole economics represents opposition within complicity, a concept I will take up in the next chapter.

CONCLUSION

As Patrick's case suggests, and as anthropologists have long demonstrated, local economies are not detached sites of production, exchange, and consumption where laws of supply and demand act without reference to local values and beliefs. Economic activity is embedded in a network of relationships and in the values and practices within the local context. Striking evidence of these realities is apparent in virtually every study of culture change.

Consider the last 500 years of outside economic influences on nonwestern cultures: European colonization, planned "modernization" efforts after World War II, and, most recently, the trend among multinational corporations to move production and factories into non-western areas. Wherever major, externally induced sources of economic change have occurred, local accommodations to this change are mediated by other attempts to resist it. In the Trobriand Islands, residents resisted attempts by British missionaries to eliminate their erotic dances during harvest by incorporating such pleasures into inning breaks during the missionary-introduced substitute of cricket. Young women in Malaysia resisted the unfamiliar discipline imposed by capitalist-run factories by becoming possessed by spirits on factory floors and provoking work shutdowns.[89] Slaves resisted their bondage through everyday acts of resistance such as stealing tools, slowing work, feigning illness, or poisoning the master's food.

The point is that local cultures are complex, interconnected webs of meaning. Fundamental change in one area is likely to impose stress on other aspects of culture. For this reason, the application of an outside economic logic (e.g., nurturing incipient entrepreneurs) without comprehension of the inside system risks distortion or, worse, failure. Today, many scholars of development agree that the way in which local societies are drawn into the global forces of capitalism hardly resembles the promise of modernization envisioned in the postwar era. Instead, attempts to incor-

Cultural Economies

porate non-western societies into the logic of western economic systems are likely to be "fragmentary, incoherent, and dissimilar."[90]

Culture does not explain everything. Economic practices clearly respond to the types of political and economic systems that present incentives and disincentives. But the sweeping, bird's-eye view provided by a traditional, neoclassical account of an informal economy can only predict that people will avoid compliance when the regulations are too heavy. To understand more about why people choose the path of noncompliance that they do, we need other insights generated from close-up observations, on-the-ground.

FOUR

Afro-Caribbean Identities

POSTCOLONIAL TENSIONS
AND MARTINIQUE'S
CREOLE *DÉBROUILLARD*

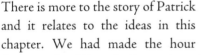

STRIVING TO BE BOTH EUROPEAN AND
BLACK REQUIRES SOME SPECIFIC FORMS
OF DOUBLE CONSCIOUSNESS.

—Paul Gilroy, *The Black Atlantic*, 1993

There is more to the story of Patrick and it relates to the ideas in this chapter. We had made the hour drive north of Fort-de-France in order to have lunch with his mother. The swimsuit interlude was entertaining and, it turned out, a window into the social world of men in Martinique. The next many hours had less to do with Patrick's show of economic cunning than with his fluid transitions between creole and French systems of meaning. Through "code switching," or alternating between languages and the cultural expectations tied to each, Patrick revealed that distinctly creole and French identities remain vital in Martinique today. The recognition of separate but interdependent identities ultimately helps make sense of creole economics.

Patrick's mother was expecting him for the usual Sunday meal. On opening the door, Madame Bonheur's face lifted and her eyes smiled as she looked at me and said, "Ah, son, you have brought a friend?" Her skin was a creamier version of Patrick's deep golden hue. As I looked at mother and son standing next to each other, the biological legacy of Patrick's father was apparent, despite the few social traces he had left on Patrick's life. "Yes, mother, an American girl," he replied, explaining how he had rescued me from the mysterious French public phones in town. Madame Bonheur led us inside, where an ample living space opened onto a smaller dining area one step up. With only two leather chairs in the living area, she quickly secured an upright dining chair with rattan seat and back, scooting it up to the oil-finished wooden coffee table. She instructed each of us to relax in the leather chairs as she vanished into the kitchen.

She returned shortly with a tray holding a bottle of champagne, three *coupes*, and a plate of crackers. Patrick opened the bottle without fanfare and poured. She wanted to hear all about my family and life in my world. She had been schooled in Paris and pointed proudly to the shelves of books she treasured from her days there. After an hour or so of stories about Paris and Texas, Patrick announced that he and I would be leaving and return later. I wondered where he was taking me this time. It turned out we walked only a few blocks to a neighborhood restaurant and bar.

The casual, open-air restaurant was perched right on the water, and following Patrick into the establishment, I could feel the soft ocean breezes on my skin. He led us past the view and the breezes into an enclosed, bamboo-walled bar where a half-dozen young men were comfortably installed at tables. After taking our seats at the bar, I realized that I was the

only woman there. At first, Patrick said little. The buzz of conversation had stilled, leaving a conspicuous quiet. He wanted to order me a tourist's rum drink, but I insisted on having what he was having, a *'ti (petit)* punch, the ubiquitous local drink of white rum, cane syrup, and lime peel, cut to form a round of peel and the smallest sliver of fruit. He ordered a plate of fried cod fritters. Patrick turned to the other men, engaged with them in Creole and gradually the polite hush relaxed into an animated rhythm led by Patrick. Soon, there were belly laughs and snorts. I followed nothing, but smiled all the same, reassured that my presence had not stifled their communication. In fact, Patrick seemed to soak up the attention generated by having arrived with an American guest. He then connected with his friends by telling a story, which, I suspected, yielded yet another type of status.

After our drink, Patrick walked me back to his mother's house. Seamlessly, he shifted back into French and explained to me why his friends had erupted into rounds of laughter at his story. He was recounting an incident that had taken place in the wholesale fish shop where he works. A metropolitan man had come into the shop, surveyed the colorful display of various fish on ice, and then proceeded to endlessly question the merits of different varieties, revealing both his complete ignorance of fish and his social ineptitude as he bogged down the line of customers waiting to place their orders and leave with plastic wrapped, ice-packed specimens. The humor, I decided, must have been clearer in the Creole telling, but it was obvious that no Martiniquais man would have made the same blunder.

Back at the house, I resumed conversing with Madame Bonheur while Patrick disappeared and remained gone till dinnertime, another two hours later. She brought the focus to French literature and cuisine, and pulled off the shelf several books for me to inspect closely as she moved between our conversation and the kitchen. She would accept no help, but by the time we actually ate, I had grown restless with hunger. I imagined an exotic fish would be our centerpiece, since Patrick worked at a fish shop, and of course, fish was so near at hand in this town. But to my surprise, after our course of potato soup, it was beef that arrived on the table, along with a starch called *cristophine* (a local tuber she had boiled, pureed, and prepared with local spices). It was a simple but delicious meal, served with red wine in familiar, French stages.

On the drive back to Fort-de-France, Patrick asked me if I liked classical music and dance. I replied yes, but that actually, I was more interested in local music and theatre. He didn't seem persuaded. I wondered: did he want to signal something about himself by anticipating an American's taste or perhaps make a statement about Martinique's high culture? Was he hoping to show me off in a prestigious, public venue? Whatever he was really asking, I sensed the need to head off any questions about future dates and switched the subject. "So, once you sell all those swimsuits," I asked, "what do you use the money for?" "Oh, for everything I want!" he replied. "I keep an apartment in town where I can entertain my friends. I can take someone to a nice restaurant or to a concert, and the apartment is there for later. I use it to buy nice clothes too, and you already know I like to travel."[1]

For people like Patrick, who seek to prove his worth both as a respected Frenchmen and as a successful Martiniquais, status requires an energetic

mix of assertions. Yet, like other islanders who model Frenchness to varying degrees, moving between French and local systems of meaning occurs
naturally, like code shifting between separate languages that serve different
needs. And, while having a good job or taking a woman to a fine restaurant
can earn status in both French and creole systems, often the values and
meanings of each system remain distinct, and at times they are in conflict. For this reason, local identities are not best described as "hybrid."[2]
Rather, my experience suggests that Martiniquais carry simultaneously
distinguishable or "plural" identities: part creole, part French, and, to the
extent that cultural meanings overlap, part blended. For just as French
Creole and French remain distinct languages, mutually unintelligible to
one another, and used separately,[3] so creole and French identities remain
largely distinguishable from each other.

Creole identities are themselves an invention of distinct African and
European cultural influences, as well as more recent influences from Indian, Syrian, Lebanese, Chinese, and other migrants to the area. The meaning and implications of mixed identities has become a central concern in
postcolonial studies, leading many scholars to consider the Caribbean region as the world's most useful metaphor for the cultural fragmentations
and fusions that are rapidly characterizing other postcolonial areas of the
world.[4] In this chapter, I will discuss the "miracle of creolization" within
the Caribbean,[5] the daily practices and domains of life that became animated by these creolizing forces, and the efforts of local intellectuals and
outside scholars to grapple with the meaning of creoleness in the context
of postcolonial relations, and, in particular, Martinique's increasing assimilation to France. Finally, I will show how the creole version of *débrouillardism* in Martinique points to the continuing separation of creole and French
identities, leading us into the territory of creole economics.

LOCATING THE CREOLE CARIBBEAN

Like volcanic eruptions that form brand new earth, creole societies of the
Caribbean were fundamentally new constructions spewed out of both resistance and accommodation to alien pressures from which there was no
ready escape. In the context of the longest-running and most brutal labor
system in human history, New World slaves produced and reproduced

adaptations to endure and to resist the indignities of their shrunken humanity. The New World phenomenon of creolization was thus provoked by circumstances unique in world history: the forced displacement, transatlantic relocation, and lifelong enslavement of millions of Africans at the hands of a few thousand Europeans. For nearly two centuries of slavery, "creole" adaptations were born from this collision of African cultural systems and New World impositions. These new constructions of creole thought and practice permeated every aspect of life.

Creole identities continue to shape the way Caribbean peoples tell stories, play sports, establish households, and perform the arts. In the case of Martinique, resilient creole identities that were forged in history continue to evolve in relation to powerful and enduring connections to France. The French identities that residents of Martinique can claim are thus negotiated through their own creole identities. The complex relationship of Martiniquais people to their adopted "motherland," France, is a relationship that feeds creole economics. To clarify this situation, we need to look inside the islanders' creole world.

The term "creole" means many things, especially in popular culture. In the US, "creole" is a term people associate with a type of food preparation or a style of language. Many associate the term with New Orleans jazz and jambalaya, and a local dialect that is charming but hard to follow. In many areas of Latin America, creole is an ethnic term that refers to someone of European ancestry who is born and raised in the Americas. In the Caribbean, a "Creole" person also refers to someone who is native born and raised in the islands, but irrespective of ethnic background. "Creole" in the Caribbean context thus applies to the *békés* of Martinique, the white *Afro-Caribbean* descendants of slaveowners, as well as to the descendants of their slaves *Identities* and to others who have grown up in creole society. The origin of the term is in fact Portuguese, where "*criollo*" simply means "raised in the home."[6] I use the term creole in ways that match Caribbean usage: to designate homegrown in the islands, including people who are born and raised here, folktales that got passed on during slavery, types of food and food preparation, performance styles, music styles, religious traditions, and plantation-derived language patterns. These creole phenomena incorporate African and European elements, but are wholly neither. My central point in this book argues for the extension of creole life to include the realm of economics when economic behavior fulfills values associated with creoleness.

THE EMERGENCE OF CREOLE IDENTITIES:
WHAT PART AFRICAN?

The origin of creole identities sprang from life on the plantation, where ordinary Africans, captured and transported to the Americas against their will, faced traumatizing changes. Slaves were made to submit to brutal labor regimes and to endure severe alienation from all they had left behind: family and kin, community ties, orienting rituals, recognized hierarchies, and the security of being surrounded by others speaking their native language. On the New World plantations, slaves from different language and culture areas were thrust together and forced to reinvent the meaning and strategies of survival: linguistically, culturally, and economically. For the more than 200 years that slavery endured in Martinique, slaves adapted in areas of work and worship, song and folktale, courting patterns and status hierarchies. These inventions—Old World knowledge and practice adapted to New World realities and European influences—became known as "creole" culture. Because of these painful and long-term adaptations required by slaves to meet the demands of New World life, creole cultures cannot be understood as simply a mosaic of reconstituted African ethnicities. Instead, plantation histories forged creole societies into irreducibly new cultures, as bound up in European as they were African influences.

In the last fifty years, scholars have advanced the understanding of the role of African influences in contemporary Caribbean societies. In the 1940s, anthropologist Melville Herskovits and sociologist Franklin Frazier argued respectively that survivals of African culture did or did not exist;[7] we now admit a more nuanced reality. Our current understanding of the role of Africanness in Caribbean societies remains indebted to the work of Sidney Mintz and Richard Price, who suggest that the evidence for African influences need not be reduced to concrete "survivals" such as food and music. Their more robust approach recognizes the continuity of African-based "cognitive orientations," or mental maps that have contributed form and meaning to creole adaptations.[8]

The model proposed by Mintz and Price uses the dramatic evidence of creole languages and cultural inventions to position New World creativity at the center of Caribbean social analysis. Manifestations of such creativity argue against the view that coherent African "ethnicities" remained viable in the New World context.[9] The extreme cultural and linguistic diversity of West Africans on New World plantations suggests that whole African languages and cultures could not have survived. But, as their model suggests, the diversity of African peoples certainly contributed to the many forms of creolization. Sometimes, they argue, these creole forms involve primarily a synthesis of ideas and practices drawn largely from the different African groups represented, resulting in what Price calls "inter-African syncretisms."[10]

Slaves thus invoked the resources of deeply held African sensibilities and, to varying degrees, incorporated these underlying principles of meaning into their new lives on the plantation. Yet the endurance of certain African-derived principles among slaves was incomplete and contingent, as was their integration of European forms. As Mintz noted, "Caribbean communities exhibit neither the elaborate linealities of African kinship on the one hand, nor the town meeting atmosphere of New England on the other."[11] Increasingly today, scholars are approaching the processes of creolization as phenomena that vary considerably in form and timing according to precise circumstances and settings.[12]

In the development of New World creole languages, for example, most linguists recognize important contributions from native African languages spoken by slaves, though the nature of this contribution varied according to local factors.[13] Unlike ordinary languages, which typically evolve gradually into new languages, creole languages emerged in response to a rupture in the natural course of language development, a "linguistic violence."[14] The different native African languages these captives spoke shared common rules of syntax and grammar, but they were mutually unintelligible. In order to communicate, fresh slaves (known as "bozals") captured from many language areas of West Africa were often forced to learn a rudimentary pidgin on the coasts of West Africa and in the holds of slave ships.

Through the process linguists call "creolization," a rudimentary contact pidgin language became elaborated into a fully complex "creole" language in a remarkably rapid time frame. Linguists debate exactly how creole languages emerged from pidgins,[15] but unlike pidgins, creole languages become the native language for many speakers.[16] Once creole languages had emerged as a mix of European and African contributions, experienced slaves taught the newly arrived bozals the local plantation language during their "seasoning" period.[17] Since a single plantation might comprise bozals speaking a dozen or more distinct native languages, the new plantation language of Creole supplied the vital link of communication, both among slaves and between slaves and master.

Many linguists hypothesize that elements of the native West African languages of slaves can be identified in Creole grammar, while the languages of the dominant planter class comprise the more visible contributions to Creole vocabulary.[18] Although these ideas remain debated, Creoles in the French-, English-, and Dutch-held areas exhibit such distinctive vocabulary that they are not mutually intelligible. Meanwhile, the relatedness of French, English, and Dutch Creoles is apparent in many shared aspects of syntax and grammar.

Apart from language, many other aspects of creole culture appear to draw part of their energy from African-based "mental maps" as well as from European-based models. Contemporary belief systems such as Vodou, Santería, and Candomblé reveal creole syncretisms (blends that imply new forms) of African and European content. Adaptations to New World pressures forced many slaves to worship their gods in a clandestine manner. Depending on the length of colonization and the demands placed on slaves to convert to Christianity, the belief systems that emerged among slaves in the New World varied. The short tenure of French colonization in Haiti, for example, gave rise to only superficial adherence to Catholicism as slaves worshipped their own deities from the pantheon of West African gods using the Catholic saints as substitute icons. The practice of Haitian Vodou is recognized today as far more African than European in form and content.

In those areas with long-running French colonization, a deeper acceptance of European Catholicism seems to have resulted, though without erasing separate forms of belief. While living in a low-income neighborhood near the heart of Fort-de-France, I learned that alongside many people's rather unenthusiastic commitment to orthodox Catholicism (learned by and passed down from their ancestors during French colonization), there also exist strongly held, African-inspired beliefs in sorcery. In time, I came to realize, as others have,[19] that the coexistence of apparently incompatible systems of belief resulting from colonization do not necessarily compete; nor are they contradictory. Instead, for many local people, irrespective of socioeconomic status, these distinct systems of belief simply coexist, offering alternative sources of supernatural power for the individual at different moments. After several months of residence in this neighborhood, I was taught to recognize certain reclusive neighbors as effective sorcerers. In the local newspaper, it is common to spot mug-shot advertisements of African practitioners of sorcery and magic. Over the course of my years of study in Martinique, I met a dozen or more professional

women and men who told me that for those who can afford the trip, the place to find the most powerful sorcery is Africa. I have talked with many people and heard of dozens more who have fallen victim to someone's act of sorcery.

In addition to systems of belief, African-inspired influences appear in the local aesthetics of performance: in the domains of music, dance, and storytelling. The traditions of African drumming, rhythms, and interactive call-and-response voicing are strongly apparent.[20] Such African-based patterns became modified to relate to the demands of the New World environment and, in some cases, to offer another set of possibilities for the channeling of values not embraced by European practice. In creating creole music, dance, and folktales, slaves relied extensively on African rhythms and forms to interpret, cope with, and find opportunity in New World environments. In Martinique, for example, several dance styles demonstrating strong African resemblances have been cited by local experts, including the "*calenda*," the "*laghia*," and the "*bélé*" (or *bel air*, in French).[21]

Just as creole drumming styles echo an African beat, and many dance forms recall African dances, creole folktales too bear many resemblances to African tales. Many of the same animal characters and their recognizable traits traveled from West African societies with captive slaves across the Atlantic. However, key features of the African stories changed in the New World context to meet the realities of plantation slavery. Whereas in Africa the trickster tales ended in securing the community good, the Caribbean versions favored outcomes that benefited the individual.[22] In stories of New World trickster animals like Compère Lapin (known in the US as Brer Rabbit) or Anansi the Spider,[23] the triumphs of cunning became self-serving, not oriented to saving the group from outsiders. With the shift from a focus on the community to a focus on the individual, these creole tales signal new moral boundaries of behavior.[24]

In my explorations of bookstores in Martinique, I saw that creole folktales, replete with lessons that run counter to the standards of "respectability" in France, continued to be reprinted and sold at a steady pace year after year.[25] Teachers and parents use the tales routinely to teach youngsters about their own folklore. Traditional storytellers still enchant throngs of local residents at ritual events in the countryside, recounting the wiles of tricksters like Rabbit and how they dupe more powerful (but less clever) adversaries. The enduring power of creole values and identities is also apparent in the scores of individuals (some of whom you will meet later) who claim to pursue undeclared income as a way to realize their own initiative, cleverness, and success, just as Compère Lapin did. As discussed in Chapter 5, local scholars have noted how the Rabbit was the original creole *débrouillard*, the one who through individual cunning and sometimes deviousness figures out how to get what he wants by going around the rules and avoiding getting caught.

EVOLVING THEORIES OF CARIBBEAN IDENTITIES

The special difficulty for African-descended peoples in the Americas, says Paul Gilroy, is that they are "in but not of" Western society.[26] With their mixed African and European ancestries (and sometimes Indian, Chinese,

Syrian, or other combinations), a "black" person's creole identity is not rooted in a single, coherent heritage. Moreover, in contrast to other colonized, but indigenous, peoples of India, Africa, or Latin America, African-descended peoples in the Atlantic societies could not launch "anticolonial" struggles in terms of calling for a return to precolonial identities and social formations. The memories of their ancestors do not summon Africa; they begin and end on Caribbean sugar plantations.[27] Afro-Caribbean peoples, therefore, have no "indigenous" past to which they can symbolically or literally return. At the same time, as will become apparent from the following discussion, people who attempt either to reject fully or to imitate wholly the influences of European values and practices face a self-defeating prospect.[28]

DOUBLE-CONSCIOUSNESS AND BLACK IDENTITY

How does one "feel" the fragmentation of double or multiple identities? How does one embrace a mixed heritage which continues to call on separate sensibilities for outside validation? W. E. B. DuBois, perhaps the most prominent black American writer at the turn of twentieth century, championed black dignity and, at the same time, recognized the tug of assimilation to Euro-American culture. Much of what he said applies easily to being black and French in Martinique. Prolific and passionate, DuBois wrote about the terrible "split" residing in every American black person, calling it the insidious and irreconcilable pain of one's "double consciousness." According to DuBois, "One ever feels his twoness—an American, a Negro; two souls, two thoughts, two unreconciled strivings; two warring ideals in one dark body, whose dogged strength alone keeps it from being torn asunder."[29]

DuBois did not sympathize with the "Back to Africa" solution to this dilemma, however, as was promoted by Jamaican Marcus Garvey.[30] In 1914, Garvey left his Caribbean home to go to Harlem, New York, where he founded the United Negro Improvement Association (UNIA). In leading the UNIA, Garvey pioneered a plan to return African Americans to Africa, where, he claimed, they belonged and would find the dignity that eluded them in the US.[31]

At about the same time that Garvey's plan for a return to Africa was crumbling under the weight of financial and legal troubles, Aimé Césaire was growing up in Martinique. Césaire would become a poet and leader of a different movement to reclaim the conflicted "soul of black folk." In the 1920s, most people of color in Césaire's island home were still engaged in sugarcane production or other agricultural work. Aside from the already privileged class of mulatto professionals, merchants, and government officials, few in Martinique had found opportunities for upward mobility. However, the colony's Frenchness fed hopes of prosperity for larger numbers. Local schools became replicas of metropolitan schooling, and the lessons were taught in the respectable language of standard French. All children, black and white, in the French West Indies and in French Africa were taught the same lessons as their counterparts in Paris: that the Gauls were their ancestors and that figures such as Charlemagne and events like the Crusades represented histories they could take great pride in.

As a fourth grader, Césaire likely read the following passage, cited from a 1926 textbook which all French schoolchildren his age would have read on the same day of the school year:

> France is one of the world's greatest powers . . . Heroism shown and services rendered to humanity have enriched its national patrimony and radiance. And yet, in population France is very inferior to the great rival nations. If, in spite of this very grave inferiority, we could keep a considerable place on the earth's surface, it is because of the admirable vitality of the race exhibited in a *brilliant manner*, the expansion of the language outside of France, and the successive formation of two colonial empires. French is the auxiliary tongue of all civilized peoples. Among Europeans, it remains the preferred language of cultivated society . . .
>
> It is every French person's duty to contribute to his full power in propagating our language by which are spread throughout the world the generous ideas that make people love France and increase her moral authority. Beyond that, the spread of our language helps greatly the spread of our products.[32]

Césaire was being prepared for life as a proud Frenchman.

NEGRITUDE AND CARIBBEAN IDENTITY AS AFRICAN

Most children in Martinique during the 1920s would have been considered lucky to get a primary school education. But Césaire grew up in a family where education had always been stressed and where educational success meant the possibility of continuing French scholarships. In the early 1930s, having won just such a scholarship, Aimé Césaire traveled from his home in Martinique to the capital of France to further his schooling.

What Césaire had learned about the power of a universal French identity collided with the different reality he experienced in Paris: the shock of encountering racial prejudice. For the first time in his young life, the hypocrisy of colonial rhetoric sank in: the ideals of *liberté, égalité, fraternité* seemed to have no relevance to a black man in France. The French ethic of assimilation became, to Césaire, a lie.[33] This revelation provoked a focused new mission in Césaire—to reconceptualize the meaning of being black in the modern world.

During his years in Paris, Césaire met and befriended other blacks from French-colonized countries in Africa and the Caribbean. Key among Césaire's contacts were Leopold Senghor, from Senegal, and Léon Damas, from French Guiana. Together these young poet-scholars developed the concept they called Negritude.[34] The poets of Negritude rejected insidious European stereotypes of the day about Africans and the assumptions about race, color, and mental and physical attributes which bourgeois West Indians had largely internalized. They also rejected the lure of French identity, realizing it was an impossible goal for colonized peoples. Césaire held up African identity as the single great alternative to a European identity, the sovereign remedy for the alienation provoked by European colonialism. Negritude, said Césaire, is "the simple recognition of the fact of being black, the acceptance of this fact, of our black destiny, history and culture."[35] The founders of Negritude thus encouraged the African-descended Caribbean individual to become assimilated into the African cultural sphere. Their suffering, their devaluation by the white race, became the passport to kinship with a newly valorized African world of cultural difference.[36] Although Negritude did not invoke a physical return to Africa, as Garvey had proposed, it embraced an African psychological and cultural identity.

Afro-Caribbean Identities

GLISSANT AND THE SEARCH FOR A MORE LOCAL IDENTITY

For decades after the breakthrough ideas of Negritude were published in the 1930s, intellectuals and artists around the world rallied around the international movement for black liberation. But identifying oneself as African never gripped the imagination of most people in Martinique. For one thing, as more West Indian intellectuals had the opportunity of actually visiting Africa and realizing how different their societies were, many began to express doubts about the psychic integration of Caribbean with African peoples. In addition, the political evolution of the African colonies shattered hopes of a pan-African unity. In the 1960s, the majority of African countries gained independence, and each country retreated behind its borders, focusing on its own development and cultural preservation. At the same time, in the Caribbean, English-speaking islands were becoming independent, one by one.[37] The French islands, having become politically integrated overseas departments of France in 1946, were hardly in a position to lead the charge for cultural identification with Africa. And, finally, Martiniquais had for generations been socialized to aspire to being French: *liberté, egalité, fraternité* for all.

For all these reasons, by the late 1960s and early 1970s, Negritude and pan-Africanism had both waned as a viable solution to the identity problems of French Caribbean peoples.[38] As a consequence, the all-powerful notion of race became replaced over the years with a more focused concern about culture. Leading the scholarly probings into new conceptualizations for local, Caribbean identity was Edouard Glissant, a social theorist and writer from Martinique.[39] Glissant's alternative, "Antillainité" (Caribbeanness), asserts a West Indian cultural specificity.[40] To Glissant, Negritude relied on a futile backward search for African roots that were too remote to identify with. He believed that Caribbean identities needed to correspond to the distinct histories and influences that have shaped these societies. His ideas challenged the false sense of universalism based on race, mapping out the basis for a new, inclusive sense of identity

based on *métissage*— heterogeneous influences. So, where Negritude asserted a connection of Afro-Caribbean peoples to an "essential" African identity and conceived of this in terms of a homogeneous, single root tree, Glissant conceived of Caribbean identity as a "relational" construct, more like a rhizome: open, transformative, and multidimensional, spreading sideways and outward in a movement signifying its relationship and interaction with other multiracial New World cultures.[41]

CRÉOLITÉ: PRESCRIPTIONS FOR CELEBRATING CREOLENESS

The historical realities facing Césaire and, a generation later, Glissant, were different, yet both authors grappled with the problems of identity for

African-descended peoples in the New World. Both asserted a local cultural difference from France. Yet neither made a significant impression on the vast majority of Martiniquais. Françoise, a fifty-year-old brown-skinned, professional woman I knew as a gobbler of local literature responded to my question about Glissant's ideas with "Oh, no! Not that! No one reads that kind of thing. No one I know!" In recent years, several younger writers have attempted to launch a new identity-based movement they call *créolité*. One of the explicit goals of *créolité* (creoleness) is to reach a broader public by calling for a celebration and renewal of creole culture in all its forms.

The ideas surrounding *créolité* first appeared in 1989, when two prolific young Martiniquais writers, Patrick Chamoiseau and Raphaël Confiant, and a linguist, Jean Bernabé, outlined their thoughts in *Eloge de la Créolité* (In Praise of Creoleness). The notion of *créolité* represents the most explicit attempt to date to redefine creole culture through the language and folk traditions that are the common denominators of a diverse population in islands as far flung as the Seychelles, Mauritius, and la Réunion, islands in the Indian Ocean off the east coast of Madagascar. *Créolité* thus focuses sharply on Martinique and other Francophone plantation-colonized areas resembling it.[42] Creole culture, unified by creole language, is seen as the result of a process of adaptation that started with plantation days: a mixed culture that arose from the forced, non-harmonious confrontation of different languages, customs, and worldviews. These views of creole identity reject the notion of a fused "hybridity" commonly employed in postcolonial studies. For them, *créolité* "expresses not a synthesis, not a *métissage*, or any other kind of unity," but a "kaleidoscopic reality."[43]

The public take on *créolité* translates easily as a celebration of all variety of creole culture and language, wherever it occurs. Thus, although *créolité* is dismissed by some western as well as West Indian intellectuals as male-biased, ego-centered, and simplistically groping, unlike the sophisticated and nuanced ideas of Glissant, *créolité* is a concept to which more and more people in the local environment seem to relate.[44] Françoise was much more familiar with the work of these younger writers. And, though she is quick to defend her creole ancestry, she does not credit *créolité* with her sense of pride.

THE CARIBBEAN PARADIGM OF CREOLE "REPUTATION" AND EUROPEAN "RESPECTABILITY"

Whereas Martiniquais intellectuals have focused their attention on the problems of multiple identities in a creole context, outside researcher Peter Wilson approached the tug of fragmented heritages differently. From 1958 to 1961, this anthropologist studied a tiny Caribbean island called Providencia.[45] Wilson's ethnographic research of men and women from black and white families on the island suggested to him that many Afro-Caribbean people act in ways that do not attempt to emulate European standards of behavior. Wilson hypothesized that the creole adaptations of slaves to their environment had resulted in their seeking prestige in ways that defied European teachings about ideal behavior. Through an ethnographic lens, Wilson provided a specifically Caribbean view of DuBois' concept of "double consciousness."

Briefly, Wilson contended that, contrary to prevailing scholarly opinion,[46] Caribbean peoples did not necessarily aim to achieve European standards at all. Some people prefer to follow creole standards, and some could operate within both systems of status simultaneously. Wilson proposed that two coexisting systems of status operate among Afro-Caribbean peoples of the Caribbean: European "respectability" and creole "reputation."[47] The European system of respectability, he argued, stresses clean, responsible living, hard work, and loyalty to family and church. Respectability is internalized in varying degrees by different segments of Caribbean populations. According to Wilson, women are especially likely to judge themselves and others against the measures of respectability. The creole-based prestige system, called "reputation," in contrast, promotes status through such means as public performance and verbal and sexual prowess. According to Wilson, reputation is more commonly pursued by men than women.[48] For Wilson, understanding a person's behavior, therefore, requires an understanding of the rewards a person is seeking—whether someone is interested in advancing a creole "reputation" (as Patrick did by selling chic but undeclared swimsuits) or a European-styled "respectability" (as Patrick did by maintaining a regular, taxpaying job, earning steady income, and supporting his aging mother).

Wilson concludes his book with a "solution" to help resolve the double consciousness and conflicted loyalties of Caribbean peoples. He exhorts Caribbean people to purge themselves of European influences and to embrace fully their own creole values and practices. If history is any guide, however, Wilson's solution will probably fare no better than Garvey's or Césaire's.[49] Moreover, as the longstanding "love child" of France, Martinique's material comforts make shedding the relation to France look like a remote possibility indeed.

According to some, the notion of a family romance aptly describes the relation between France and her overseas "love children."[50] Mother France,
they argue, lavishes gifts on her DOM children in order to remove for them
the hardships of independence. These parental gifts include subsidized
imports, tax exemptions, salaries for government functionaries that are 40
percent higher than those on the continent, and low-cost daily flights to
Paris. France also ensures metropolitan standards in local schools, hospitals, clinics, roads, and public buildings and spaces, as well as universal
access to higher education, to basic health care, and to unemployment
insurance. That Martinique and Guadeloupe maintain perhaps the highest standards of living in the Caribbean is not because of a thriving local
economy; it is because French transfers have made it so.

In this romance, the family's true home is the metropole, not the Caribbean. Most families I met have at least one relative living in Paris, and it is
common for middle- and even moderate-income people to make regular
visits during the year. Georges, a twenty-seven-year-old copper-skinned
Martiniquais man, is married, has a small child, and is on his way up in the
world. When I asked how he thought about living in the Caribbean but
being a part of France, Georges replied,

> We don't relate to our geographic region at all. Not with the Carib-
> bean, nor with the Americas. One thinks of France. That's where
> people travel, that's where they move to. It's true that the *békés* send
> their children often enough to universities in the US or Canada. But
> the rest of us are oriented to the metropole.

*Afro-Caribbean
Identities*

Claims of being French, however, meet a disturbing obstacle when
Martiniquais travel to the "family home." Here, in metropolitan France,
Martiniquais find that their color disqualifies them from being taken as
French. Just as literary scholar Stuart Hall reported being defined by
blackness and by "the gaze of the Other" when he moved from Jamaica
to Britain,[51] so many researchers have documented similar problems for
Martiniquais, made worse by their heightened assumptions about being
French (recall Aimé Césaire's shock in the 1930s). In Paris, Martiniquais
find that they are commonly taken to be foreigners from Africa, are mis-

taken for illegal African immigrants in police sweeps of the metro,[52] are routinely denied access to housing and to private sector jobs, are generally treated like second-class citizens, and are regularly reminded of their "outsider" status.[53] This widespread popular racism haunts the gap between a universalizing rhetoric of Frenchness and the lived experience of Martiniquais in Paris.

One of my upper-income informants expressed this problem clearly. Pascale, a psychologist for the state hospital, has a white metropolitan father and a black Martiniquaise mother. She explained that when she was young, going to France with her well-off parents never exposed her to the pervasive racism she later encountered as a university student looking for housing in Paris.

When you try to find a job or locate housing, that's where Antillean people have problems. We don't feel so French then. After living there by myself, I encountered problems I hadn't seen before, and now I no longer trust a metropolitan person instinctively as I used to.

Considering that this woman's own father is metropolitan, her experience in being treated as "black" rather than "French" was confusing and frustrating to her. Her story was one I heard often, especially from middle- and upper-income people, who have the highest expectations for their own Frenchness and who travel frequently to the metropole and send their children there for advanced schooling. When islanders realize that their skin color undermines their acceptance as authentically French, they feel alienated and demoralized.[54]

Even on their cultural home ground, Martiniquais are sometimes required to endure the wagging finger of metropolitan French living in Martinique. Assuming a self-appointed role as proxy "parent," some metropolitans stiffen their backs and puff their lips in disdain of Martiniquais, whom they regard as inept, lazy, and dependent on the gifts of mother France. According to a metropolitan man who owns a lumber production company and has lived in Martinique with his wife and teenage sons for more than fifteen years, Martiniquais are terribly spoiled people, precisely because of the money France has sunk into the island's standard of living.

> In effect, they are big children because they went through too rapid an evolution, without stages—from a society that had virtually nothing, to a consumer society. They like to appear as though they have more than they have. Its not the vulgar negro, it's the "evolved" negro. He wants to make himself seen. He buys a beautiful car, but he puts in only 10 francs of gas.

For Martiniquais, then, there is a cost associated with mother France's gifts to ensure that the island inherits in equal proportion to all other French departments. Unlike the departments in continental France, the former colonies overseas are regarded as "welfare children" of France. Only they must suffer the indignities of their widely recognized dependency and their outsider skin color. Some analysts further argue that these DOM societies are made to feel as though they are, in perpetuity, indebted to the French state for these benevolent gifts. Even many local intellectuals agree that the dependency of Martinique on France has allowed islanders to stagnate in a state of perpetual adolescence that stunts their growth and future potential as a mature, independent people composed of capable, productive individuals.[55] According to Glissant, because assimilation has proven to be a false ideal, Martiniquais people suffer from a kind of psychic dispossession.[56]

The paradox of identity facing Martiniquais plays out in the Caribbean context as well. When local residents look across the water at neighboring islands, they compare, frequently in obsessive detail, their own prosperity and "Frenchness" to the economic hardships and lack of European sophistication or infrastructure they see elsewhere. The material difficulties of St. Lucians, Dominicans, Haitians, and others are visible to Martiniquais as they travel to these islands and as they come in contact with those who visit or live in Martinique. But many Martiniquais privately conveyed to me their envy of the pride and clarity these "independent" Caribbean people demonstrate. For although Martiniquais can claim Frenchness at home and in the wider Caribbean, when they are in the family home (metropolitan France), they remain unable to overcome their outsider status.

Creole identities in the French Caribbean thus appear hinged to the expectations, promises, and disappointments of assimilation to France. These contradictions of assimilation stoke an ambivalence about Frenchness. For this reason, creole habits and ways of thinking are reinforced as both an assertion of and a refuge from local "difference."

CONTRADICTIONS OF IDENTITY, SUBVERSIVE TACTICS, AND THE CREOLE *DÉBROUILLARD*

IN MARTINIQUE, HE
WHO RESPECTS THE LAW
IS AN IMBECILE.

—M. Guillaume,
local state prosecutor

Relief from the tensions and ambiguities of creole and French identities finds expression in Martinique's widespread, cross-class informal economy. The Martiniquais sense of dispossession, identified by both Glissant and Fanon, is precisely the contradiction of identity that opens what literary scholar Homi Bhabha calls a "third space,"[57] a space in which subversive acts are valorized. The practice of creole economics represents just such a subversive "third space" in Martinique: an escape from the rules of the Other and at the same time an exercise of personal autonomy and cultural difference. Thus, in the guise of conformity with French norms and laws, people with legitimately declared jobs routinely engage in undeclared work on the side.

Michel de Certeau's concept of *"la tactique"* (the tactic, or calculated action) can be used to help explain how creole economics constitutes a subversive act of resistance to French control. According to de Certeau, subordinate people resort to "tactics" to undermine another's power. Recourse to this "art of the weak," says de Certeau, means that a tactic may depend on trickery and "must accept the chance offerings of the moment . . . It must vigilantly make use of the cracks that particular conjunctions open in the surveillance of the proprietary powers. . . . It is a guileful ruse."[58]

In Martinique, cultural histories of subordination and creole adaptations to the lack of autonomy feed the practice of trickery and opportunism embodied in *débrouillardism* and creole economics. Even work inspectors and prosecutors frequently recognize that the tenacious quality of undeclared activity is related to local histories and strategies of survival, as indicated in the previous chapter. The state prosecutor from metropolitan France has lived in Martinique for several years. For him, the problem is intractable because it includes tradition and culture—factors that do not change just because a law exists. Resigned, he said,

> It's the Antillais spirit: "It is not a sin to be a *débrouillard.*" This spirit exists at all levels of the economy. He who respects the law is an imbecile. People here do not accept being forbidden or constrained. They commit crimes without having the impression of having violated the law.

"Is this not the same in metropolitan France?" I asked.

> It's not the same mentality or culture. It's the *débrouillard,* but with a clear conscience about having crossed the law.

The prosecutor's reference to the clear conscience of the local *débrouillard* hints at the economically subversive character of a *débrouillard* in Martinique. In fact, I learned over time that the French term *débrouillardism* has been extended and bent in the local setting to mean something more than it means in standard French. No one suggested that the local meaning of *débrouillard* contradicts the metropolitan meanings of being dynamic, smart, self-reliant, and resourceful. However, the term is widely perceived to carry more muscle and more nuance locally, typically being associated with *le travail noir,* working off the books, and with the personal qualities of being sly and cunning in an economic sense.

Micheline, a forty-four-year-old financial consultant who is married with two teenage children said:

> To call someone a *débrouillard* is, well, stronger than in France. In Creole, we mean someone smart, cunning, shrewd—they are people who know how to land on their feet. It's a great compliment, but at the same time, it has a malicious connotation. A *débrouillard* has devious ways, he doesn't do things by the books.

When people devise strategies to earn money off the books, they frame their activities as a form of *débrouillardism* and many consider themselves to be *débrouillards* in a creole sense. A young construction manager echoed many of my male informants, saying,

> A *débrouillard* is someone who is always looking for solutions for personal profit on every plane: physically, financially. They try to be more cunning than others . . . You search systematically to avoid the normal steps, to skip some. It happens all over. It's is a compliment to be called a *débrouillard*. A professor will give classes that are not declared. He will put money in his pocket without declaring it. He will do business on the black market. Professors and doctors will be chauffeurs at night. That is *débrouillardism*.

Metropolitan French living in Martinique are also quick to point out the particular meaning assigned to *débrouillardism* locally. Jannick has a dental practice in Fort-de-France. He is metropolitan French, but has lived in Martinique for eighteen years and is married to a Martiniquaise woman. They have two children. In his view, it is not only clear that there is a different local meaning of *débrouillard*, but it is a meaning that he finds shameful.

> Here in Martinique, a *débrouillard* is someone who is more cunning than others. In France, being known as a *débrouillard* simply means that you are clever enough to find the best deal for something— that's clever.

Of course, my metropolitan informants acknowledged that the under-reporting of income in continental France is considered a national sport. Many also referenced the rather open political practice of "system D" (D for "*débrouillard*"), in which someone plies his personal networks to effect a desired outcome, as described by French anthropologist Laurence Wylie in his classic ethnography of a town in Provence.[59] However, metropolitan versions of economic self-interest are not strategies that resemble the strategies or the motivations of the creole *débrouillard*. Moreover, metropolitans who routinely defraud the government are not accorded prestige for their accomplishments.

Consistent with informant accounts, dictionaries of standard French indicate narrower and more straightforward meanings for this term than those specified by dictionaries of French Creole. In the Larousse *Dictionnaire de Français*, for example, *débrouillard* is defined as *ingénieux, astucieux* (ingenious, astute) and illustrated with the following phrase: "ils sont assez débrouillards pour y arriver" (they are resourceful enough to make it).[60] In the Harrap's French/English dictionary, *débrouillard* is simply defined as a "resourceful person."[61]

In the French Creole dictionary, however, the creole term *"débouya"* is defined as *"malin, habile, roublard,"* terms which mean respectively, "crafty," "clever" or "skilled," and "wily" or "cunning." In a second usage, *débouya* is defined as *débrouillardise, roublardise* and is illustrated in usage with the decidedly non-metropolitan phrase *débouya pa péché*, meaning, "it is not a sin to be a *débrouillard*."[62] This entirely local proverb reveals the morally complex character of the creole term. We will come back to the issue of morality in relation to creole identities shortly.

Although the origin of the creole usage of the term *débrouillard* is not known, linguists and historians point out that double meanings for gestures, folktales, song lyrics, and words carry a long history of adaptive practice in Caribbean societies.[63] Just so with the word *débrouillard*, a French word that was perhaps bent by slaves to justify an illicit edge on behavior the French merely associate with resourcefulness within legal boundaries.

The practice of creole economics may offer some islanders a way to earn status by both asserting their intelligence and, at the same time, displaying a "tactic" to express their "difference." This "reputation-oriented" status depends on illicit but productive activity because here, unlike in a legitimate job, one is required to demonstrate economic initiative and success while taking illegal risks. In these material and symbolic ways, the practice of creole economics represents an unmistakable form of opposition within complicity.[64]

Perhaps, unconsciously, such practices also constitute a way to subvert the homogenizing assumptions of Frenchness promoted by liberal politicians in the metropole. As we have seen, the premise of assimilation that presupposed absorption of local cultural identities into a melting pot of Frenchness would prove impossible. Through creole economics, Martiniquais not only advance their own material interests, but also assert their autonomy from the French state and, effectively, tax it back.

CONCLUSION

In addition to the burden of sorting out a sense of cultural identity in the Caribbean context, the identity struggles of Martiniquais and Guadeloupeans suffer from the added weight of their choice to become a part of France. Today, nearly sixty years after being brought formally into the bosom of France through departmentalization, many Martiniquais claim their Frenchness proudly. These claims to Frenchness are not delusional imaginings, but follow logically from assimilationist orientations promoted by both the French state and by many colonized peoples themselves. More recent economic infusions that have hoisted island standards of living to metropolitan levels reinforce the sense of assimilation to France: grand and modern government buildings, well-maintained roads and roundabouts, French boutiques, Peugeots, Renaults, and Citroëns—all provide visible evidence of the Frenchness of Martinique. Supporting these concrete manifestations of Frenchness is the rhetoric of a universal French identity, one which effectively casts a net over the dispersed "confetti of empire" to claim a familial bond among all who speak French and carry a French

passport, a bond transcending color, culture, and geography. Yet the realities for people of color in metropolitan France tell a different story.

The continuing intensity of intellectual concern around conceptualizing local identity today signals the still-unresolved dilemma that Martiniquais face: wanting the prestige and material promise of being French, yet falling short of the symbolic capital needed to become fully French—whiteness.[65] Creole identities in the French Caribbean are, for this reason, in constant tension with the expectations and promises of assimilation to France. Martiniquais poets and literary artists have since the 1930s poured their energies into the project of negotiating a meaningful local identity, different from the European identities many islanders aspire to internalize and project. The contradictions these writers attempt to expose—and in

The mountains of northern Martinique

some measure, resolve—articulate what many in the society simply act on instinctively: their local difference. Assertions about local difference have remained in the forefront of local writing, from essays and social theory to poetry, plays and novels. In fact, as one western scholar recently noted, Martinique is a place so deeply conflicted it seems to give birth to a disproportionately large number of writers and artists.[66] Their respective arguments are distinguished by historic context and by the particular vision of local difference each author claims. But the arguments are bound by a central point: Martinique's identity cannot be subsumed by French identity, despite the "universalizing" rhetoric of Frenchness.

Ocean view in southern Martinique

1950s French currency depicting Martinique after incorporation as overseas department

Sugarcane worker in contemporary Martinique

Mechanized cane harvesting in Martinique

The prefecture in
Fort-de-France, seat
of the French state in
Martinique

Cathedral Saint-Louis
in Fort-de-France

Bibliothèque Schoelcher, city library of Fort-de-France

Typical French road in the rural interior of Martinique

Departmental archives library in Fort-de-France

Patisserie (pastry shop) in Fort-de-France

Street on bayside edge of downtown Fort-de-France

Street bordering downtown Fort-de-France

*Chamoiseau's Texaco neighborhood in background overlooking
Fort-de-France center with informal vendors in foreground*

Overlook of low-income neighborhood

Habitation de Loyer Modeste (HLM), *French subsidized housing
for moderate-income families*

Elegant new Martiniquais home under construction

Home of upper-income Afro-Martiniquais family

Parc Savane monument of Empress Josephine intact, before 1991

Same monument of Empress Josephine decapitated and bloody, after 1991

PART THREE

Practices

FIVE

Adaptations of Cunning

THE CHANGING FORMS
OF *DÉBROUILLARDISM*

ONLY RARELY DID A VIOLENT PHYSICAL
CONFRONTATION RESOLVE THE TENSIONS
THAT UNDERLAY THE SLAVE'S AND THE MAS-
TER'S PERPETUAL STRUGGLE FOR AUTHORITY
AND POWER ON THE PLANTATION. MUCH MORE
TYPICALLY THE SLAVE USED A KIND OF MEN-
TAL JUJITSU, SIMILAR TO THE TACTICS OF THE
SLAVES' FOLK HERO, BRER RABBIT, TO DECEIVE
OR DIVERT HIS OPPRESSORS, THEREBY SEIZ-
ING MASTERY OF THE MOMENT AND GAINING A
MEASURE OF OPPORTUNITY AND FREEDOM.

—William L. Andrews and Henry Louis Gates Jr., *The
Civitas Anthology of African American Slave Narratives*, 1999

The original wound of slavery conditions both the fact of creole-style
débrouillardism and its form in the
contemporary economy. So, however much islanders may claim they are
French, the indignity of their histories, the continuing stigma of their skin,
and the subsidized dependency of their material lives prevent the final
healing of that original wound. In this gap of assimilation, local versions
of *débrouillardism* affirm a creole identity of autonomy and cleverness in the
face of another's power.

To explore the idea that creole identities can be discovered in economic
practice, we need to consider the historic context in which creolized slaves
learned to assert their humanity through regular attempts to undermine

the master and to secure for themselves even the slightest gain. In this chapter, we will travel back in time to see how this profound ideology of economic survival and need for respect was born out of the conditions of slavery in Martinique. The heart of this ideology is symbolized in folktales of the individualistic, creole rabbit, who, in human form, is the *débrouillard*—smart and unorthodox, scheming, and successful on his own terms. Although the opportunities and constraints have altered in form over time, the spirit of the creole *débrouillard* lives on because the tensions he is striving to resolve live on. At all levels of society, the legacy of the *débrouillard* continues to express the energy of people who are proving their worth by making smart, self-interested economic choices.

SEEDBEDS OF *DÉBROUILLARDISM* AND CREOLE ECONOMICS

SLAVE STRATEGIES OF RESISTANCE

The French slave system in the New World was a construction of colonists who shared a cultural identity, a language, and common economic interests. In contrast, the slaves whose labor enabled colonists to realize their fortunes from sugar had been ripped from many areas of Africa and transported to the New World with their various native languages and cultural traditions. Beyond this imposed alienation from home and family, slaves were further denied any claims to their own ancestors, relatives, and even their own children. In a life that sociologist Orlando Patterson called "social death,"[1] the isolation slaves endured served the interests of colonists well. The social divisions they created and the linguistic divisions they reinforced among slaves precluded early revolts by minimizing communication within and across plantations. Such controls were especially important in plantation society as the proportions of slaves increased to more than eight times the number of whites.[2]

Slaves did not passively accept their drastically shrunken, alienated new lives as property of white masters on sugar plantations an ocean away from home. Yet because of the brutal consequences for resisters (whipping was a standard means of coercion, and punishment with physical torture was not uncommon), it was in the best interests of slaves to keep resistance below the radar, to refrain from interfering with the power structure of the

PRACTICES

120

plantation. Indeed, the odds of staging a successful revolt were very low; only in Haiti was the white planter class overthrown and kicked out.[3]

Apart from the sporadic occasions of violent revolt, slave resistance took the form of hidden acts of defiance that coexisted with apparent acts of compliance. Thus, on the one hand, the highly supervised, compliant work of slaves enabled the white planters to accumulate handsome profits from the sale of sugar in Europe. On the other hand, slaves found discrete ways to resist their exploitation by plotting sabotage and devising ways to serve their own self-interests. The "everyday tactics" slaves used to oppose the system included "work-stops," disorganization in the fields, lying, mocking those in control, pretending to be sick, serving poisoned food, and stealing farm tools, supplies, and food.[4] In addition, recorded incidents of infanticide and abortion suggest that some slaves withheld their reproductive potential from a system that would only imprison new life.[5] Over time, slaves became increasingly adept at exploiting weaknesses in the plantation system and incorporated "industrial sabotage" to their repertoire of resistance tactics. These latter strategies included, for example, setting fires in the canefields, killing cattle for meat, and destroying carts, machines, and tools.[6]

Such acts of resistance by slaves represented a crucial assertion of self in the midst of its denial within the plantation system. Yet because resistance could not directly confront the power structure, it occurred indirectly, in the context of slaves' accommodation to the system.

Political scientist James C. Scott elaborated de Certeau's idea of the tactics of the weak to conceive an insightful framework for understanding how slaves and other subordinated groups coped with their involuntary subjugation.[7] Subordinated groups, he says, engage in both public and private ways of speaking and behaving. In the kind of public situation where powerholders are present, Scott identifies the communication strategies of slaves as following the logic of "public transcripts" where solicitous behavior is oriented to the "flattering self-image of elites."[8] Yet, "offstage," in the privacy and relative security of their own quarters, slaves engaged in "hidden transcripts," speaking "the words of anger, revenge, self-assertion." A third type of slaves' political discourse, according to Scott, straddles these public and private realms. This, he called a

Adaptations of Cunning

politics of disguise and anonymity that takes place in public view but is designed to have a double meaning or to shield the identity of the

121

actors. Rumor, gossip, folktales, jokes, songs, rituals, codes, and eu-phemisms—a good part of the folk culture of subordinate groups—fit this description.[9]

Resistance within accommodation requires a keen sense of both the workings and limits of duplicity. Thus, the morality of duplicitous be-havior, involving simultaneous accommodation and resistance, afforded the only path to dignity: by feigning complicity, slaves could cope and also remain human. As Caribbean scholar and literary critic Richard Burton notes, "The whole point of 'psychological' resistance was to show and not show nonacceptance of the system and above all *not to be caught* in the act of maneuver, deception, or defiance."[10]

The adaptation of duplicity helps explain many apparent contradictions that encourage Martiniquais today to benefit from both the economic and social advantages tied to assimilation and the cultural validation embed-ded in creole identities.

THE MATERIAL MEANS TO EXERCISE AUTONOMY

The material basis for creole economics began with the small garden plots on the margins of the estate given by masters to their slaves for the pur-pose of provisioning themselves. Generally, slaves were allowed as much land as they were able to work. This practice, which began with slavery itself in the French colonies, included a custom of "free" Saturdays for the slaves to cultivate their food. Although the French Code Noir, enacted in 1685, required the slaveowners in the French colonies to provide their slaves with a given level of food, shelter, and clothing, the law was poorly enforced. And despite various subsequent attempts to require planters to provide rations for their slaves, slave gardening for subsistence came to represent established practice in French colonial life in the eighteenth and nineteenth centuries until abolition in 1848.[11] Historian Dale Tomich cites the Colonial Council of Martinique as acknowledging that "the slave is the sovereign master over the terrain that is conceded to him," and the smooth functioning of island plantations came to depend on the rights of slaves to these provision grounds.[12]

For the already overworked slaves, gardening on the side meant more work and also saved slaveowners the costs of purchasing and distributing rations.[13] But cultivating small provision plots gave slaves a way to realize the fruits of their labor and to do so without supervision by the master.

Moreover, various accounts suggest that the slaves regarded their individual plots as a unique space of autonomy and freedom, dignities they were denied in the primary work of their lives.[14] Tomich notes that these proto-peasant activities

> offered a space for slave initiative and self-assertion that simply cannot be deduced from their economic form. Through them, the slaves themselves organized and controlled a secondary economic network that . . . allowed them to begin to construct an alternative way of life that went beyond [the plantation].[15]

Historical archives indicate that slave gardens were well kept, bountiful, and often quite profitable. The staple crop was manioc supplemented by vegetables, potatoes, yams, and bananas. By selling manioc flour and other surplus produce to plantations and at Sunday markets in the towns, slaves were able to realize a source of income. This income or barter power allowed them to obtain manufactured goods including clothing, shoes, jewelry, furniture, and other dry goods. For the industrious slave, the ability to acquire material goods, especially high-quality clothing, helped signal his economic independence and, consequently, his status among other slaves.[16]

Although tending the provision plot comprised a relatively small proportion of a slave's working life, it was steeped in significance for the development of creole economics: to a slave, his private garden represented an opportunity to earn a profit from his own labor and "reputation" among his peers. This side economic activity also offered a unique source of autonomy and of the individual status that such buying power made possible.[17] As Roger Bastide and others argue, these provision grounds permitted slaves to exploit a niche in which creole culture could take shape.[18]

Adaptations of Cunning

Individual gardens constituted an officially sanctioned place for slaves to do productive work for self-gain. However, slaves found other, more clandestine, opportunities to profit at the expense of the master. For example, an entry from a Jamaican slaveowner's diary described an exchange with a slave caught stealing sugar. When confronted, the slave maintained that he had not stolen it at all: he had merely "taken" the sugar:

> "As sugar belongs to massa, and myself belongs to massa, it all de same ting—dat make me tell massa me don't tief; me only take it!"
> The master asked, "What do you call thieving then?"
> "When me broke into broder house and grond, and take away him ting, den me tief, massa."[19]

123

Stealing food or tools from the master was not considered immoral or wrong by slaves; to the contrary, it was smart, survival behavior.[20] Any strategies that exploited the system to one's own advantage were admired. Tricking the master and not getting caught increased a slave's reputation among other slaves. In his historical novel *Texaco*, Patrick Chamoiseau (who helped develop the notion of *créolité*) recounts how clever slaves learned to "disappear" from the plantations without being noticed. One scene recalls the visit by a field slave during broad daylight to a slave laundress washing at the river.

> [He] blew her a few words then came back the following day, then another, then a whole day, careless of the overseer's eye. "So how is it you don't work?" [she] asked all astonished. "I haven't left work," he would answer opening his eyelids wide around his eyes. And when [she] asked around, no one had ever seen him leave his post or sabotage his cutting. The overseer who accounted for the number of slaves at work never fell upon his missing backside.[21]

Stealing, lying, and other forms of exploiting the system were common tactics employed by slaves at all levels, from the mass of field slaves performing the most undesirable work to the small minority of "higher" slaves with less odious jobs and better chances for favors. Higher slaves served as artisans—carpenters, mechanics, and masons; drivers and field supervisors; and domestics who worked inside the Great House. But despite the relative advantages of "higher" slaves, they too leveraged their respective positions to advance their individual interests in whatever ways possible, winning for themselves better food and shelter, occasional holidays, and gifts of cloth.[22]

Female slaves sometimes sought the advantages of concubinage with their master. The advantage to such a relationship involved the potential to "whiten" themselves through light-skinned children, thereby improving their own social standing.[23] Moreover, their mixed-race children, especially males, would typically inherit special privileges and often win their freedom in the slave-based economy.[24]

In a material sense, therefore, clever slaves seized on whatever opportunities they could to improve their lot. Because the degradation of their lives was so severe, distinctions between self-serving activity that was licit (as with provision plots) and activities that were illicit (as with stealing food or tools) were not meaningful. The point was that those who were alert and able to create even small advantages for themselves in spite of their victimization became the models for others.

THE CREOLE RABBIT AND FOLKTALE MODELS OF AUTONOMY

The pursuit of music and storytelling occurred in the niches outside plantation work: at nights and on Sundays. During these times, slaves could exercise control over their lives and demonstrate individual prowess, all the while helping to humanize a shared painful existence. The cracks of opportunity for such self-expression provided key avenues for reproducing the survival values coded in folktales. According to folklorist Roger Abrahams, in oral cultures, the power of words in public performances is undervalued by people in literate societies. In addition, he says that "in oral cultures, storytelling is a fundamental way of codifying hard-won truths and dramatizing the rationale behind traditions."[25]

Ultimately, these survival values would have a far-reaching impact in the mental maps that slaves took with them after abolition. In a collection of contemporary creole folktales, Chamoiseau introduces their historical context:

> At the foot of the hill, in the slave quarters, someone emerges from one of the huts. The slaves are waiting for him, expectantly, beneath an ancient tree . . . By day, he is merely a field hand who works, suffers, and sweats, living in fear and in stifled rebellion.
> At night, however, . . . he will become the Master of Words . . . the Storyteller.[26]

Adaptations of Cunning

According to an analysis of creole folktales by Maryse Condé, a prominent Guadeloupean writer, more than 70 percent of these tales involve the use of trickery to escape conditions of "grinding misery."[27] Chamoiseau explains that these stories reinforce the value of cunning as indirect resistance in a system that precluded direct resistance: "The Creole tale reveals that overt force guarantees eventual defeat and punishment, and that through cunning, patience, nerve, and resourcefulness (which is never a sin), the weak may vanquish the strong or seize power by the scruff of the neck."[28]

Whites were aware of these storytelling rituals, but were not generally able or willing to recognize that the tales, filled with "exaggerated deference, disguised satire, and outright cunning, duplicity, and mendacity," were not harmless banter, but fodder for the subterfuge of everyday life.[29] In the Caribbean generally, the folk hero in these trickster tales was either a spider (Anansi) or a rabbit. In the French Caribbean, the most enduring and popular trickster character is the rabbit, Compère Lapin (or Brer Rabbit, as he is known in the British Caribbean and American South), a direct ancestor of our own Bugs Bunny.[30]

In stories recounting how Rabbit outwits an animal more powerful than himself, such as Lion, his superior intelligence frees him from the imposition of the Lion's will.[31] Rabbit is known for his cleverness at outsmarting bigger and stronger animals in order to turn impossible odds to his favor; his powerful intellect more than compensates for his small size.

In their new creole language, as described earlier, storytellers rewove their African folktales to fit the terrible new plantation environment.[32] The rabbit, which had been a hero for the collective good in African folklore, became, in the context of New World slavery, the hero for an individual's own good. Because slaves were routinely separated from their own kin, there was no stable community of relatives to consider. The slave was accountable to his master, and the most important social unit was oneself. One's best hope was to watch out for him- or herself, to plot individual strategies of survival and resistance. When slaves managed to escape, they did so in twos and threes, not in large groups, since groups could be too easily spotted and controlled. The fear and insecurity brought about by these drastic social changes was profound by all accounts, and the transformation from a community-minded to a self-interested rabbit is a vivid illustration of this changed mentality.[33]

Chamoiseau echoes this point as he cautions that the tales, though they involve trickery and deceit, do not incite group revolution. On the contrary, they prescribe individualistic solutions: "The hero is alone, and selfishly preoccupied with saving his own skin."[34] Other folktale scholars have noted that the creole trickster strategies "involve the maximization of short-term (economic) gain at the expense of long-term social cohesion."[35]

One tale, from Martinique, recounts how Brer Rabbit tricks Brer Tiger out of his dinner. The story begins with Tiger cheating Firefly out of the fish they both caught. Firefly complains to Rabbit, who decides to outwit Tiger himself. Rabbit tempts Tiger with the promise of a big pig dinner, but when Tiger comes to collect his meal, Rabbit sneaks out, steals Tiger's basket of fish, and returns home before Tiger knocks on the door. Rabbit greets Tiger with tears in his eyes. "My pig's been stolen! My pig's been stolen!" he cries. Disgusted, Tiger sighs and returns home. That night, Rabbit fries the big fish and enjoys a tasty dinner.[36]

Rabbit represents a folktale "archetype" of cunning and maneuverability. His superiority lies not only in his ability to spot opportunity, but also in his ability to avoid getting caught.[37] The survival lesson of duplicity was thus codified in creole folktales, replete with hidden meanings. James C. Scott used the example of Brer Rabbit stories to point out how slaves were able to communicate double meanings without raising the suspicions of masters:

> At one level these are nothing but innocent stories about animals; at another level they appear to celebrate the cunning wiles and venge-ful spirit of the weak as they triumph over the strong . . . Thus, . . . folktales of revenge are the infrapolitical equivalent of open gestures of contempt and desecration . . . aimed at resisting the denial of standing or dignity to subordinate groups.[38]

Rabbit's success provides a model for behavior which emphasizes the use of intelligence and alertness to find opportunities for gain where others see none.[39] John Roberts' analysis of trickster tales among African descendants in the New World holds that these tales involve "the use of wit, guile and deception to acquire material rewards. [The trickster's] actions became the model for getting what they needed with minimal risk."[40] Chamoiseau agrees that the tales became models for living: "These tales provide a practical education, an apprenticeship in life—a life of survival in a colonized land."[41]

Local scholars are quick to point to the fact that the human *débrouil-lard* in Martinique is drawn from the character of Compère Lapin.[42] As Martiniquais-born psychiatrist and author Frantz Fanon noted in his 1952 book, *Peau Noire, Masques Blancs* (Black Skin, White Masks): "These sto-ries belong to the oral tradition of the plantation Negroes. Therefore, it is relatively easy to recognize the Negro in his remarkably ironic and wry disguise as a rabbit."[43]

Like the rabbit, the *débrouillard* embodies the "strength of the weak" by using his superior intelligence to trick the dominant system and turn it to his own purpose.[44] The appeal of *le lapin* is his ingenuity and guile at getting what he wants, no matter the odds. Today, creole folktales, still replete with the devious plots and generally victorious outcomes of Com-père Lapin, continue to be reproduced orally by traditional storytellers, and published and circulated in schools and in homes.

Because of the master's control over a slave's name, clothing, hairstyle, body marks, and religion, slaves had been allowed very few public opportunities for self-expression. Only with emancipation in 1848 were these controls lifted, giving freed persons the right to wear hats, shoes, bright colors, or other adornments in public.[45]

However, abolition changed very little of the structural arrangements of life, and for this reason, the requirements of survival after abolition acted to validate and reproduce slave-based habits of exploiting opportunities for economic gain wherever they could be found. In addition, as one historian of slavery noted,

> The autonomous provision-ground cultivation and marketing elaborated within slavery provided freed people with an alternative to plantation labor after emancipation . . . Probably few could escape the plantation entirely after emancipation, but provision-ground cultivation and marketing networks enabled the great majority of freed slaves to struggle effectively over the conditions of their labor.[46]

Nevertheless, the majority of freed men and women remained poor. Meanwhile, the white *béké* planters, who continued to control arable land and the resources needed to make it profitable, also controlled wages and migration. The plantation economy continued to flourish and dominate local production into the 1920s, when new sources of sugar and then the Great Depression created rapid drops in the demand for Caribbean sugar. From abolition through the next 100 years, neither the former slaves who left the plantation to become independent peasants nor those who stayed on as wage workers could survive without pursuing multiple occupations.

The small mulatto class with mixed blood and light skin occupied a middle-class position, a status inaccessible to darker-skinned descendants of pure African heritage. Recalling the strategies of "higher" slaves whose opportunities for self-gain on the plantation were of a different variety than those available to field slaves, mulattos mined the veins of French guilt by pressing the state for political favors at the same time they used it to enhance their own economic standing. As a group, they claimed new rights and increasingly insisted on achieving for Martinique equal living standards as well as levels of development equal with those of metropoli-

PRACTICES

tan France. This political pressure to gain what they viewed as their economic right was accompanied by economic pressure to be assigned administrative, teaching, and political positions in the colonies. Clearly, mulatto attitudes about what was due them by the French state helped to model new ways of thinking about "payback."

As a logical conclusion of historical patterns and strong popular movements for assimilation to France, in 1946 the island colonies of Martinique and Guadeloupe and the South American colony of French Guiana became fully incorporated into France as overseas departments. In pressing for this outcome, the mulattos operated out of the same understanding that their slave ancestors had: to move up in the world, one had to move into the white man's household, where respectability and power lie. The only avenue to true political power and social mobility at that time lay in Martinique's full assimilation to France as an overseas department, or DOM (*département d'outre mer*). Neither independence nor status as a territory could offer the same benefits.

With DOM status and the full economic benefits of political integration, islanders became eligible for good jobs in the metropole. In the forty years following departmentalization, the search for work in the metropole became a pronounced strategy, and by 1990, there were approximately 350,000 Martiniquais or Guadeloupeans living in mainland France—nearly one French Caribbean person in the metropole for every two persons in the islands.

Although one outcome of full political assimilation was the increased stigmatization of creole language, dress, and diet, the underlying mental maps of creole culture were being actively reproduced in the economic sphere. During World War II, for example, just before departmentalization, the world system which had linked sugar produced in the French islands to France for 300 years came to an abrupt halt. The four-year Vichy occupation of France led Allied forces to blockade France's Caribbean islands. No imports could be received and no exports could leave the dock; the lifeline was cut off. Isolation from France, the single source of economic connection and the hope for assimilation, left Martinique alone in the world. In a sense, these years tested the Martiniquais ability to tap their own cultural resources to survive the difficult odds. People still remember vividly these years of ingenuity in the face of austerity. Today, the Vichy period is commonly referred to as a triumph of self-reliance and, for that reason, a period which evokes great nostalgia.

From 1947 to 1970, rural dwellers, suffering from the decline of sugar markets, migrated en mass to urban areas of the island. Urban studies scholar Serge Letchimy[47] indicates that these rural dwellers brought with them to Fort-de-France their longtime economic practices of exploiting multiple occupations. What had begun in the fields as "informal" profiting from personal gardens, he argues, diversified into new "undeclared" economic activities including construction work, craftmaking, and sewing. For him and other local scholars, the contemporary notion of doing jobs "on the side" represents the continuity of an adaptive cultural habit dating to slavery.[48]

Together, the struggles of slavery, post-abolition subsistence, the Vichy period, and the heavy rural-to-urban migration after World War II all required the still-poor masses of Martiniquais to adapt by exploiting a system they did not control. The structural realities of political and economic institutions clearly differed over these periods. Yet because each set of institutional arrangements precluded the possibility of upward mobility for most, economic opportunism remained adaptive and structures of enforcement were too weak to hinder its development. From the slave-era schemes to enhance personhood and improve life to the multiple economic strategies after abolition that migrated with population movements into urban areas to the entrepreneurial inventiveness during the Vichy period, Martiniquais have demonstrated their embrace of all kinds of opportunities in order to exercise and display personal autonomy. The success of these opportunistic adaptations to hardship over time have contributed to a status system that accords prestige to those who exploit whatever cracks of opportunity possible to come out ahead.

CREOLE-STYLE *DÉBROUILLARDISM* TODAY

Just as economic practices and creole folktales of slaves operated with one foot in compliance, one foot in opposition, so the language of the master could be twisted and used by slaves to secretly serve their own ends. The term *"débrouillard"* is French, but its Creole usage has long carried a more shaded, layered meaning in Martinique than in standard French.[49] As I indicated in the previous chapter, comparisons in dictionaries of standard French and French Creole indicate that unlike the French connotation of a resourceful person, the common understanding of *débrouillard* in Martinique reaches well into the illicit zone of resourcefulness, to include ideas of cunning, dishonesty, and trickery. It is possible that the positive connotations of resourcefulness and ingenuity inherent in the metropolitan term were strategically co-opted by slaves to express their own ideas about resourcefulness.

Scholars have established that in adapting to the demands of slavery, slaves bent many French words and phrases (just as they bent traditional African folktales) to make them fit the circumstances they were confronted with.[50] Indeed, slaves became masters at linguistic duplicity. As noted in the previous chapter, the weaving f double-edged meanings into songs and stories and gestures allowed slaves to express themselves openly with each other without being understood by their masters. For slaves, *débrouillard* would have doubled as a reference to initiative and hard work in the eyes of the master, while a more subversive meaning might simultaneously be communicated to fellow slaves. The term might well have acted as a code for the allowable breaches of morality (stealing/"taking" tools, time, etc.) required to negotiate a labor system void of direct opportunities for advancement or freedom.

Adaptations of Cunning

Today, the term *débrouillard* still carries a complexity not found in metropolitan France, putting Martiniquais in the enviable position of using this word to mean anything they want within the full range of standard French to French Creole cultural understandings. Because Martinique is home to thousands of metropolitan French and because it remains strongly connected to metropolitan France on a daily basis through media, commuter flights, and families with residents in both places, the local meaning for a term like *débrouillard* is constantly juxtaposed with the conventionally positive meaning people convey in standard French. In a symbolic way, this potential for verbal play allows Martiniquais to indulge in a small act of resistance to the dominant culture, which has not fully embraced Martiniquais as French.

The informal economy in Martinique today remains a stage on which cultural history and creole adaptations are expressed and reconstituted, just as the creole language is itself reconstituted each time it is spoken. To say that Martinique's informal economy is characterized by economic values and practices that recall slave-based adaptations to work is not, however, to say that the same economic behaviors have mindlessly repeated themselves over generations and centuries. The slave who "took" the sugar could not even imagine the world in which Patrick sells swimsuits. Rather, it is to say that despite changes in structural factors since slavery, Martiniquais have continued to face serious obstacles in realizing the most important quality denied them during slavery: autonomy. Thus, in addition to earning profits, the values underlying creole economics supply Martiniquais with a kind of moral permission to violate expectations of the state in order to achieve what is rightfully theirs. From a local perspective, the Martiniquais *débrouillard* has no reason to set aside the practices that do him good and do no real harm to anyone else.

Of course, not everyone agrees that trickster behavior has a place in economic exchange. However, the fact that the detractors express such passionate objections to creole-style *débrouillardism* suggests something about the success of creole economics. To clarify the varied perceptions of behavior evoked by this powerful local term, I will introduce you to three broad groups of people according to their views of the morality of *débrouillardism*. These are people I met along my own journey of discovery.

MY JOURNEY TO DISCOVERY

THE CENSUS INTERVIEWS AND "ROUNDING OUT THE MONTH"

By the second month of fieldwork, I had completed another round of edits for the census interview that I had prepared and revised with the help of local volunteers. Since I wanted to ask about people's income, assets, and debts in order to stratify the sample for later in-depth interviews, the imposing first round of questions needed to be especially carefully worded and ordered. Finally, with my sixth major edit, my helpers agreed that the interview now made sense and flowed smoothly. By then it was late August: the long summer break had ended and the routines of school had reasserted their authority and discipline over daily island lives. This exciting annual surge of change and anticipation coincided with the change and anticipation I too was experiencing. Over the next several months, I would knock on the door of every fifth household in three neighborhoods of the city.

The census was aimed at establishing a baseline of information about each household and its members: their ages, relations, who did what for income, what rent and utilities cost, what appliances they owned, and whether they owned other property. I had no real expectations for encountering major insights into how people worked off the books during this stage. I already knew, from my earlier work in French Polynesia, that for as useful as census questions are in laying a foundation of information about households, they are not particularly exciting interviews. The beefy questions I was eager to ask about earning off the books would have to wait until later, in the next round of interviews. But I was in for a surprise.

I had barely begun my first week of census interviews when an informant voluntarily mentioned his undeclared work on the side, as a way to *"arrondir la fin du mois"* (round out the end of the month). Quickly, I incorporated this idiom for side earning into a census question. Once people told me the kind of work they did and what they earned from it, I asked, "Is there anything else you do to 'round out the end of the month?'" Adding this simple question generated much more data about informal earning than I imagined possible at this early stage of research. More importantly, posing a delicate question in idiomatically familiar terms had the effect of signaling my awareness and acceptance of the practice of generating undeclared income. And my perceived acceptance of illicit economic behavior no doubt lowered defenses and provided the latitude for many people to speak candidly, not only of their unofficial economic lives, but also of their attitudes about this work. Thus, it was during the census interviews that many people asserted without hesitation their own involvement in earning undeclared income. As often as not, these same people expressed the rationale for their actions in terms of *débrouillardism*. "Je suis un débrouillard" (I am a *débrouillard*) was an assertion I heard again and again.

At first, I assumed that when people spoke of themselves or others as *débrouillards*, they were simply referencing the qualities of someone who is resourceful and self-reliant, as the French meaning denotes. Yet the more I noticed the contexts in which people used the word, the more I realized the meaning could not be glossed by reference to standard French usage. The more people I talked to, the more shaded and complex the word seemed to be. I began noticing, too, the use of certain idioms I did not know as people described their *débrouillardism*. So, one night in early November, when I was just halfway through the census interviews, and three months into my fieldwork, I seized an opportunity to test out my hunches with a group of people who had invited me to a festive dinner/dance affair.

FLOATING AN IDEA IN ROUNDTABLE COMPANY

The full day and evening event took place high above Fort-de-France at a beautiful overlook setting where many elegant parties are held. The occasion was the annual celebration of a mutual society headquartered in Fort-de-France. According to the society's president, who had invited me, a majority of the members are over age forty and most are moderate to middle income by island standards. As people arrived in their polished cars, smiling and proudly outfitted, I took note again of the fact that island standards of relative affluence were nearly as high as those in the US.

Events of this kind are a treasure for anthropologists because they provide an opportunity to see how people perform in public for each other, how the cultural meanings of pleasure and status are practiced in group settings, how people follow protocols for dancing, mingling, and eating. Fortunately for me, I would also strike a cultural hot button, something that is not easily hidden once the button is pressed and people are relaxed.

The setting and displays of food and flowers provided many clues about the aesthetic markers of an elegant event. Under a huge roof, the open-air space was filled with at least twenty round tables, a large wooden dance floor, and an elevated bandstand. The tables were dressed in starched white linens with elegant place settings. The sensual colors and exotic textures of tropical flowers arched naturally from the table centers as if they had grown there.

As I learned was customary for such events, the day began with *des apéritifs*, including various juices and the ubiquitous 'ti punch (white rum, cane syrup, and a twist of lime) and hors d'oeuvres, a buffet of delicious ham and salami finger sandwiches. The band of seven men had been hired to play the music many older islanders love best—classic Martiniquais tunes from styles known as the *biguine* and the *bélé*, as well as European waltzes and some contemporary *zouk*. Their madras-inflected, all-white outfits and the upbeat, rhythmic sound of their music created another dimension of the evening's aesthetic.

Besides the cloudlike perch of the setting, the lush display of colorful foods and flowers, and the warm energy of Antillean music, the event also seemed to explode with visual human interest, at least for an outsider. Men of all ages wore suits, some with madras cumberbunds. Many older women wore the traditional, freshly starched white lace dresses, some with madras-covered skirts. Younger women wore fashionable, fitted dresses that accentuated their femininity.

The sheer variety of people's skin colors could have advertised Martinique's distinctively fluid color spectrum. Absent the white skin of *békés* and metropolitans, a nearly full range of skin shades was represented, from people with deep ebony skin to those with a skin tone of medium-dark reddish brown, copper brown, yellowish brown, or creamy mulatto. The largest proportion of people had skin tones in the medium-brown range. In Martinique, the correspondence of skin color and class is no longer as predictable as it was during slavery and in the post-abolition period. However, despite many exceptions, it remains true that darker skin colors are more common in lower-income families, and lighter skin colors are more common in families with higher levels of income and education. At this event, the smaller numbers of very light or very dark skin shades certainly echoed the broad island pattern for middle-income people.

Everywhere I looked, I also noticed how carefully people's hair had been styled. Unlike skin color, hair presents an opportunity to assert one's own statement about class. As others have reported for Afro-Creole peoples elsewhere in the Caribbean,[51] "good hair," like fashionable clothing, shoes, and accessories, helps mitigate the stigma of dark skin and elevate the perception of one's class standing. At this event, hair treatments fell into three broad categories: short-cropped afros on some women and most men; chemically smoothed, fashionably styled, and sometimes lightened or highlighted hair on many women and a few men; wavy, curly, and shiny hair on the handful of women and men who appeared to have inherited naturally "good hair" from their East Indian or European ancestry. To be sure, the guests were a diverse looking group.

I had wondered whether I might become restless after hours atop a mountain from which there would be no escape, but the event proved to be a special gift for me. After several turns on the dance floor, politely in-

Adaptations of Cunning

135

dulging whatever old or young man had asked, I took my seat at the host's table of ten and began to engage with the other people loosely gathered in anticipation of beginning the meal. Not long after settling in, I began thinking about the question that had been circling in my brain for days. Would I work up the nerve to ask? Would it offend anyone? I was, after all, a guest of the event's host. I pondered.

We had just been served the opening course and everyone was cheerful, animated, and eager for the main dish to arrive. Several at the table had been busy learning all about me and what I was doing in Martinique. I explained my research as an attempt to understand how people organized their lives economically. After answering many questions, I decided it was the right moment to exchange the curiosity. I turned to the charming, middle-aged man seated next to me. I could use some help making sense of something I had heard in my interviews, I said to him. He smiled and said, "Bien sûr, vas-y!" [Of course, go ahead!]. I asked if he could explain to me what people meant when they said, "Se débrouiller c'est pas pécher?" (it is not a sin to be a *débrouillard*). At that point, I did not yet realize that I had inadvertently Frenchified a Creole expression, *débouya pa péché*.

He looked up, scanned the faces of others at the table, and repeated the correct phrase, "*débouya pa péché?*" Yes, that's it, and what, I asked, might be an example of something you would do and then use that phrase to describe it? Two of the men broke out laughing, while others at the table fell silent. The question I had raised acted like a vortex, suddenly sucking in all the diffuse energy and focusing it in a single instant. Like awakened fountain pots at Yellowstone, people's faces and voices became full of intensity.

I felt my head swiveling in different directions, trying to hear each interjection, which was quite impossible. Oh, for a recorder, I thought. I took copious mental notes and scribbled details during a bathroom break.

The dinner arrived and people's attention turned to the plates of lamb chops and roasted potatoes before them. Then someone said, "Se débrouiller c'est pas mechant" (to se débrouiller is not a mean thing) and others, already tasting their first bites, offered nonverbal agreement with vocalizations of recognition and enthusiastic nods. Someone added, "It takes intelligence to be a real *débrouillard*, because alternate routes are not always available." One man offered a story to illustrate. It was about a man who wanted badly to get into a big soccer match but could not afford the ticket. "The man goes outside the stadium and waits till he spots someone he knows. Then he walks in beside that person, standing tall and proud with nothing to hide, and slips right in."

Near the end of the evening, after a buffet table of desserts was present-ed, one member of my table came back with a napkin full of several desserts, intending to take them home. "Débouya pa péché!" she cried. Everyone laughed and laughed. This example offered another illustration of the con-cept—taking something for use in a way it was not intended, but hurting no one in the process. I left this genial event realizing I had located a local zone of intensity. The mini-focus group interview conveyed both the com-plexity and energy evoked by a single phrase, *débouya pa péché*. If the actions of a *débrouillard* were a little shady, they were also defensible, and moreover, a display of intelligence. The clues and insights would help me plan how to get more information on the topic in the second phase of research.

MORAL JUDGMENTS OF *DÉBROUILLARDISM*: CONTESTED VIEWS OF DEFENDERS, RELATIVISTS, AND OBJECTORS

As my experience with Patrick on that first Sunday in Martinique had forecast, the census interviews revealed early on that I had indeed found a place where many people who had regular jobs also earned undeclared income and were not reticent to claim the activity as positive. How many others might admit to performing illicit earning strategies, I wondered, if I could make them feel relaxed enough about me to be honest? Over the course of these interviews, I figured out a plan. I had become acquainted with several idioms people used to explain their undeclared earnings on the side. More often than not, the explanations revolved around the no-tion of *débrouillardism*. I decided that if I could fold these ideas into a sys-tematic linguistic investigation in the next set of interviews, I might be able to elicit informant responses in the abstract that would create a relaxed environment for the eventual discussion of the informant's personal eco-nomic strategies. Thanks to my tablemates' enthusiasm about discussing *débouya pa péché* at the dinner/dance event, I had learned that broaching a sensitive topic is easier in the abstract. By the time I was ready to begin the next set of interviews, I had devised a strategy for probing informants to teach me more about the meaning of key words and phrases.

On the basis of my census interview data, I selected seventy informants for follow-up, in-depth interviews, people who represented the range of socioeconomic status in Fort-de-France. My primary goal in these inter-views was to learn about the role of informal activities in a household's economic strategy. Did any members of the household participate in buy-ing or selling undeclared goods or services? What was the nature of these

Adaptations of Cunning

137

activities and how much did they contribute to one's income? What meaning did this involvement in illegal economic activity carry for those involved? Knowing these questions were personal and potentially offensive, I began the interviews by asking informants to help me understand some expressions I had encountered over the last many months during my first interviews. Specifically, I asked for their help in explaining the four idiomatic phrases I had heard repeatedly through the census interviews. These phrases included the following:

1. *On a plusieurs cordes à son arc.* (Literally—He has several strings for his bow.)
2. *On a un roue de secours.* (Literally—He has a spare tire.)
3. *Il faut se débrouiller.* (You have to work hard, be resourceful and self-reliant.)
4. *Débouya pa péché.* (It is not a sin to be a *débrouillard*, to do whatever it takes to make it.)[52]

This plea-for-help strategy to open interviews worked extremely well in creating an immediate sense of interest in the interview. As I had hoped, talking about sensitive issues in the abstract appealed to almost everyone. People were eager to offer their opinion of these expressions and to provide examples to illustrate them. The simple act of giving people the space and attention to explain a local phenomenon in their own way seemed to open the floodgates. The strategy not only generated a vast amount of information about the extent to which common local expressions were similarly used and understood or not, but also set a supportive tone for people to segue into talking about their own informal strategies. I will focus here on responses people gave in regard to phrases three and four, which generated the most energetic and long-winded responses.

When I asked people to explain the phrase *il faut se débrouiller*, I learned that how people relate to *débrouillardism* is typically explained in terms of their view of unorthodox economic activities on the side. One of the most interesting findings from this interview technique involved learning how often the examples people gave in the abstract actually corresponded to their own life experience that they eventually shared. Following are some highlights of how various people explained the concept of *débrouillardism* in terms of their own relationship to creole economics.

Philippe is a forty-five-year-old man with cappuccino skin, designer glasses, and a head of thickly curled black hair. He owns a legitimate company that imports and locally distributes paper goods. In the course of our interview, Philippe revealed that in addition to his declared employees, he also keeps a number of people employed off the books to shelve, take inventories, run errands, and clean his cars. Outside of business, he routinely hires undeclared craftsmen who build custom furniture for his beautiful home. Phillipe echoed the views of many middle- and upper-class men I interviewed: "The Martiniquais *débrouillards* do everything to arrive at their ends. It happens at every level, every social sector. They work on the black market. They are gifted. They *se débrouiller* and manage to make ends meet."

Michel, a copper-skinned forty-year-old high school principal, responded to my question about what it means to be a *débrouillard* with "celui qui reussi ce qu'il entreprenne" (he who succeeds at what he undertakes). Michel currently pursues nine distinct types of undeclared economic activities, from hiring undeclared workers to making undeclared money from real estate deals on the side of his functionary job. Interestingly, Michel's portrait of the *débrouillard* is a self-portrait.

"Who are they?" I asked.

> Everybody would like to be a *débrouillard*, but not everybody is. They are people who have several sources of income, that's what a *débrouillard* is. For example, a functionary, he has several houses he rents in addition to his salaried income, and lots of other things that earn him money. The *débrouillard* is someone who finds small but worthwhile niches to operate in.

Edouard, an insurance executive, is a tall, unusually dark brown man for his class. His Caucasian facial features, however, reveal his European heritage. Edouard emphasized the intelligence of a *débrouillard* and how a side activity can affirm this intelligence, which doesn't get expressed in one's primary work. He said,

> Everyone has a definition of a *débrouillard*. I defend my interests, that's it. A *débrouillard* is the most intelligent person, who succeeds in solving a problem first. For example, a professor gives courses on the black market to complement his salary. He must find something on the side to complement. It is degrading to not be able to use your intellectual capacities. This is why many people do work on the side that they like.

Charles is a very dark man with African facial features and a moustache. He is a fifty-year-old taxi driver with a lighter-skinned wife and three teenage daughters. In addition to his taxi work, which is officially licensed but not entirely declared, he also performs odd jobs on the side

that he does not declare as income. In explaining the meaning of a *débrouillard*, Charles described himself in the abstract: "[A *débrouillard*] has three jobs. He is a gardener, mechanic, and something else. If he is a teacher, he can give classes. The more money you have, the better your life is."

In Martinique, people who tend to pursue entrepreneurial, income-generating activities that are not declared are very likely to call themselves *débrouillards*. As side work separate from one's regular job, such activity is highly valued, even by many in comfortable, professional jobs, because of its association with personal freedom and the intelligence required to make such activity profitable.

Asking people to explain the phrase *débouya pa péché* (it's not a sin to be a *débrouillard*) was what best established my credibility as a knowing insider. Almost without fail, this moment in the interview generated the most energy—nervous laughter, intense explanations, pride, anger, defensiveness. *Débouya pa péché*, I was told, offers a defense of a *débrouillard's* actions—being a *débrouillard* is not a sin because even God is said to understand. Interestingly, few of the metropolitans I interviewed who are living in Martinique recognized the *débouya pa péché* phrase unless they interacted regularly with local residents.

Because the phrase effectively asserts one's innocence in the face of God, people tended to reveal their emotional and moral biases about *débrouillardism* as they explained its meaning. Some segments of Martiniquais society fiercely deny the morality others accept in the local style of *débrouillardism*. The vast range of examples and reactions people exhibited in explaining this phrase sorted into three loosely bound points of view about creole-style *débrouillardism*: the defenders, the relativists, and the objectors. The first group believe that creole-style *débrouillardism* is justifiable in almost any context defined by need; the second believe many illegal acts are defensible, so long as they fall within the normative limits of society; and the third group objects to the ideas that both of the other two groups defend. These variations in understanding can lead us to see more clearly the stakes involved in an act of "opposition within complicity" as described in Chapter 4.

DEFENDERS: NOTHING A (NEEDY) *DÉBROUILLARD* DOES IS A SIN The defenders support a broad range of behavior associated with *débrouillardism* as long as it is necessary. This small but vocal set of Afro-Creole people cluster in low- and moderate-income households. Their similar class positions inform two key views about *débrouillardism*: first, they relate *débrouillardism* to neediness; and second, this orientation to need leads some of them to criticize higher-income people whose side work threatens the livelihood of people of lesser means. Both of these strongly held views suggest that class differences in Martinique remain a source of local tension.

Adaptations of Cunning

A very dark-skinned thirty-one-year-old low-income tailor named Yves expressed the opinion that people with few resources must be given the latitude to make ends meet, however they can.

> Someone who is taking care of his needs in life is not a sinner. There are commandments in the Bible, but these laws have been adapted. Many people are forced to steal.

René, a low-income mason with dark skin, used an example from his own experience to frame the idea of *débouya pa péché*:

You work for the city. The mayor leaves early to go to another job. You go to another job during business hours, but you can't stay there a long time. *Débouya pa péché. Débouya pa péché* is always a good thing.

And while a collective sense of difference from France creates a certain solidarity that binds people across their socioeconomic differences, it is perhaps this very solidarity that is being invoked as lower-income people attempt to protect the work that others like them depend on. Guy is a dark-skinned twenty-four-year-old man who repairs radiators on vehicles from his Ermitage neighborhood and lives an entirely undeclared economic life. He contrasted two examples that point up his class-based perspective. The first example clearly relates to someone of modest means. Whatever he must do to get by is acceptable. On the other hand, it is a sin for affluent people with regular jobs to pursue side work that might jeopardize someone else's livelihood:

> Because having clothes to wear is a basic need, it is not a sin to do whatever you must to ensure you are at least able to dress yourself simply. On the other hand, let's say you already have a good job, like a functionary, and you do something on the side for extra money, like grow crops for resale. If you take your produce to market and undercut the prices of those who make their only living selling crops, then you are no longer a *débrouillard*, but a sinner because you have hurt others.

Béatrice, a very dark-skinned woman who is the head of her matrifocal household of seven and a charcoal vendor for forty years, agreed that "people who keep others from making a living are sinners." Smiling nervously, she continued, "People like functionaries do this. Politicians also have three jobs, even more. They shouldn't have three jobs."

Roger is a reddish-brown-skinned fifty-five-year-old factory worker. He too complained about the space these people of means take up in a society with too few jobs to go around: "When you earn a good salary, you have houses to rent, you shouldn't come intrude on the less fortunate by doing work on the side. You already have a lot of money. You keep people who depend on it for a living from selling things. That is not good."

People who assert class-based distinctions of *débrouillardism* tend to support the call of economic need in whatever form it takes, so long as that form is not "reprehensible" behavior. Because people with higher incomes do not face these same needs of survival, their own acts of *débrouillardism* are denied legitimacy, particularly if it appears that they compete unfairly.

RELATIVISTS: CIRCUMSTANCES DEFINE A SIN   The most frequently cited views I heard on *débrouillardism* cohered loosely around "relativist" ideas. People who express these perspectives apply no absolute standards of morality to most behaviors they associate with *débrouillardism*, suggesting that the key to judging such behavior is understanding the circumstances. Unlike the previous group, those who support relativistic views show no predictable involvement in undeclared activities and no class biases about what constitutes acceptable limits of *débrouillardism*. For example, an employed city welder who uses city equipment to furnish work for his private clients on the weekends is a model of *débrouillardism*, as is a banker who supplies rural meat markets with undeclared beef from the livestock he raises on family land outside the city. For many in the "defender" group, the banker might not be viewed as a good *débrouillard* because his side activity could be seen to undermine someone's full-time livelihood.

Relativist views are common among a broad spectrum of Martiniquais, sweeping nearly all income levels, from low to high. Only the very wealthy *békés* or metropolitan French, both of whom strongly disapprove of creole-style *débrouillardism*, are not represented.

According to relativist views, the local *débrouillard*'s schemes frequently violate state law, just as they reach well beyond the conventional meaning of a *débrouillard* in metropolitan France. Legal violations do not necessarily trouble people in this group. Instead, circumstances determine whether a given act can be called by the positive term *débrouillardism*.

Unlike defenders, who justify a broad range of low-income activity under the label of *débrouillardism*, relativists agree that at some point, there are important moral limits to a *débrouillard*'s practices, whatever the circumstances. For them, *débrouillardism* is a proudly held ideal best reserved for a special set of clever behaviors, often illegal, but *"pas grave"* (not serious).

For example, any behavior that makes someone a victim of violence or personal theft of significant value is considered by relativists to be inappropriate for inclusion in the designation of *débrouillard* behavior. People with these views do not hesitate to express their disgust with activities such as prostitution, drug dealing, and contraband smuggling. These "serious" illegal activities are seen to contribute to social problems and trying to pass them off as *débrouillardism* is morally out of line, they argue.

On the other hand, most relativists tend to dismiss small theft such as roadside picking from a plantation or petty pilfering from an employer's office since there are no real victims. The rich will not miss a few bananas;

the employer owes extra to the employees since he pays them so poorly. As a fifty-year-old hairdresser reported to me,

> If you take fruit from the tree of a *béké*, you aren't depriving him. He doesn't use them. You can take them and resell them. It's a small thing. It doesn't make much money.

Among this group of people who accept *débrouillardism* within limits, their explanations in terms of what makes some kinds of activities acceptable varies. For some, the notion of honesty, the open pursuit of a better life without cheating others, is the key. Bertrand, a forty-year-old banker, asserted the difference he sees between the "honest" kind of undeclared work he does (selling items he builds, such as picture frames and aquariums) and other activity that should not be considered *débrouillardism*.

> When you have something on the side, it is not a sin. The goal is to have something undeclared on the side and to also have a declared job. It is a way to make money, to make ends meet. It is not a sin to make ends meet by different means provided that you are honest. The damage that you do to others is not terrible. They are little details. Thieves have a different philosophy.

A twenty-three-year-old female student who lives with her seven brothers and sisters in a moderate-income household also expressed validation for the honest kind of *débrouillardism* that she associates with work off the books:

> People here are never content because they don't want their neighbors to be more successful than they are. There is always a little something on the side, even if you are honest. There are a lot of people who are honest, even the most honest have something on the side.

Others expressed the view that *débrouillardism* can be defended if the scale of activity is small and there is no "hurt" to society. Léon, who teaches auto mechanics, spoke for many people who are able to justify small theft as an acceptable form of *débrouillardism*. His ideas point up the complexity of situation-based ethics:

> A worker takes two bricks from his workplace without asking his boss. It is dishonest. It is a theft, a sin. But, seen in a different light, it is small, too small to hurt the company financially. *Débouya pa péché.*

He goes on to show how this same kind of behavior performed on a larger scale becomes a different phenomenon.

A well-placed banker will not take bricks, he will do something else. Maybe he travels to another country and buys fifty cases of whiskey. He goes through customs without declaring it. He will then try to sell it. This is called traffic, not *débrouillardism*.

A thirty-year-old construction worker for the city, Lucien, works on weekends to build shelves or decks. He, too, emphasizes scale in distinguishing *débrouillardism* from serious crime.

You take something from work—sand or cement. You need just one bag to build something. You take it without the intention of stealing. You do it out of need. In this sense it would not be a real theft. If you take a whole truckload of bags, then it could be taken as a theft. A real thief will take everything.

Michel, a high school principal, effectively defined *débrouillardism* as work off the books. In his view, true *débrouillardism* does not "hurt" society and simply earning money on the side, as he does, is no sin. Saying *débouya pa péché*, he explained that

It is not a sin just to be a *débrouillard*. The *débrouillard* believes that he has not stolen from the society. He does what he can. His actions aren't bad. One defends oneself as one can. The main thing is that the activity earns money and that it doesn't hurt society. That's the Martiniquais mentality.

Michel continued by explaining that *débrouillardism* boils down to another creole expression, "bwé duvan bov lo prop," which translates to French as "le beouf de devant boit l'eau propre" (the first ox to reach the lake will drink clean water). In this single proverb lies an expression of an ethic I found again and again in various aspects of social life—it pays to be first, to be ahead, out in front. Even when there were clearly not enough people to fill a bus, there was always a scramble to be at the front of the boarding line once the driver had arrived. Michel himself said,

You have to be ahead. This is really the mentality of Martiniquais. One is very individualistic. Him first, the others after. Even in the family. This attitude is really Martiniquais, it's not French.

Débrouillards are generally admired by others; those who don't consider themselves *débrouillards* regularly commented that not being one can cost them. I asked Yvonne, a middle-income functionary with the customs office, to explain what a *débrouillard* is. She said,

> A *débrouillard* is tricky, intelligent, sharp. They see everything. It is always good to be a *débrouillard*. Not everyone can be a *débrouillard*. When you are a *débrouillard* in life, that is to say that he seizes opportunities to augment his salary without hurting anyone.

I asked her whether she considered herself to be a *débrouillard*. She replied,

> I don't know. It is difficult to say. For us, it is a good thing, but we are not as talented. You see people who are more cunning, more intelligent, sharper. My husband is sometimes. He has his occasions.

As Yvonne suggests, having a reputation as a *débrouillard* is testament to a person's intelligence and cunning. Among relativists, the *débrouillard* is regarded as a positive force that a few people try to stretch too far. With a cultural ideal that carries such power and status, it is easy to see how *débrouillardism* can influence economic attitudes and practice.

OBJECTORS: THERE ARE NO EXCUSES   The third group includes those individuals whom I call objectors. They do not accept the creole version of *débrouillardism* at all and cite their own moral standards, whether religious or personal, to condemn such behaviors. Adventist and Evangelical Christians, *békés*, high-income Afro-Creoles oriented to metropolitan values, and French metropolitans in Martinique all find a common target in those islanders (e.g., the defenders and the relativists) who accept and often practice creole-style *débrouillardism*. Objectors include many individuals who do not recognize their philosophical kinship with each other because they are positioned in such different places in local society. Thus, while low-income Evangelical Christians are not likely to converse with conservative, upper-income elites about *débrouillardism*, these individuals are nonetheless allies in their contempt for behavior they see as rampant and wrong. Each of the constituent groups of people who express objector views is strongly influenced by European or western standards—whether through the preachings of evangelical religions, through cultural orientations to Europe, or through (in the case of the *békés*) continuing economic domination of island resources, modeled on the control of their colonial French ancestors.

One young, low-income male Adventist described a typical situation for which someone would say *débouya pa péché*:

I have a job. The boss goes out to eat and while he is gone, a client comes in. He says, "I have a problem." So I fix it for him. He asks, "How much do I owe you?" I say 150 Francs. I take the money and put it in my pocket. That is when I say *débouya pa péché*. When you do that, it is not a good thing. Someone who was raised well doesn't do those kinds of things. The Adventists are forbidden to do that because it is a sin before God.

Maurice, a fifty-year-old Afro-Martiniquais man, was one of the very few middle-income people I met who expressed strong objector views. The fact that he spent most of his youth in metropolitan France may account for his passionate disapproval of Martiniquais-style *débrouillardism*. As the former owner of a failed refrigeration company, Maurice said that his employees stole from him and called themselves *débrouillards*. This, he complained, caused him to fail. His bitterness became especially clear when I asked him what he thought about the idea of *débouya pa péché*. He responded energetically,

Good people don't say that. It means that if you are not caught or if no one sees what you did, then *débouya pa péché*, it is not a sin. But it is not honest. He is just excusing himself. Most people are more or less *débrouillards*. They have that mentality. It is rare that people don't do this. It has entered into morals like it is something normal.

Interestingly, as the examples from both Maurice and the young Adventist suggest, judgment about local-style *débrouillardism* requires no consideration of scale, "hurt" caused, or neediness. Like others in the objector group who are white, these men of color associate all creole-style economic behaviors with dishonesty. Naturally, for them, there is no status derived from Martiniquais-style *débrouillardism*.

In my interview with a metropolitan building contractor who has lived with his metropolitan wife and three children nearly ten years in Martinique, I asked him if he would like to be called a *débrouillard*. "No, no, not at all. For me it is something negative. In general, it is not very good. They do something that they shouldn't do. To do something and then say *débouya pa péché* means it is a sin. You say that to excuse yourself."

A metropolitan dentist who has lived in Martinique eighteen years and is married to a Martiniquaise woman expressed contempt for the lack of morality of the local *débrouillard*: "I would not like to be known as a *débrouil-lard*. I prefer to remain in line and wait my turn. Those people irritate me."

The financially elite, endogamous group of white Creoles, *békés*, who are descendants of original French slaveowners, do not embrace any system of values they believe to be practiced by *le peuple* "blacks." Although I met a number of *békés* casually, and from them learned of their disdain toward the crafty Martiniquais man, only one *béké* agreed to be interviewed for this study (the reason I was unable analyze *békés*' relation to creole economics).

Laurence is a very wealthy *béké* business owner, age forty, with wife and children. When I mentioned to him upon arriving at his home that he was the only *béké* who had agreed to meet with me, he smiled knowingly and explained that he was more open-minded than many. Clearly, he intended to make a good impression on this North American researcher. His wife appeared on the porch shortly after we had settled in to the questions I was posing. She handed Laurence a tray with champagne and crackers. Without loosening his tie, he unceremoniously popped the cork and poured the champagne, all the while responding in a bemused way to my questions.

Near the end of the interview, I asked what he thought about *débrouil-lardism*. The unexpected question caused his posture to stiffen and his voice took on a different tone. He did not want to discuss this topic and seemed disturbed that I would be interested in it. Among other objectors, I had frequently noticed that my questions on this topic provoked body language of discomfort. I asked Laurence if he considered himself a *débrouillard*, to which he replied abruptly:

The black man is a *débrouillard*: the *béké* is dynamic.

Laurence declined to elaborate and the interview ended shortly after that. But his simple phrase communicated a powerful message. Because *débrouillardism* in Martinique carries the potential for pejorative connotations, he rejected any association with this kind of behavior. In effect, he was arguing that among his fellow *békés*, business is conducted with a sense of morality that a "black man" perverts into illegality and dishonesty. By couching his dissent about *débrouillardism* in racial terms, he suggested that there is a "naturally" higher standard of white, European morality, unpolluted by the trickery and deceit of the local *débrouillard*.

The "objectors" remind us that in circles of people more thoroughly assimilated to European values (whether cultural or religious), true respectability demands a standard of absolute morality. The variation of these views of *débrouillardism* suggests that the space for opposition within complicity shrinks in proportion to one's internalization of European values.

VIEWS OF *DÉBROUILLARDISM* FROM LOCAL SCHOLARS

The scholars and writers I spoke with over many years in Martinique offer somewhat different explanations of the practices I call creole economics. Yet, there is striking consensus about the fact that these practices are rooted in slave-based histories and adaptations. According to Raphaël Confiant,[53] Martiniquais novelist, the slave-born ethic of *débrouillardism* was coded in the tales of the Rabbit, who used his guile to outwit bigger animals. Echoing Fanon from decades earlier, he said, human rabbits do all sorts of things in the economic realm because nothing is sure. Young and old Martiniquais alike, said Confiant, feel strongly that "life is fragile, precarious. At any moment, one can fall to having nothing. There is a fear of finding oneself with nothing."

In other words, it is not wise to have just one career, because one never knows what might happen. Especially with unemployment so high, people need to know how to do many things, to cushion themselves.

In our interview, Roland Survélor[54]—an erudite *homme de lettres* and historian who has authored several definitive works on the history of Martinique—echoed Confiant's philosophical convictions about his people's deep, unresolved insecurities, imprinted by the conditions of slavery. "We are a people of fear. Fear of God, of masters, of France, of Europe, of our women with other men."

Ultimately, this profound insecurity, coupled with a cultural ideal which promotes self-interested behavior, creates a compelling explanation for the prevalence of undeclared economic activity. Fear drives people to make decisions that will protect them. The rabbit *débrouillard* provides a clear role model for how one can overcome the odds and win for himself what others might not have the courage or cunning to do. At the bottom of this complex psychological profile is one's desire to gain true autonomy, freedom from fear. Being "autonomous" or "independent" was offered most often as the reason the qualities of a *débrouillard* were positive and enviable. As Confiant pointed out, since the grandparents of today's older Martiniquais were among the first slaves freed, memories of hardship and of being disenfranchised are still quite fresh.

The contemporary Martiniquais often goes outside the law in his business dealings, but this poses no crisis of conscience for him, Suvélor insists, because "it's payback, so they're not embarrassed to accept what they can get. It's something they've earned. All is recuperated in the form of the *débrouillard*." Suvélor points out that because *débrouillardism* is indeed viewed as an entitlement, the *débrouillard* is free to seek profits for himself though the channels he wishes, legal or not, to arrive at his goals.

CONCLUSION

Work was the central feature of slavery, and it was during this time that the opportunistic attitudes and strategies embedded in creole economics were first formulated. Slave-era strategies of cunning, oriented to subverting the master's control and achieving economic gain and personal autonomy, have continued to prove adaptive precisely because of structural factors associated with French colonial and postcolonial policies. These habits of economic duplicity (coded in still-popular trickster stories) lend support to the impulse among many local people to better their incomes while ignoring the laws of a state to which they feel only a partial sense of allegiance.

Perhaps this attitude of proper compensation for centuries of mistreatment helps explain why people were rarely reticent to talk about their undeclared side activities or second careers. The law in all its manifestations is of French design, not Martiniquais, so people here do not necessarily feel compelled to act within it. Making money from informal activities does not raise a moral problem for most people I talked with, even if they are not themselves benefiting. In fact, a large share of my informants seem to feel no need whatever to conform to the law if their only "crime" was not sharing their earnings with the state in the form of fees or taxes. And, while objectors of *débrouillardism* criticize such local practices and hold them up against European or religious standards of economic morality, those who defend *débrouillardism* may be positioned best to survive adversity in uncertain times.

SIX

Opportunism by Class

THE PROFIT AND STATUS OF UNDECLARED WORK

> THE EXPERIENCE OF SLAVERY HAS SHAPED
> CARIBBEAN SOCIETIES AND STILL DICTATES
> BEHAVIORS THAT HAVE APPARENTLY NOTH-
> ING TO DO WITH THE ACTUAL PERIOD . . . IT
> IS AS IF AN INVISIBLE WOUND WERE STILL
> BLEEDING IN THE MEMORIES OF THE DESCEN-
> DANTS OF MASTERS AND SLAVES ALIKE.
>
> —Marie-José N'Zengou-Tayo, "Exorcising Painful Memories," 2000

The practice of creole economics occurs in an animated landscape of meaning and activity, a landscape that has been shaped organically by the past. Without this understanding of context, the informal economy in Martinique could easily be misunderstood as a simple reaction to the high costs of doing business in France legally. And while these costs certainly do account for the widespread scale of undeclared income schemes, they do not help explain why people want to work on the side, as so many do. Understanding why people work on the side matters to development planners and economists, who are prone to assume that informal economies exist as a survival strategy and that therefore informal operators are eager to make the transition to formal sector employment given adequate inputs of training, credit, or aid.

To make sense of the local patterns in how people earn informally, we need to see creole economics from an insider's perspective. In the preceding chapters, I have focused on the building blocks for such a view, including the following:

- the longstanding and uninterrupted weight of France in island life;
- the seedbeds of *débrouillardism,* the continuing value of these adaptations over time, and the contested meanings of *débrouillardism* by different segments of local society;
- the difficulties Martiniquais still face in claiming their Frenchness and the related invigoration of creole identities that valorize illicit economic activity.

With this landscape of social histories, adaptations, identities, and attitudes toward economic morality, it is now possible to see how strategies differ by class. In this chapter, we will meet many practitioners of creole economics, each situated differently with respect to household income and needs, workplace opportunities, and social networks.

TRACKING THE BUYING AND SELLING RANGE OF INFORMAL ECONOMIC ACTIVITY

PRACTICES

Unlike metropolitan French, Martiniquais in significant numbers and at virtually all income levels accumulate extra, undeclared income by engaging in productive activity. Usually, exchanges of undeclared goods or services occur between pairs of buyers and sellers. Very often, these buyer/seller dyads connect patrons and clients across socioeconomic groups. In contrast, when people simply underreport their earnings or use contacts to effect an administrative outcome, as in metropolitan France, there is no productive activity. The distinctively productive form of informal economic involvement in Martinique appears to be linked to the "mental maps" that have long channeled economic self-interest in locally prescribed ways.[1] Cheating on taxes surely occurs in Martinique, but this activity would not fulfill the non-economic needs for autonomy and status generated from *débrouillardism.*

To better grasp the broad range of people who participate in undeclared activities, I performed a cluster analysis of the 200 households in my sample. I chose to analyze households rather than individuals, despite the fact that Martinique is a very individualistic society, and household members do not generally pool resources except at survival levels. Still, individuals who pursue undeclared earning schemes often do so in response to household rather than individual needs, a social reality that neoclassical economics tends to ignore. In addition, the household base typically supplies an individual with the information, social networks, and time needed to participate in an informal activity on the side. Understanding the relative affluence of a person's household helps make sense of his or her economic choices. On the basis of collective resources, debt, and income, each household was sorted statistically into one of four clusters: low-income, moderate-income, middle-income, and upper-income.[2]

When involvement in undeclared work (creole economics) is viewed through the lens of class (and in the next chapter, gender), it becomes much easier to see how it is fitted to the opportunities and resources available. It will also become apparent that in spite of the variations spun by individual needs, opportunities, and success, participation in undeclared economic activity is meaningful beyond the benefits of income. Even those who generate negligible amounts of money from their side activities enjoy doing something of their own making.

Viewing households according to their resources also allowed me to separate buyers or consumers of undeclared goods or labor from sellers or producers according to socioeconomic levels. Figure 2 condenses these findings to illustrate three key pieces of information: (1) how overall buying and selling patterns shift by class; (2) how specific types of activities characterize undeclared earning strategies by class; and (3) how women and men engage in informal earning in distinct ways.

The undeclared activities of poor and moderate-income people generally involve selling informal goods and services. Undeclared workers perform odd jobs such as hauling and delivery, as well as car and home repair, construction work, domestic work and yard work. Most of these jobs serve a higher-income patron or buyer. Low- and moderate-income people also act as street sellers and resellers of produce and manufactured goods. Many middle-income professionals also sell their work on the side of their formal work in order to earn extra income. I met architects, engineers, accountants, and schoolteachers who moonlight on weekends, selling their services to other middle-income people. Some pursue a side business for extra income unrelated to their formal employment (selling products like cakes or services like coaching).

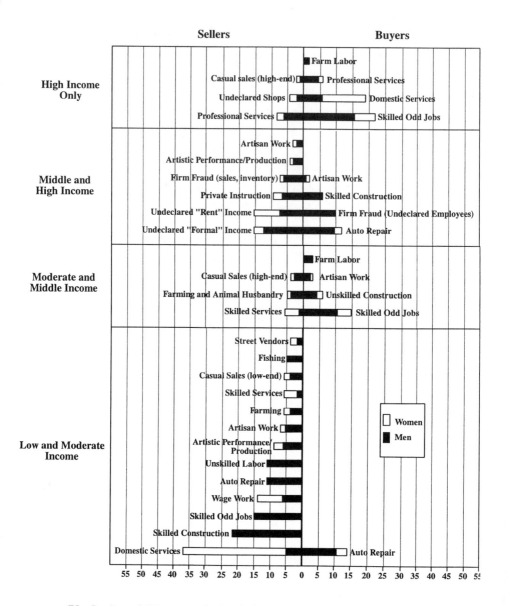

Sellers   **Buyers**

High Income Only
- Farm Labor
- Casual sales (high-end) / Professional Services
- Undeclared Shops / Domestic Services
- Professional Services / Skilled Odd Jobs

Middle and High Income
- Artisan Work
- Artistic Performance/Production
- Firm Fraud (sales, inventory) / Artisan Work
- Private Instruction / Skilled Construction
- Undeclared "Rent" Income / Firm Fraud (Undeclared Employees)
- Undeclared "Formal" Income / Auto Repair

Moderate and Middle Income
- Farm Labor
- Casual Sales (high-end) / Artisan Work
- Farming and Animal Husbandry / Unskilled Construction
- Skilled Services / Skilled Odd Jobs

Low and Moderate Income
- Street Vendors
- Fishing
- Casual Sales (low-end)
- Skilled Services
- Farming
- Artisan Work
- Artistic Performance/Production
- Unskilled Labor
- Auto Repair
- Wage Work
- Skilled Odd Jobs
- Skilled Construction
- Domestic Services / Auto Repair

□ Women
■ Men

55 50 45 40 35 30 25 20 15 10 5 0 5 10 15 20 25 30 35 40 45 50 55

Undeclared Economic Activity by Frequency of Participation

© Browne, 1996   F I G U R E 2   *Numbers of individuals who buy and those who sell off the books, mapped by their gender and the socioeconomic status of their households. Patterns show that men dominate all informal activity and that undeclared production dominates in low- and moderate-income groups, while more affluent groups buy as well as sell off the books. This table does not include non-cash exchanges of goods or services.*

Very often, middle- and upper-income people act as buyers of undeclared labor when they hire lower-income workers to perform household or business services or to produce goods such as custom-built furniture or clothing. I also met professionals (like Patrick) who buy undeclared, high-end clothing and accessories imported and sold by casual retailers in undeclared suitcases of goods brought from Italy, Venezuela, or Brazil. Government functionaries frequently hire undeclared laborers to build their new or second homes. Two functionaries revealed to me that they act as "hidden" entrepreneurs behind a host of apparently independent street vendors in Fort-de-France. As this variety suggests, the forms of informal activity pursued by people at different ends of the socioeconomic ladder often connect middle- or upper-income buyers to low- or moderate-income sellers in one-to-one economic relationships that circumvent the state.

The analytical separation of buyers from sellers accomplishes two purposes. First, it recognizes the theoretical importance of the demand (buying) side of economic activity, a side that is rarely mentioned by those studying informal economies. Second, it casts light on the relationships that link sellers to buyers of undeclared goods and services. As I discussed in Chapter 3, many studies have assumed that the informal economy is a self-contained phenomenon in which poor informal producers provide cheap goods and services to other poor people. My research suggests, however, that the buyers and sellers of a given service or commodity often represent people in different class positions. Consider, for example, people who use undeclared construction or domestic workers. The people selling their services are not working for clients of their same socioeconomic background. These kinds of cross-class links are a vital part of the resilience of informal economies precisely because they are built on dyadic, personal relationships between buyers and sellers.

Opportunism by Class

INFORMAL INCOME PATTERNS BY CLASS

LOW-INCOME CREOLE ECONOMICS

During my original fieldwork, I lived in the two-room basement quarters below the garage of a large home in the neighborhood where most of my low- and moderate-income informants came from. Although my cold-

water shower was located outdoors in rather plain view of other households, my living arrangement was comfortable by neighborhood standards. Ermitage, as the neighborhood is called, is a relatively small, self-
contained area which occupies the lower portion of a *morne* (mountain)
that (via a separate road) rises upward to the higher perches of middle-
and upper-income neighborhoods. Ermitage is a convenient location for
those without cars. It is just a mile walk to the center of Fort-de-France
and only a few blocks from the central bus terminal, which fronts one side
of the town's main cemetery, a wash of white, above-ground tombs dotted with colorful flowers and photos. To reach Ermitage from the center
of town, one passes by the bus terminal and cemetery, and then a long
stretch of produce vendors who line the edge of the park where the city
arts-and-crafts teaching center is located. Beyond the arc of vendors lies
a bridge which crosses an inland canal where traditional fishermen dock
their small, brightly painted wooden fishing boats. On the bridge, one is
likely to encounter several other Ermitage residents, coming home or going into town.

The entrance into the neighborhood requires a steep climb, one I made
many times a day for more than a year. Modest wood homes line either
side of the street. This neighborhood is one of the oldest in Fort-de-
France, having been built back when the town center of Fort-de-France
itself was also just developing in the early 1900s. The main street up into
Ermitage feeds several small, one-way streets that turn east and cut the
neighborhood into a stacked set of rectangles. Each of these streets is lined
with homes, mostly modest, but well kept. Many of the dwellings one
sees from these small streets are the original wood with wood shuttered
windows. Where the old structures have been demolished, new homes of
concrete have been constructed on the lots, making the neighborhood a
densely packed assortment of wood and concrete, the old and the new, the
neglected and the meticulously maintained. Some blocks include a small
dry goods shop; one houses a kindergarten school. The main road up
boasts a resident family patisserie.

But the density of households in this compact area is far greater than
one can observe from the street. For between the vertically staggered finger
roads, there is an abundance of modest dwellings, invisible to vehicular
traffic, dwellings that have absorbed the spaces since the original neighborhood was developed. To view them, one must walk down the concrete
 footpaths that lead off several of the small streets. On either side of these

footpaths lie more wooden homes and some structures built of galvanized tin. At least two dozen that I counted are so hidden from the main roads that the census takers do not know they exist. Identifying undeclared homes is easy—they do not bear the ubiquitous white-on-blue address plates that mark every recognized French address. Generally, these un-marked dwellings are little more than crude shelters, built of tin scraps and wood or unpainted concrete blocks. The squatters residing in them access running water and electricity by poaching off the legitimate lines of neighbors. In most cases, these pitiful dwellings belong to immigrant families—people from Haiti, neighboring St. Lucia, or Dominica. Many households in this neighborhood keep livestock such as pigs, chickens, and other fowl confined to small areas in the yard.

My cluster analysis sorted forty-three households into the "low-in-come" category. No single earner in these households is likely to earn as much as a minimum wage. The average monthly income per producer (income earner) in these households (including both formal and informal earnings) is 3,380F ($676US), higher than the average income officially re-ported, but still well below the official minimum wage for Martinique.[3] According to my research, nearly 67 percent of working women and 56 percent of working men in low-income households earn their entire in-come in the informal sector. Undeclared economic activities also supply 50 percent of the income generated each month in households at this low-income level (see Figure 1). But although low-income households struggle to make ends meet, it should be pointed out that "absolute" poverty is rare. Generally, the poorest people in Martinique are confined to illegal immi-grants who come to perform the kinds of manual labor that Martiniquais do not seek.

The vast majority of people in low-income households have basic utilities such as indoor plumbing, running water, electricity, and phones. However, they only sometimes have cars or amenities such as washing machines. Although they are not at risk of starvation because of substan-tial French welfare programs, low-income people often live in unhealthy, even dangerous, conditions with few comforts and without any economic cushion that others in the society routinely enjoy. The children from these households also experience lives of economic vulnerability. Few had adult role models for achieving at school or for learning marketable skills with which to compete on the job market. A third of low-income households in this group are matrifocal, that is, headed by women with no resident male partner. Another third are households composed of extended families that rely primarily on women's earnings. Matrifocal and extended family households are commonplace in lower-income segments of Caribbean societies, where nuclear families represent only one of many adaptive living arrangements. Both of these structures impose especially severe constraints on the women who bear the burden of supporting them. With so few resources available to household members, older children often end up dropping out of school in order to earn enough to keep the family going. It is then easier for younger brothers and sisters eventually to follow suit, rather than face the uphill struggle of keeping focused on their studies. To make meager resources go as far as possible, it is also common for family members to disperse and locate temporarily in other households, so that the composition of households in this group frequently shifts.

In these households a reliance on informal work can be self-perpetuating. This pattern relates not only to low levels of education and skills training, but also to the limited social networks one can access. With no other source of contacts, the networks of parents and other relatives present the only effective entry point for the young adults of the household. By contrast, as I have shown in other work, better-endowed households are better able to encourage family members to achieve a good education, which helps them form the kind of new social networks that can help them leverage their own upward mobility.[4]

With less education and fewer marketable skills than others in society, low-income workers are severely limited in the types of formal, declared work they are able to find and keep. Even if someone locates a job in the

formal economy, it is frequently insecure and subject to termination without notice. Those who find low-wage work in factories or warehouses, in grocery stores or large retail centers, are often the first to be laid off in pressed economic times. Sometimes, the only work men find is temporary, undeclared labor on construction sites or in service stations and garages. Women are most often forced to take undeclared clerical or housekeeping jobs.

Low-income people routinely collect state aid for unemployment, indigence, or single parenting. Many informants confessed to me, however, that they had figured out how to manipulate the system to their advantage. "It's best if I keep my work undeclared," said a construction worker, "because if they find out, I'd lose all the allocations I'm getting now from the state." Of course, state allocations do not alone constitute an adequate basis for survival, for in the consumerist society of Martinique, any income is quickly absorbed.

The low-income households I visited included the following people: Angélique, a fifty-year-old single mother of ten who supports her household on a part-time cleaning job for a private company as well as whatever side jobs she can find; Victor, a forty-year-old man who lives with his elderly, invalid mother and does masonry work for construction companies when they call him; Paul, a twenty-two-year-old man who paints exteriors for any clients he can find and lives with his brother in a bare, two-room dwelling hidden from the street; and Alexison, a twenty-six-year-old who repairs car radiators and the only one of his siblings who generates income for the household, which is headed by their mother. Since she quit her undeclared housekeeping job after being diagnosed with glaucoma, she has no unemployment insurance and cannot afford the operation necessary to recover use of her eyes.

In the following case study, I will show how, despite the survival orientation of low-income households, informal earning cannot be viewed in economic terms alone. The values of and concern for autonomy operate at this level, even if there are fewer opportunities to express it.

LOW-INCOME CASE STUDY: MARIE AND JEAN-MARC, ODD JOBS, AND HOUSEKEEPING   Marie and Jean-Marc's household shows how total dependence on informal income can paralyze economic advancement, since informal sources of income are typically unpredictable and insecure. Undeclared workers are unprotected by laws requiring proper notification of job termination, unprotected by the full range of social security coverage, and unable to access unemployment benefits if they lose their jobs. For people who pursue informal activities on the side of their declared work, this lack of protections holds no meaning. But for people like Marie and Jean-Marc, working hard to earn enough to sustain their family consumes time and energy that might be otherwise directed at learning new skills. When fundamental economic insecurity pervades a household's livelihood, the endless frustration and low pay become hard to escape. At this level of earning, creole economics is less a strategy for profit than a strategy of mere survival. Even in this context, however, as we will see, men who consider themselves *débrouillards* regard their informal work as a source of personal autonomy.

Marie and Jean-Marc are a recently married couple with three young

Opportunism by Class

159

children. The dark skin of family members is typical for low-income people, though Marie's straightened hair helps her look stylish and pass as someone with more income when she is out alone, running errands for her employer. Both Marie and Jean-Marc have a primary school education. They live in the Ermitage neighborhood in a small, crowded, two-room house, self-built with wood planks and tin roof. Anyone wishing to visit the family must approach their living quarters through an alley. Once inside the chain link gate, which is usually locked, there is direct access through back stairs to the large home belonging to their patrons, the Augustin family. The Augustins' home is two story, well furnished, brightly painted, and one of several imposing exceptions in this older and primarily low- and moderate-income neighborhood. Marie has been the domestic servant of Madame Augustin for many years. Her work is undeclared. For her employer, Marie's calling-distance proximity is a great convenience since she is almost always available to assist the household—whether weekend, holiday, or middle of the night. Her work consists of cleaning the large house, cooking for the family of four, doing laundry, shopping, and walking to town to run errands.

Jean-Marc finds what work he can in construction, but his income is irregular. He is often recruited by the retired husband of the patron household to perform odd jobs, repair work, or painting for their home or for their rental property in the neighborhood. To help make ends meet, Jean-Marc leaves the city on the weekends to fish or collect food from the gardens in the rural area nearly two hours south of town where his mother and brothers live. To get there, he must pay for a *taxi collectif* each way since he has no car. Despite the uncertainty of his income, Jean-Marc uses his freedom from set working hours to continue work on a grand project he recently began. On a small piece of family land near his mother, he is working to build his own house. "I'm free," he said, "because I can do almost everything myself and with my friends—electricity, plumbing, roofing. In two years, I'll have my own house." His rudimentary skills are those he has learned informally and so tend to be disregarded by employers. "I know enough," he argued. The personal autonomy that Jean-Marc displays is something others around him notice and admire. As one of his brothers said, "He's a born *débrouillard*, that's for sure."

When the project is finished, Jean-Marc and Marie may be able to alter their lives, out from a rent payment that leaves very little income to live on. For now, though, the challenges they face are complicated by emotional as well as economic ties to the Augustins, who occasionally give small gifts like books or toys to the children. Meanwhile, there is little incentive for the Augustins to help their clients advance their skills, broaden their contacts, or find better opportunities elsewhere. For now, Jean-Marc and Marie are stuck.

This example points up the sober implications of undeclared work for people who must depend on it for their entire livelihood. Full-time informal operators may face serious compromises and sacrifices with respect to working conditions, hours, and benefits—all problems that do not affect those whose informal work operates on the side of a regular job. The reality for low-income people thus raises a question about whether or not the cultural values embedded in creole economics as side work also operate at this survival level. When working off the books is simply the best way to scratch out a living, how likely are people to see their work as an opportunity to exercise economic cleverness or personal autonomy?

I didn't expect the answers I heard. Few men, including Jean-Marc, complained to me about their undeclared work lives. When I asked them if they would accept a full-time, declared job with predictable income and benefits, more often than not, men said no, responding with the phrase, "J'ai besoin de mon liberté" (I need my freedom). In contrast, however, when I posed the same questions about taking a formal sector job to women dependent on informal income, most of them said yes, they would. This difference in gendered attitudes relates to my finding that men are much more likely than women to participate in creole economics, a phenomenon I take up in the following chapter.

Marie and Jean-Marc's predicament may seem like a clear-cut case of performing undeclared work to meet survival needs. But Jean-Marc's attitude about his work helped me see that even when earning one's entire income off the books seems like a last resort, there are culturally meaningful reasons to prefer it. The handyman jobs he is assigned by his patron, said Jean-Marc, allow him a wide degree of latitude to come and go according to his own schedule, to carry out each job according to his own plan, and to spec and purchase materials he needs. In addition, Jean-Marc's secret homebuilding project supplies a crucial source of personal autonomy and control over circumstances that otherwise constrain him. When he talks about it, his face lifts and he smiles with unabashed pride. By building his own house, completely off the books, Jean-Marc demonstrates to his family and his male friends that, whatever else may be true, he is his own man.

Opportunism by Class

The moderate-income households I visited were located in the Ermitage area as well. Often, the slightly better off households were obvious to a passerby because they were larger, often new homes of concrete construction, and more likely to be painted. The size of the home, however, is not necessarily a good indicator for the relative standard of living, since several larger, even two-story homes were occupied by poor residents.

There are sixty-seven households from my sample that fall into the category of "moderate income." In these households, unlike the low-income group, material assets are likely to include a car and a washing machine, and earners produce higher formal and informal incomes. The total monthly income generated per earner (including formal and undeclared sources of income) in these households is about double that in the low-income group (7,129F or $1,425US). About 72 percent of men and 69 percent of women in the moderate-income group of households have a formal sector job, which provides a steady if modest income. Far fewer people from moderate-income households, therefore, depend wholly on informal income, but many men (42 percent) and some women (15 percent) pursue informal income as a supplement to their regular incomes to make ends meet. Women in this group are half as likely as women in the lowest-income category to be the sole head of their households.

People in moderate-income households make about 34 percent of their income from informal work (see Figure 1 and compare to low-income earners, who earn 50 percent off the books). However, while the percentage

PRACTICES is lower, the raw income from informal activities is higher in this group. Here are some of the people I met in the moderate-income households I visited.

Jean-François is a young man of thirty-two who lives with his mother (who bartends) and his step-father, a clerk at city hall. Through his father's network, Jean-François got a job in the city's garage, where he repairs engines on city vehicles, and on weekends he does undeclared repair work for his own clients.

Olivier is forty-six and lives with his mother (a part-time retail clerk) and sister (who has a job with social services) in a three-room home with few amenities. Olivier drives a taxi belonging to his cousin when it is available; the rest of the time, he does undeclared plumbing work in the

neighborhood.

Brigitte, thirty-eight, lives alone and works full time at the Red Cross as a declared secretary. To earn more, she does hair styling in clients' homes as well as in-store promotional marketing for large consumer stores.

In most of these cases, creole economics plays an important role in generating income, even if one is regularly employed. In the fuller case discussed below, the role of creole economics can be seen as a vital way to leverage one's economic position while achieving the satisfaction of running one's own business.

MODERATE-INCOME CASE STUDY: JULIAN, FURNITURE REPAIR   The potential of creole economics to improve someone's living standard becomes apparent when there is at least a minimal base of resources to build upon. Julian's case shows how the practice of creole economics advances an individual's economic position without compromising his sense of security or violating his strict religious code of morality. Julian's single-family wood home is small but well kept. Tropical bushes line the walkway to his front steps, where an ample front porch with wood rocking chairs greets visitors. The driveway, made uneven from shifting soil, leads to his garage workshop. It was in the garage where I heard the whir of a band saw and where I sat for the interview as he continued to rebuild a chair for a neighbor client.

Julian is a retired furniture maker, a handsome man with bright eyes and deeply reddish-brown skin that made it hard to tell his age. Like Marie and Jean-Marc, he lives in Ermitage. Unlike them, Julian possesses a valuable skill that his record of employment attests to. Before his retirement, his declared job gave him access to a broad range of affluent clients who made it possible for him to leverage his economic position. For twenty years before his retirement, he managed the furniture inventory and repairs for the largest bank in town. The steady job and access to those more affluent enabled him to borrow enough money both to build on to his own modest home and to purchase and renovate an abandoned adjacent property. He now rents out this neighboring property to an immigrant Haitian family and does not declare the additional income. Throughout his tenure with the bank, he performed undeclared activities on the side for various high-level employees who sought his carpentry skills for a lower, informal price. Generally, they hired him to build custom pieces of furniture for their private homes. "Officers of the bank came to me," he said with pride. "A lot of people wanted me to build things for them on the weekends. It was good for everyone."

Opportunism by Class

Although he is retired, Julian continues to build and repair furniture for higher-income clients who came to know him through the bank as well as for friends in the neighborhood. Maintaining clients of various socioeconomic means has allowed him to supplement his formally earned retirement benefits with income he does not declare. Did he consider himself a *débrouillard*, I asked? "Yes! I'm a good *débrouillard*," he said. "And God appreciates my work," he added.

As I looked around the workshop for more clues about Julian, I noticed the organized tool racks, supply pegboards, stacks of raw wood, sheets of leather, and several icons of the Virgin Mary. Julian made clear to me that he is a religious man and despite his ready openness to discussing his long-term illicit income earning, he peppered our conversation with numerous scriptures he knew by heart. Mostly, he used these scriptures to denounce the corrupt world around us and to emphasize the need for young people to embrace a clearer moral guide. At no time did he apologize for or indicate any misgivings about his extra undeclared earnings over the last twenty-five years. For him, as with so many others I met, there was no contradiction between leading an emphatically "moral" life and earning illicit income. "It's God before all for me. I get along with everyone—poor and rich alike. If I can do a service for someone, I do it. I am content with myself, with who I am."

The conviction that creole-style *débrouillardism* does not compromise one's honesty or morality recalls the "relativist" perspective of those who consider circumstances to define good or bad behavior. Because Julian works hard for his money and does not cheat others, he considers that he is acting with the kind of morality that "counts" in the eyes of God.

MIDDLE-INCOME CREOLE ECONOMICS

The neighborhood where I located my middle-income informants is a bustling area of "upper" Fort-de-France. From the low- and moderate-income areas huddled close to the town center, one drives up the *morne* to the more exclusive neighborhoods. Not surprisingly, the road up does not pass through Ermitage, but around it. At the top, one reaches a plateau culminating in one of the busiest roundabouts in town. Spokes off the hub channel drivers variously to large commercial shopping areas, private schools, medical clinics, and newer residential areas; to older, middle-income residential areas; or to the oldest and most exclusive residential area, called Didier, where the *békés* (mostly gone now) built their urban colonial estates and once held dominion. At various points from the roads that circulate at these heights, one can view the spectacular lookouts over the bay of Fort-de-France and the Caribbean Sea beyond.

Taking the spoke that heads to the upscale shopping area known as Cluny, one bisects neighborhoods that are dotted with newer as well as older homes. Typically, the newer homes reveal architectural concerns with security—from imposing privacy fences to iron security gates. Many older homes have also been retrofitted to add iron enclosures on doors and even windows. Guard dogs are increasingly common in these areas, as are home alarm systems. The contrasts with the low- and moderate-income areas below are striking but familiar. In addition to the obvious differences in home construction materials, privacy measures, and well-tended landscaping, middle-income residential areas are also visually distinguished by the near absence of pedestrians and the ubiquity of SUVs and high-end sedans. Compared to Ermitage, where people fill the streets and most people know not only their neighbors but also many others in the neighborhood, residents of Cluny are detached from each other and generally unaware of each other's comings and goings.

Compared to households like Jean-Marc's and Julian's, which generate informal income as a primary source of earnings or as a vital source of secondary income to meet basic needs, more affluent islanders practice *débrouillardism* and creole economics to improve their already good living standards. There are thirty-two households in my sample which fall into the middle-income socioeconomic group. These households have fewer members and more resources, including an average of two cars and property other than their homestead, averaging $3,416US per primary household earner per month. Incomes are substantially higher among people in this group than in the two groups just discussed, but the range of incomes is large. In these households, an average of 25 percent of total household income generated comes from undeclared economic activities (see Figure 1).

The middle-income householders I visited include the following. Martin, thirty-five, lives with his wife, a high school teacher. He owns a shoe boutique and returns from buying trips with suitcases full of undeclared clothing and electronic goods he resells locally.

Chantal, forty-six, is a lab technician at the city medical research clinic; she lives with her husband, who is in management for a metropolitan firm.

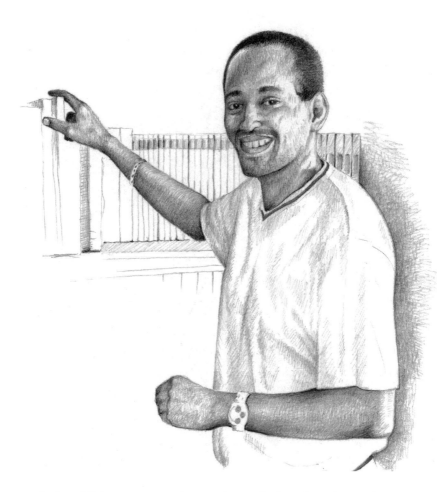

PRACTICES As her children were growing up, she worked on the side one day a week for a private lab.

Régis is a fifty-year-old mid-level functionary at the Prefecture, the local seat of French government. With his good income and stable job, he easily secured a bank loan to purchase a fancy fishing boat that he uses to indulge his passion, dazzle his friends, and earn a nice second income off the books. His hired crew of two help him collect the catch each weekend and distribute it for sale in Fort-de-France.

Henri, fifty-one, is a banker who lives with his wife and two teenage children. At least twice a week, he visits his acreage in the country, about forty minutes outside Fort-de-France, where he has two hired workers who help him most of the year cultivate fields of vegetables that he will hire others to sell in rural town markets.

MIDDLE-INCOME CASE STUDY: MARTIN, OWNER OF SHOE BOUTIQUE   Martin and his wife, Michèle, are a handsome couple each a shade of copper brown, she with short, platinum-bleached and straightened hair. They were married early by local standards, at the ages of twenty-four and twenty, respectively. In the four years since then, they have lived in a comfortable, six-room, two-story home that Martin inherited from his parents upon their marriage. The exterior is freshly painted in a dusty rose with white trim and enclosed within a handsome but imposing iron fence and gate. Inside, the home is well equipped with color TVs, washing machine, stand-alone freezer, and an elaborate stereo system. They each own a late-model car.

At the time of their marriage, more than ten years earlier, Martin had been employed for several years as an accountant for a private firm. Michèle was economically secure in her teaching job at the middle school. But after several years of work in this capacity, Martin realized that his real chance for economic growth related more to the informal economic activities he had been performing for years on the side. While still a young man living at home with his parents, Martin had traveled to Brazil and to Italy. He realized that by taking an empty suitcase and bringing it back full of clothing, he could resell the items locally for a large profit, as he knew others had done. Explaining to me why he ultimately decided that the world of retail suited him better than behind-the-scenes work of an accountant, Martin said, "To be good in retail, you have to know how to build networks and this comes naturally to me." In Martin's case, it probably did not hurt that he is also good-looking and charismatic. As became more evident through the course of my fieldwork, building and maintaining social networks is a critical skill for anyone performing undeclared activities, since finding and keeping clients for one's services or goods is the key to making money.

The year before I interviewed him, Martin had decided to abandon his accounting career and launch himself in retail. He opened a high-end shoe boutique in town, where he sold the newest fashion shoes from Brazil and Italy. Maintaining his retail life as a shop owner requires a great deal of time, Martin said, but fortunately, his experience with accounting helps him keep things on track. To manage the shop on an everyday basis, Martin relies heavily on a paid (and declared) employee. The legitimate status of the shop and his manager provide Martin ample room to pursue his undeclared economic life undetected. Moreover, his shoe buying

Opportunism by Class

167

trips provide the occasion as well as the personal networks to locate other goods which he imports but does not declare. In effect, for Martin as for many others in Martinique, the mix of declared and undeclared economic strategies he pursues is a virtually seamless whole, well integrated and interdependent.

Martin makes six buying trips a year to "buy shoes," alternating his destinations between France, Italy, Brazil, and Venezuela. He orders the shoes, which are generally shipped, but brings back with him high-end clothing and gadgets—everything from exclusive brand clothing, handbags and belts, to cell phones. Each trip becomes a tax deduction. According to Martin, he pays himself $3,200US/month from his boutique, but this income is supplemented by another $2,000 a month on average that he generally nets from his undeclared sales to friends, family, and shoe clients. He pours his energy into these side activities not only because they yield such high returns, but also because they increase his importance and status among sellers abroad and buyers locally. For so many middle-income Martiniquais men and women who strive to display their economic status through physical appearance, the demand for lower-cost luxury goods and expensive clothing is very high. In fact, part of Martin's strategy with the shoe shop was to create a new set of clients whose demand for designer shoes would translate easily into a potential clientele for his undeclared goods.

The profitability of his strategies cannot be disputed, but the reputation he gains for economic wit is also a great source of pride for Martin. "I'm good at this and I enjoy it. It's much more exciting than doing accounting on the side. I've gotten to know a lot more people and once the right people want to buy from you, others follow them." In the small world of Martinique, nurturing a wide circle of contacts also positions *débrouillards* like Martin and Patrick to show off their success. For Martin, earning undeclared income on the side is a kind of sport. Martin also acts as a buyer of undeclared goods, using people in his network to supply him with undeclared car and home repair services.

HIGH-INCOME CREOLE ECONOMICS

From the busy roundabout at the top of the *morne*, instead of veering off at the Cluny spoke, drivers can take the one that leads due north and further up the *morne* to Didier, once the most exclusive residential area of all

Martinique. Until departmentalization of Martinique, white *béké* families,
the original French colonial slaveowners, located their urban estates here.
Most have since moved out, prompted by the gradual desegregation of
the area as successful mulattos and, later, darker-skinned people began to
move in during the 1960s. The old colonial mansions still anchor either
side of the narrow Route de Didier that demarcates this neighborhood.
Today, some of these grand estates have been bought by prosperous private companies; others belong to Martiniquais of color who have claimed
their place among the island's elite; still others are corporate homes, owned
by metropolitan firms that turn over the residences to their management
elites who come from France to live and work for several years with the
local branch office. Didier thus remains an elegant residential area, testify-
ing all the while to the changing face of affluence and ambition that has

radically altered the demographic landscape since departmentalization in 1946.

There are fifty-eight households in my sample which represent the high socioeconomic level. Most of these households have at least one car per earner, as well as luxuries like dishwashers, air-conditioning, and full-time domestic help; incomes are significantly higher among members of these households than among the middle-income group. The average monthly income per earner is $4,201US, 23 percent of which is generated through informal economic means (see Figure 1). Generally, members of high-income households are supported by earnings in the private sector, but as one example below will illustrate, through creole economics, a cunning functionary can propel his earnings into this level.

At the high income level, participation in creole economics more often involves buying undeclared goods and services than producing them. People who already earn high salaries generally invest so much time in their careers that they have little time left for additional productive work on the side. For them it is more efficient to act as patron to the undeclared work of others, which effectively increases their earnings by cutting their expenses. High-income earners include high-level government functionaries, private sector executives and entrepreneurs, and doctors, lawyers, and accountants. Interestingly, however, among the high earners who are not in business for themselves, many do pursue side work and explain it as a need to feel "autonomy."

Some of the high-income people I met who routinely practice creole economics include men like Edouard, Philippe, and Joseph. Edouard is a

very successful insurance executive who lives in Didier with his wife and an infant girl in a sprawling estate on a half-acre. Although his primary work is a declared, salaried position with a reputable company, he increases his income by engaging in multiple forms of creole economics. To earn extra money that he does not declare, he conducts on-the-side business consulting for a number of personal clients. "It's my chance to really be in charge," he said. Edouard also routinely hires casual, undeclared laborers to save money on custom furniture, outdoor fences, heavy installation projects, and hauling and delivery errands. His entire new home and many of the furnishings in it were built with informal labor—skilled as well as unskilled.

More typically, high-income producers who participate in creole economics do so only as patrons. Philippe owns a large paper distribution company; his wife is a schoolteacher. For all sorts of personal and professional tasks, Philippe hires undeclared laborers. They stock inventory, make deliveries to clients, service his nine vehicles, and build beautiful custom furniture for his home.

Joseph is a radiologist who hires undeclared workers to perform home repairs, build add-ons to his home, and work on his fancy sports cars. Within his medical social circles, he and his family also trade services with other doctors so that none declare their earnings from each other's visits.

Through the story of Michel, a high school principal, we can witness the continuing grip of the *débrouillard* ethic among people who have created for themselves a life of affluence, despite more modest beginnings. Michel's economic life also clarifies how one's strategies in the realm of creole economics are likely to shift with changing economic pressures and opportunities.

HIGH-INCOME CASE STUDY: MICHEL, EDUCATION FUNC-
TIONARY AND *DÉBROUILLARD* PAR EXCELLENCE   Michel's household presents a useful frame of reference for what others in this class view as the ideal—successful, entrepreneurial, self-made, the true *débrouillard* that defines the model to which many Martiniquais, like Martin, Julian, and Jean-Marc, aspire. Today, at age forty, he is a highly paid, salaried functionary in the education system. The affluent profile of Michel's household might not be apparent at first glance. The home he built, where they have lived for more than twelve years, is large but not imposing, and there are no fences or guard dogs like those that stalk the grounds of certain sections of Cluny and Didier. It might appear in fact that this is a typical middle-income family. But the wealth Michel has managed to accumulate goes beyond what is apparent even in his employment situation, which holds no particular growth potential. By pursuing other income from a web of related undeclared economic activities, he continues steadily to increase his assets and resources year by year. They now own their home outright, as well as several other income-producing properties. They have full-time domestic help, air-conditioning in most of the house, and two late-model luxury cars.

Michel, the oldest of four children, grew up without ever knowing his father. His mother alone raised him and the others with modest means, herself working full time at washing, ironing, and cleaning jobs to earn what she could to support them. Michel said that she was a strong disciplinarian,

Opportunism by Class

devoted to their getting a good education. Before they went off to school every morning, she made them go over their lessons with her, correcting their mistakes and drilling them on problems they were expected to solve. He said all four earned their BAC (baccalaureate), a level of academic accomplishment still valued as significant today. With the help of a scholarship, Michel was able to continue his schooling in metropolitan France.

Following two years of training in education in the metropole, Michel returned to Martinique at age twenty and secured a highly sought after government "functionary" position, working as a teacher in primary school. At age twenty-eight—eight years after beginning his career in education, three years after marrying, and the year his first child was born—Michel oversaw the building of his family's first single-family home. He had purchased a lot in Cluny well before the new development area had begun to gain momentum. He saw the property as an opportunity to buy low before the area had become attractive to large numbers. He does not regard his risk as having been a gamble, merely as foresight and planning. Today his neighborhood is one of the stylish, high-end areas in Fort-de-France.

Considering his modest family background, Michel was unusual in being in a position to parlay his education into a secure and well-paying job. But he has worked to improve his social standing in other, ingenious ways, and his strategies have evolved as his economic position has changed. For the first ten years of his career as a teacher, Michel earned extra money from furniture he built to order on the side. At the same time he was earning income from this side activity, Michel was also busy increasing his exposure and range of acquaintances by organizing neighborhood property owners to address certain concerns regarding city services. He became president of the development area and used his position to expand his social networks among the affluent, who respected his volunteer efforts to help their community.

A few years after settling in his new home, he was promoted to principal of his school, and in the same year, named *adjoint au maire* for an affluent city near Fort-de-France, a plum position he claims he got through his strong social networks. This job requires him to manage the city's land and property concerns and, thus, gives him access to all the prime residential and commercial properties owned by the city, properties which are to be sold off in order to raise needed local revenues. His management of the information and the properties in question puts him in the enviable position of having control over a large portfolio of resources.

Michel is a careful, pragmatic strategist who thinks constantly about what economic opportunities he can exploit now or arrange for the future. With his new position at the city and with increased responsibilities at work, Michel's informal earning schemes have adapted so that they require less of his personal time; increasingly he takes the role of the buyer of the undeclared work of others. On both his current home and the second new home he is now building, for example, Michel declared himself the *entrepreneur* of the construction project. This status makes him responsible for hiring all the labor and for paying the state-mandated TVA (value added) tax. By using an undeclared architect as well as undeclared workers, he has rendered the entire project effectively invisible to the state, enabling Michel to evade the stiff TVA tax, which in Martinique amounts to 7 percent of the value of the home. Since the various arms of French taxing authorities are notoriously poorly coordinated, this is a relatively low-risk option, according to Michel.

All the workers on his construction projects are also undeclared, though most of them have declared jobs with construction companies during the workweek. Some take off from those jobs to work his project; others work there in the evenings and on weekends to earn extra money they do not declare. For Michel, the undeclared status of the work both saves money and keeps the project low profile, which is important in avoiding certain taxes. In addition, because he has strong social networks, he is able to find highly qualified workers who will work on the side for less, but offer the same expertise as their respective firms would charge much more money for. The list of laborers he uses in this way includes masons, ironworkers and welders, carpenters, plumbers, and electricians.

Opportunism by Class

In addition, there are other undeclared aspects of the work he does on his new home. For one thing, he said that he is keeping files on all materials receipts in order to qualify for *défiscalisation* tax breaks. Under this law, passed in 1986 (and since renewed), investment in building and other capital activities was encouraged to boost local employment. In the process, new home construction became eligible for large tax breaks.[5]

So, Michel has found a way illegally to secure significant tax advantages, and because of the stated value of the construction, he is deducting all these expenses from his taxes, a deduction that virtually eliminates all personal income taxes for five years. Since the project is in fact being built by undeclared workers, the only way he is able to access the benefits of this law is to present receipts of materials and work done, and hope that the various branches of government (such as tax and labor inspectors) do not swap files. Michel has a strong bet on this risk considering France's lumbering, inefficient bureaucracy and the "rights of man" law, which prohibits trading computerized data on individuals between different arms of the government.

The range of undeclared activities Michel pursues includes a virtually seamless web of productive entrepreneurship and blatant fraud. By his own account, which I suspect to be conservative, he regularly participates in at least nine distinct forms of undeclared activity. Some of these involve his political office, some his rental properties, and some his construction activities.

Apart from the small number of Evangelicals, Adventists, *békés*, and metropolitans, who view with disdain the creole version of *débrouillardism* that Michel models, few Martiniquais of color would accuse him of violating norms of acceptable behavior. What he has, he has worked hard to get. The defenders and relativists described in the previous chapter (and who represent the majority of my sample) would likely respect his energy and his cleverness at getting what he wants by being alert and seizing an opportunity the moment it presents itself. If his only activity off the books were private schemes to defraud the state, Michel would not be recognized as the *débrouillard extraordinaire* that he claims to be. True *débrouillardism* is a public performance, one that has no real value if others don't see it. Thus, Michel actively displayed his polyvalent abilities to do carpentry, plumbing, masonry; to understand a set of plans; to manage his own undeclared construction workers; and to use his city office to advantage without causing harm to anyone. These are skills others can witness and therefore admire.

PRACTICES

CONCLUSION

The case studies in this chapter offer testimony to the fluid, cross-class character of economic exchange that occurs without state awareness. These exchanges are largely personal and dyadic in nature and, as often as not, connect people of distinct socioeconomic groups. The activities discussed are not exceptions, but typify both the kinds of undeclared activities people at different income levels pursue and the structure of economic relationships that characterize these exchanges.

This study tells a story about the way creole economics anchors certain kinds of local economic activity to a culturally distinct system of values. Some of the patterns I found include the following:

+ undeclared economic activity is a cross-class phenomenon—a survival strategy for some, a strategy of accumulation for others;
+ vertical links connecting informally operating patrons (buyers) and clients (sellers) bind people of different class positions in a single informal economy;
+ underlying cultural values on cleverness and being your own boss, constituent elements of *débrouillardism*, shape the form of many local informal economic activities.

In sum, the local practice of creole economics belies accepted wisdom in development circles about the survival orientation of informal economies.

Informal economies are not constructions of economic and political factors alone. The variability in their form and the organization of informal economic actors are also patterned along lines of cultural history, social relations, and local values. These findings challenge the assumptions of those development planners who expect low-income undeclared operators to be willing candidates for legitimate entrepreneurship.

SEVEN

Women, Men, and Economic Practice

DIFFERENT ROUTES TO AUTONOMY AND STATUS

DON'T LIVE ON NOBODY EYELASH SO
THAT WHEN THEY WINK YOU FALL

—traditional "vinegar story," recounted by
Merle Collins in "Sometimes You Have to
Drink Vinegar and Pretend You Think Is
Honey," 1998

Relations between Afro-Caribbean women and men in Martinique (and in the Caribbean generally) are notoriously complicated and have been since life on the plantation. Many women today complain regularly about men—about their laziness, their lack of responsibility, their infidelity, and their continuing assumption of authority over women. The particularities of gender relationships among people of color in Martinique bear directly on the differences in how women and men organize their economic lives. In this society, both sexes express a desire for economic autonomy, but the nature of the independence they cherish is different in kind.[1] Unlike men, who talk in terms of wanting freedom to move about as they please and to be their own boss, women

talk about wanting to be taken seriously as economic operators as well as a need for economic independence from men, whom they find unreliable. In addition, a woman's drive for economic independence is tied to her concern for her children and her home. These common female priorities on family and children condition how and when women practice creole economics. In this chapter, I discuss the ways in which the shaping influences on women's and men's lives play out today in distinctly gendered economic identities and practices.

CREOLE HISTORIES AND WOMEN'S ECONOMIC INDEPENDENCE

The genesis of women's understanding of the necessity for economic independence dates to their lives as plantation slaves. Slave women learned to rely on themselves for what they and their children needed, but at the same time, they learned that any advantages they could secure would come from their status as women in a world controlled by white European men. It is these linked historical realities for Afro-Creole women that today figure in distinguishing women's economic lives from men's: on the one hand, the context of creole life as slaves forced women to assume roles as primary providers for children; on the other hand, to improve this situation, women oriented themselves to European values. Because the economic pressures and opportunities for male slaves were different, their sensibilities about economic life developed differently.

In the French- and British-colonized areas of the Caribbean, women were central economic actors during at least ten generations of slavery. Some scholars have suggested that the labor regimes of slavery were "gender blind" since female slaves worked alongside male slaves in the cane fields or in the plantation house.[2] However, as indicated in Chapter 2, slave jobs were stratified and "higher" positions such as foreman, slave driver, carpenter, blacksmith, or wheelwright were reserved for male slaves. Recent studies by historians of slavery further demonstrate that female slaves made up the majority of unskilled "field gangs," who were relegated to the hardest labor on the plantations.[3] For work in the Great House, owners also tended to keep more female than male slaves, and more mixed-race Creoles than African-born blacks. Domestic chores

Women, Men, and Economic Practice

were also assigned by sex: women typically performed jobs as midwives, nursemaids, laundresses, seamstresses, housekeepers, and cooks; domestic male slaves served as butlers, valets, barbers, tailors, watchmen, and gardeners.[4]

From their experience in the plantation homes, female slaves learned that the best way to escape the bonds of slavery was not out of but through the Great House, despite historical evidence that these female household workers were vulnerable to the master's sexual demands and that rape was a common occurrence. Sometimes, however, female slaves managed to leverage sexual favors in return for gifts from the master such as valued cloth, better food, opportunities to earn cash, or time off; a few became regular mistresses to their masters and some were even freed by them.[5] The mulatto sons (and, less often, daughters) of these unions were generally freed by their French fathers and sent to Paris for their education.[6]

For more than 200 years, generations of domestic slave women used their access to the master in his domicile to improve their lot and to secure freedom for their children. For these women and, by extension, their mixed-race sons, achieving social mobility was associated with efforts to respond to European standards. Thus, because white masters were in a position to reward behaviors that approximated their own sense of values, slave women were best able to improve their social position by imitating the values of respectability. However, even domestic slave women who managed to absorb European norms and win favors from the master could not ensure their own security. In fact, domestic slaves were especially likely to be sold when plantations were sold or when planters left their island estates to return to France.[7] A woman's initiative to leverage benefits for herself and her children also drove a wedge between her and black men that the system of slavery reinforced.

As I discussed in Chapter 2, the system of slavery all but negated the forming of stable slave families. Slaves were malnourished, often in poor health, and subject to being sold and separated.[8] Women slaves were not necessarily interested in establishing families with male slaves, who were unable to offer them any protections or rewards. Slave men were also positioned to carry out "most of the whipping," while black women did more of the hard labor in the house and fields. These gender-based power imbalances between slaves effectively "pitted black men against black women."[9]

All of these reasons combined to make male slaves peripheral to the mother/child unit. As Mintz and Price point out in their book about slave societies in the Americas,

> the matricentric cell, composed of a mother and her children, would often have constituted the practical limits of an individual's kinship network. Relations other than those between a mother and her children, and between siblings who grew up together, would likely have been haphazard; lasting ties of paternity . . . might well have been the exception rather than the rule.[10]

According to Bernard Moitt, historian of French slavery, as abolition approached, women worked hard to win their freedom from slavery and were more likely than men to pursue their cases in the courts. Yet, as Moitt notes, "It is instructive that in their struggle for family reunification, black women focused almost solely on their children."[11]

Roland Suvélor, retired professor of literature, avid social historian, and author of many historical articles on Martinique, explained that the orientation of slave women to their children was unusually powerful:

> Women were extraordinary, it's true. Women had an extraordinary devotion, that is to say they worked in the fields, and then they took care of the children. They looked after them. This is understandable from the fact that [for women] the child was the refuge and became their attachment to the world. Every being needs someone to love and thus it's for that they love their children—their children attached them to the world.[12]

In the breach left by absent or irregularly present slave fathers and partners, female slaves commonly took full charge of their children's security and health. This tendency remains in evidence today.

Women, Men, and Economic Practice

Virtually every mother I spoke to made clear that her earnings are directed first to the welfare and security of her children, whether or not a man is present. Because so many women I met have experienced disappointment with a man who proved unreliable, it became clear why they accept as true the lessons learned from their mothers and grandmothers: that the key to life is to become financially independent and that financial independence is the only way to assure a living for themselves and their children. Themes of frustration about men came up spontaneously during my interviews with women, usually long before my own questions might have channeled people to think in terms of gender relations. Rose, an aging charcoal vendor who raised five children without support from their fathers, expressed blatant antipathy for men: "Men in Martinique don't like to work. They like to drink and eat on your nickel. It's the women who do everything."

Nearly 40 percent of all households are headed by women like Rose who have no male partner in the household. Of these, most are low-income women who earn their entire incomes informally and support their children on these earnings alone. Of course, many women do not feel Rose's antagonism toward men. Instead, they simply accept their difficult lives and enjoy the company of men as they can. Some studies have shown, in fact, that Caribbean women of modest means who provide the primary support for their children would much prefer to have a male provider.[13] But while I heard this same preference from many low-income women, few considered it to be a realistic possibility. Today, increasing numbers of middle-income households, too, are not nuclear in structure and do not have a male head. Rather, they are composed of women or single mothers who may not be willing to compromise their own economic ambitions in order to make a deferential relationship work.

EUROPEAN VALUES, CATHOLICISM, AND LOCAL PATRIARCHY

PRACTICES

In the Caribbean, the authority of the black man with respect to the black woman was compromised during slavery, both by the fact that he was not the usual provider for his children and because white masters were the ones who held control. Meanwhile, the European masters practiced a different ethic between the sexes: men led and women followed. These European ideas took the strongest hold in the Spanish-colonized areas of the Caribbean, where massive-scale slavery occurred late and spanned a much shorter time frame than in the British and French areas. Today, women in the Hispanic Caribbean struggle against the "machismo" that radiates from the inherited European model in which male authority is considered a natural outcome of a man's role in providing the economic support for a household.[14] Indeed, as anthropologist Helen Safa notes about the Catholic Church in Puerto Rico, "Male control of women's labor and sexuality is maintained through an emphasis on family honor and female virginity fostered by Catholicism."[15]

The Islamic-influenced Catholicism introduced by Spanish colonizers was more restrictive for women than the traditional Catholicism brought by the French.[16] Nonetheless, France's Catholic tradition is also founded on strong patriarchal authority. Historically, this religion-based authority promoted unequal access to inheritance for women and laws which compensated only traditional mothers.[17] For this reason, male hierarchies were more strongly reinforced in the Catholic French Caribbean than in the Protestant British- or Dutch-colonized areas, where the male-dominated social bias did not impose the same degree of constraint on women.[18]

In French and British areas, European models about appropriate household hierarchies and gender roles presented a strong contrast to the plantation realities that had taught women self-reliance and bonded them to their children but less to their men. Following abolition, the concern of European officials and missionaries was strongly focused on reorganizing the gender roles that had been allowed to emerge during slavery. Free people must learn to be respectable, they argued, European style.

According to Caribbean historian Catherine Hall, "A new gender order was central to the vision of the abolitionists."[19] Bridget Brereton elaborates the nature of this European influence on gender roles, saying colonial officials, abolitionists, and clergy all shared the assumption that

> ex-slaves should model their domestic lives on the middle class Western family . . . that husbands should be the head of the family, the main breadwinner . . . and endowed with authority over wives and children . . . that wives should be dependent and domestic . . . and rear their children and provide a decent, comfortable Christian home . . . [and that] lifelong monogamy based on Christian marriage should be the norm.[20]

Colonial missionaries and officials encouraged "the wife's proper release from toil" outside the home in hopes that "as their moral ties become more sacred, so . . . may their inclination to confine themselves to indoor occupations be increased."[21] Moreover, as Smaje notes, "The willingness of newly freed female slaves to conform, at least in part, to this model of female domesticity can be seen as an act of resistance to a plantation order which had denied women the possibility of any such respectability."[22] In

Martinique, the European ideals of monogamy, the nuclear family, and male authority were strongly promoted by the Catholic Church.

Because these ideals of male authority and household headship were linked to the people who held power and resources, they easily penetrated the norms and values of upwardly striving people whose ancestors had been slaves. But they did not undo the hardest lessons of life on the plantation, lessons that have been told and retold through creole folktales and family stories. Those European standards that local people have embraced are those that make sense in a creole world. Thus, responsibility to family, hard work, and good education are all values recognized as important by most people I met. Yet other behaviors that are equally important to the traditional European ideal of respectability have proven less meaningful in the local context. These behaviors include, for example, monogamy, marriage, and maintaining separate domains of activity for men and women. Upper-middle-income informants were much more likely to express these attributes of respectability, though for a great many people who are not so affluent, many of these ideals are impractical and may, in fact, interfere with negotiating one's survival and status in Martinique.[23]

CREOLE "REPUTATION" AND EUROPEAN "RESPECTABILITY"

PRACTICES

Strongly distinct models of behavior defined plantation life. On the one hand, many slaves and free people of color were lured to seek European acceptance in order to better their lives; on the other hand, acts of theft, mockery, duplicity, and even violence against European control were strategies that could secure advantages in the midst of misery or resist power in the midst of a denied personhood (see Chapter 5). According to Peter Wilson and a long line of Caribbean researchers since, these separate orientations constitute the tension between European-derived norms of "respectability" and creole-derived norms of "reputation."[24] In his seminal 1969 article "Reputation and Respectability: A Suggestion for Caribbean Ethnology," Wilson introduced what has become the central paradigm in Caribbean studies—opposed systems of status: one creole, one European.[25] Slave men and women gravitated to these different systems in different measure and for different reasons.

184

Ideals of respectability, said Wilson, were imposed on Afro-Creole peoples by European colonial officials and missionaries. These ideals, he claimed, involve the display of behaviors that signaled legitimacy among the new middle-class segments of nineteenth-century European society[26] such as living in nuclear families, exhibiting a strong work ethic, getting a formal education, earning a high income, keeping one's home and property tidy, attending church regularly, and demonstrating self-restraint.[27] Whether or not people of color could actually imitate these behaviors, they nonetheless came to represent an ideal and to hold symbolic influence because they were (and are) linked to people with power.

By contrast, said Wilson, reputation emerged from the shared creole experience of men. This non-European system of status rewarded behaviors that stood in opposition to the European ideals of family, home, church, and hierarchy, values he indicated were more important to women. Considering that the context of plantation life funneled all expressions of personal freedom into the few hours a week that slaves could spend away from their forced work, it is not surprising that a distinctly creole basis of prestige emerged that became especially important among male slaves. Wilson argued that reputation was generally earned by men who demonstrated "manly" qualities and talents, such as performance-oriented verbal skills involved in storytelling, "sweet talking" women, and singing or playing an instrument. And while a man's status was not tied to the economic dependence of his wife, a man clearly earned reputation through fathering as many children with as many women as possible. Other sources of status were derived from drinking and outdoor skills, traveling, and making money.[28]

Wilson's binary formulations oversimplify the patterns many others have since observed. For example, historians have shown that although creole-based markers of status offered fewer advantages to women in Martinique, women did compete alongside men for prestige based on aspects of appearance, such as the quality of cloth they wore to Sunday slave markets, their shoes, and jewelry. Such physical adornments were an important basis for sorting status among slaves.[29] Other ethnographic studies in the Caribbean have also shown that women may seek reputation just as men may seek respectability and that these two systems of values are not necessarily at odds with each other.[30] On balance, however, as Richard Burton concedes, attacks on Wilson's formulation have demonstrated its resilience more than dismantled its legacy.[31]

Women, Men, and Economic Practice

THE GENDERED WORKPLACE TODAY

The economic importance of women in Martinique today is striking by any standard. Most women of working age are income producers, and the local workforce is composed of nearly as many women (48 percent) as men (52 percent). The economic importance of women in the life of a family is undisputed. But women in Martinique are not unique. Caribbean societies are well known among scholars of gender and regional experts as areas in which women are regarded as strong, independent, and economically productive.[32] In fact, many western feminist scholars look to Caribbean women as the inspiration for women worldwide who are striving to improve their social standing and sense of autonomy in their own societies.

Today, contradictory factors condition the status and economic mobility of women in Martinique. These factors include the lessons women learned during slavery about their need for self-reliance, the recent economic opportunities that push and pull more women to work, and the simultaneous persistence of resilient patriarchal attitudes. Improvements have been apparent for women in Martinique since the 1960s, including longer life expectancy, better quality of life, higher levels of education, and lowered rates of fertility. According to reports by French demographic and labor specialists, the near-equal proportion of women to men in the labor force represents an important increase since the late 1960s, when women constituted only a third of the island's workforce.[33]

PRACTICES

However, equality with men in terms of education and workforce participation has not yet signaled an end to gender stratification in the workforce or in the domain of political life. Women are overrepresented among the unemployed (54 percent), more likely than men to be clustered in the lowest-paid formal sector work (37 vs. 21 percent), and underrepresented at the highest levels of employment.[34] They are all but invisible in politics.[35] Thus, although women assume a central role in Martinique's economic life, there are structural biases that inhibit their economic mobility. In addition, the obligations felt by women and/or their desire to fulfill the role of primary caretaker in the household frequently lead them to locate their economic lives in low-risk employment.

Considering the constraints on women's time and orientation to risk, it is not surprising that few women with regular jobs seek side work in the undeclared economy. Instead, it is much more often men who devise and practice strategies to earn on the side, off the books.

VIEWING THE RELATION OF GENDER AND STATUS THROUGH ECONOMICS

Because the practice of creole economics is dominated by men, it may appear that Wilson's ideas of male reputation and female respectability play out neatly in Martinique. What men do off the books is inherently oppositional, so it seems more creole; women's choices to remain in the legitimate economy and make their families a priority seem to more clearly follow European ideals. Certainly, women and men of color in Martinique do indeed seek different goals and follow different economic practices. But there is more to the story.

Given the complexity of creole and European influences on the actions and identities of Afro-Creole people, it is a messy project to sort out who is motivated by what. By looking at how the domain of work and creole economics relates to gender-specific histories, it is possible to grasp why women and men of color are led to different economic choices that do not simply replicate Wilson's formulation. My findings suggest the following:

First, both women and men confront an "essential tension" that emerges from their specifically gender-based histories.[36] For Afro-Creole men, the essential tension relates to white bosses; for Afro-Creole women, the essential tension relates to black men. Resolving these distinct sources of tension requires different kinds of economic action.

Second, for men who seek freedom from authority figures, stepping outside the law to practice creole economics provides a good way to achieve personal economic autonomy. Women, who seek economic independence from men rather than bosses, feel no need to step outside the law to achieve their goals.

Third, the sources of reputation are themselves gendered. This insight explains why Caribbeanists have struggled to explode Wilson's unsatisfying depiction of dichotomous value systems. Rather than map female activity onto the realm of reputation as defined by men, it makes more sense to consider what women gain from the creole values they have nurtured and that carry currency among other creole women of color.

Fourth, because the behaviors that generate reputation are different for women and men, these behaviors relate differently to the realm of European respectability. For men, gaining reputation through illicit economic activity opposes European sources of respectability. By contrast, a woman's reputation is earned in part by becoming financially independent and

Women, Men, and Economic Practice

in part by devoting her resources to the household. From a distance, that devotion to family looks very much like respectability.

These different economic tendencies of women and men reveal that the relationship between reputation and respectability is not necessarily mutually exclusive, nor is it symmetrically juxtaposed. Instead, gendered economic practice in Martinique suggests that European and creole values may overlap, interlink, and mutually reinforce each other. They may also be mutually exclusive and oppositional. It all depends on the essential tension of the actors involved.

FEMALE REPUTATION AND RESPECTABILITY

It is a commonly held local perception that women in Martinique are more European than Martiniquais men. Women possess more discrete and refined manners. Georges, who is age twenty-seven, works in construction management, and lives with his wife and baby, notes:

> Women are much more assimilated to French culture than men.
> They are more worried about politeness. For example, women view poorly someone who is crude and without French education, someone we call a *gros negre* (vulgar negro).

My interviews make clear, however, that the kind of respectability women in Martinique seek and achieve is inseparable from their creole identities.[37] Since slavery, women in Martinique, and across much of the Caribbean, have tended not to depend on men to be responsible fathers and partners. Thus the European ideal of marriage, nuclear family structure, and male headship therefore still remains an abstraction for many.

When I asked informants "Who is the household head?" most women as well as men answered that the man was the head. But as Thérèse, a thirty-three-year-old taxi driver and mother of three, said referring to her partner (with whom she lives): "Mostly men are the heads here, but if you give them an opportunity to be responsible, they rarely take it."

Considering the longstanding tensions in male/female relationships, it is not surprising that nearly four out of ten working women today live in female-headed households and two-thirds of all working women are unmarried. Gender-based tensions which originated in slavery and continue to be reproduced push a great many women to fix their own economic ambition to the simple goals of financial independence. With economic

independence, women can support the needs of their households and be free from the uncertainty of unreliable males. As Professor Roland Suvélor noted in our conversation about women in relation to men in Martinique,

> There is this significant factor, above all that we have said, which is that of financial independence. That is to say that a woman who has financial independence . . . is freer. Her financial independence guarantees her independence, just so! It's a form of revenge against men who have had authority . . . and as many mistresses as they want.[38]

I heard these same sentiments in almost exactly the same language in everyday conversations with women of color. And because women place such value on their own economic independence from men and ensuring needed support for families, I came to realize that achieving these goals represents for them a source of reputation. It was a theme I heard from middle- and moderate-income women talking to each other: if you don't make your own money and keep it separate from your man, you are a fool.

As ideas often do, this one crystallized for me at the most unexpected time. I had stepped into the nearby covered market in central Fort-de-France. I needed a break from my errands, which required navigating the usual crush of cars and pedestrians that overwhelm the downtown streets. I had just begun to stroll the aisles between lush displays of produce and prepared foods when I overheard an animated conversation between two women who appeared to be in their early thirties. It sounded like an unusually public vent about men. I feigned interest in the sticks of vanilla bean and caramelized coconut strips in order to hear more. "She should have known better. If she's too lazy to make her own money, he's going to get whatever he wants." They laughed and muttered back and forth before the taller woman added, "I thank my mother for teaching me about men."

I have mentioned earlier that, with the exception of the young and in love, men and women tend to spend much of their social lives apart, moving publicly with those of their own sex. For this reason, reputation is easily reproduced in gender-specific circles. Women who are manipulated by men because they are economically dependent on them are women who get little sympathy from other Martiniquaise women of color. In the same sense, men who do not demonstrate that they are their own men are mocked by other men.

Whether female independence comes from a wage job, from working for herself, or from owning a business, women express common underlying motivations: to be economically self-reliant in the service of families. Thérèse, the taxi driver, asserted her goals for independence in ways that approximate what a great many women expressed: "There are different kinds of independence. Mine is being responsible for my children, being able to fit them into my schedule, earning my own money, and doing my own things."

Across my samples of wage-working women, a strong majority communicated their overriding concern to be economically independent, but in a manner that also embraced their concerns for family. Because women's goals of economic autonomy in Martinique are so often tied to goals of providing for children and household needs, their choices gravitate toward the secure paychecks and stable futures found in the formal sector, especially the public sector of government. Women in fact dominate the public sector, representing 54 percent of all jobs.

Middle-income female entrepreneurs, like Thérèse, also frequently mentioned that their motivation to create a business involved their desire to be able to control their own schedules so they could better manage their children or elderly parents. Many also reported that the attraction of owning a company is, in part, the ability to organize the work environment as a cooperative venture among a work-oriented "family." By creating an atmosphere responsive to the needs of employees and their children, many women made a deliberate departure from the hierarchical authority structures they claim are typical of male-run companies in Martinique. Extending their family orientation to workplaces of their own making, female entrepreneurs thus reproduce the values of both reputation and respectability.

A more explicit embrace of the values of respectability is demonstrated by the fact that female entrepreneurs commonly expressed a moral obligation to legally declare all their workers, report all their income, and generally follow the rules of legitimate business. Many of the male entrepreneurs I met, by contrast, told me that not declaring an employee was smart for at least two reasons: (1) the employee could earn money and simultaneously collect state allocations for unemployment or minimum income, and (2) he (the employer) could avoid social security payments, which allowed him to realize significant savings. In short, law-abiding behaviors that conform to rules of respectability more often reflect female rather than male priorities. In the area of economics, then, Martiniquaise women of color reveal the inseparably linked "twoness" of their creole identities and their European sensibilities.[39]

Knowing that women concerned with economic independence and accountability to family tend to locate their work in respectable, declared settings, how do we explain the fact that about one in five of the formally employed women I interviewed also generates extra income off the books? The key to understanding these apparent anomalies is that most of these women conceive their side work narrowly, as a pragmatic opportunity to help better support their households. Women who practice creole economics do so (excepting rare cases) without the same reputational motivations (to display authority and exercise freedom) that appear important for many men. Most commonly, women do not spread their informal entrepreneurial wings to become their own boss. When the nature of their formal work allows, women simply extend that same kind of work to their homes and earn off the books, a common strategy of teachers, secretaries, and sales clerks.

The small proportion of women who practice creole economics make it clear through the organization of their activity (and the way they talk about it) that they are not seeking reputation from the activity itself. Instead, women's source of local distinction comes from showing their economic independence from men. Being economically clever or operating outside the law does not appear to offer women any gains in prestige, as it does men. For this reason, very few women consider themselves *débrouillards* in the local sense of demonstrating economic cunning. Many women and men pointed out that the term *débrouillard* doesn't usually even apply to women. Micheline, a forty-four-year-old financial consultant who is married with two teenage children, said:

> To call someone a *débrouillard* is a great compliment, but at the same time, it has a malicious connotation. A *débrouillard* has devious ways, he doesn't do things by the books. I don't hear it applied to women.

Micheline not only separates women from what she views as devious behavior, she also notes that it is considered a great compliment, though a compliment that works in male circles. Because men in Martinique frequently socialize with each other at bars, sporting events, and in recreational and athletic pursuits, there are many sites that permit the reproduction of values associated with reputation. A large majority of women I interviewed recognize the value of autonomy men gain from side work. Yet for them, work on the side represents a simple strategy to earn more, not to make gains in other ways.

The intricacies of gendered economic patterns can be illustrated though language use. As I indicated earlier, the practice of creole economics tends to attract a creole-style *débrouillard* who is generally male. In a very real way, the linguistic complexity of the term *débrouillardism* (discussed in Chapter 3) expresses the tension between standard French and French Creole systems of meaning. The term can be associated with either French respectability (resourcefulness, initiative in problem solving) or with creole reputation (finding clever but unauthorized ways to profit). Most women I interviewed do not consider themselves the creole kind of *débrouillard* whose pursuits, like those of the trickster Rabbit in creole folktales, are dishonest if forgivable.

Many women explain that they are good *débrouillards* because they are able to juggle the demands of work and family by being resourceful and independent. Used in this way, the French meaning of the term is emphasized, signaling one's primary responsibility to family and thus a priority aligned with European ideas of "respectability." However, many women are actually claiming more than their ability to manage household, children, and work. They are also claiming their triumphs in generating enough income to "prove themselves," and in the process, secure their economic autonomy from men, a decidedly non-European value. Because French and Creole meanings overlap, the sense of one's usage of the term *débrouillardism* is not always clear, lending the possibility for implied verbal leverage.

Later in this chapter, I will present several profiles contrasting women and men who pursue creole economics in order to demonstrate the striking differences in gendered approaches to side work. These differences carry implications for understanding how women and men seek to fulfill their creole identities in largely distinct ways.

MALE REPUTATION AND RESPECTABILITY

Edouard, the high-income insurance executive discussed earlier, is married with one child. In our interview, he made clear that the reason he keeps his undeclared consulting business on the side is only partly about money: "The [formal] job is the sure salary. But this [side work] gives me the liberty I want; I like being in charge."

Men typically emphasize different economic goals than women, including their desire to be their own boss, to experience *liberté* in their work. Three times more men than women are self-employed and, in my sample, more than one of every two men with a declared job also participates in work off the books, compared to about one of every five regularly employed women. Thus, among those with regular jobs, men are more likely than not to have one foot in the formal economy and another in the informal economy; significantly fewer women follow such mixed economic strategies.[40] More important, though, is the meaning men attribute to their practice of creole economics. Men typically claim that there are real benefits beyond the pragmatic opportunity of earning more money.

Like Edouard, many of my male informants self-identify as *débrouillards*. As I discussed in the previous chapter, I frequently heard from men that side work offers them a sense of personal autonomy, freedom from an employer's rules, and the satisfaction of managing an activity of one's own. It is no coincidence that these commonly expressed needs for freedom and

Women, Men, and Economic Practice

193

autonomy were the very qualities denied slaves and, even after abolition, the majority of blacks.[41]

Monique, who teaches high school math, described her husband, a top-level functionary with the Treasury, as *"un vrai débrouillard"* (a real *débrouillard*). He built their elegant new home using lots of undeclared artisans, she said, and he has all sorts of side activities too, like the other men in his circle. Although Monique criticizes *débrouillard* behavior for being dishonest, she realizes that it is a fundamental part of local identity and a way men have of achieving their autonomy:

> *Débrouillardism* is a mentality here. It is like they are taking charge of their own destiny of being autonomous. When you are called a *débrouillard*, it is a quality. It is a plus to be one. It is not always honest but it works. You must turn the circumstances to profit from them, even if others have to suffer the consequences. It is truly essential. You must try to make life the least miserable as possible. Everyone does it. People who don't do it are a little bit stupid. It happens at all levels of the population. I am not at all a *débrouillard* so I criticize them.

Yet, men with the means to do so actively engage in enhancing their status in the arenas of both reputation and respectability. Edouard, the insurance executive with a side consulting business, is clear about wanting the liberty to be his own boss, but since he earns a high income, he is also careful to protect his respectability. In the course of our interview, he asked several times for reassurance that I would guarantee his anonymity. However, rather than withhold the information about his side work, he wanted me to know about it. In fact, he walked me around his house, pointing out all the work performed by undeclared laborers—a handsome rail fence around the large property, a recent installation of high-tech windows, a beautiful hand-carved mahogany chest. He also described his own undeclared consulting work as "something of my own" with obvious pride and interest. That many men of Edouard's socioeconomic level (such as those we met in the last chapter) would find satisfaction in operating outside the law suggests the continuing strength of cultural codes across classes. At the same time, these men discuss their side work with discretion.

This emphasis on protecting one's respectability appears to characterize men of means who travel frequently to France, who relate strongly to metropolitan French values, and who, like Edouard, maintain regular social and professional contact with metropolitan French in Martinique. Thus, while moderate- and middle-income men may achieve some degree of respectability through formal sector employment, affluent men of color are more easily able to nurture other markers of respectability such as achieving high levels of education, marrying and forming nuclear family households, hosting elegant parties, pledging community involvement, and appreciating "high culture." Because their broader base of respectability also increases the stakes of protecting it, these men (and those upwardly striving men who emulate them) must exercise discretion when talking about their participation in creole economics. By contrast, less affluent men with little access to high-class markers of respectability openly seek the creole form of status that is within their reach.

In sum, for affluent men, the instinct to build reputation does not wither merely because they are able to meet so many expectations of respectability. The sheer fact that so many men of high income revealed to me without hesitation their involvement in creole economics indicates that there is social prestige in claiming one's illicit economic activities, at least in sympathetic circles. Perhaps in a kind of behavioral code switching, the pursuit of creole economics allows men of means to signal their valued membership in creole society, while discretion about these personal activities in other circles allows them to claim a form of status that has currency among metropolitan French. As we have seen demonstrated in many dimensions, living inside a "double consciousness," an apparent contradiction, is standard fare for Afro-Creole people.

PROFILES OF COUPLES WHO SEPARATELY PRACTICE CREOLE ECONOMICS

We have already seen that substantial proportions of men compared to women practice creole economics. Of those men in my sample with declared, formal sector jobs, 51 percent also generate undeclared income on the side. By contrast, only about one in five women with regular jobs also pursues income strategies on the side. Unsurprisingly, the side economic activities of women are nearly always organized around household constraints.[42] If some women generate income off the books, how can these anomalies be explained in light of the much more common orientation of women to locate their entire economic lives in the formal, declared sector?

My research shows that most women who maintain an undeclared side activity have male partners who also pursue creole economics. Yet the apparent similarities in their undeclared economic practice hide the fact that the forms of informal activity practiced by men and women are quite distinct.

To illustrate how side work is itself a gendered phenomenon, I have chosen profiles from the range of household resources where one finds the practice of creole economics by design: moderate-, middle-, and high-income households. For convenience, each of these profiles involves women and men who are married or living together, but the patterns I am describing run consistently through behaviors of female heads of households and men without responsibilities as fathers. Across class, it is possible to observe how gendered expectations in the household translate into gendered patterns of work in the informal economy. We will see how these patterns in turn impact the ways in which women and men seek both reputation and respectability.

One pattern to watch for in these profiles is the way that most women do not self-identify as creole-style *débrouillards* despite their deliberate choice to work off the books to generate additional income. Often, their male partners do. Many men explicitly discuss the autonomy and freedom they enjoy through their side work, which empowers them to be their own boss. In these households, the man's side activities are unleashed from the home and do not represent extensions of their formal sector work. Their regular job may simply provide contacts that help assure a client base for their informal activity, or it may provide the time or flexibility of work schedules needed to pursue side activities. By contrast, the side work women pursue is more often a convenient extension of their formal sector work, like tutoring or typing, or it is an activity that can be done at home, like needlepoint or Tupperware parties. The following examples illustrate the ways women at varying socioeconomic levels engage in side work differently than men. Gendered ideologies about work are less transparent at low-income levels, where survival demands that women accept undeclared work (i.e., creole economics by default).[43]

Women, Men, and Economic Practice

MODERATE-INCOME HOUSEHOLDS

Nearly 72 percent of men and 69 percent of women in the moderate-income group of households[44] have a low-wage formal sector job. Many of these men (42 percent) and some women (15 percent) pursue informal income as a supplement to "round out the end of the month."[45] Unlike many women in the lowest-income category who are the sole heads of household, 61 percent of women in moderate-income households can count on some income support from a male head of household. Therefore, it would appear that these women have more choices in the way they organize work. They are, in theory, better able to position themselves for economic growth than poorer women, who work informally by default. Yet, as the following case study suggests, working women at this moderate-income level are rarely able to capitalize on opportunities for growth. Instead, their pattern of work organization favors low-risk, conservative strategies.

To increase their earnings, women of moderate means simply pour more personal time into increased economic activity. In addition, the way women construct and use their social networks compared to men indicates that they are less likely to call upon contacts to help them leverage their careers. Instead, women use those in their networks to help them manage household tasks and child care, which remain primarily their responsibility. By contrast, men at this income level, whose household chores remain relatively undemanding, find the time to use their contacts to advance their schemes for side work.[46]

MODERATE-INCOME PROFILE: PATRICIA AND ERIC   Patricia is a thirty-three-year old woman married to a slightly older man who has a low-level administrative job at the post office. She is employed at an elementary school as an aide to watch kindergarten children during their play. She has only a primary school education and in her job makes little more than minimum wage. Her husband, who has only two years of schooling beyond her, makes twice her income. They have three children, ages fourteen, eleven, and seven. Patricia is the primary caregiver for their three children and does the grocery shopping, housecleaning, and errand running. Her husband, who enjoys cooking, often prepares the family meal.

On her days off from her regular job at the primary school, Patricia works at home to earn extra income by offering child-care services to neighbors. While at home, she also embroiders and crochets tablecloths and napkins for sale to neighbors and friends of the family. Keeping her informal activities to projects she can manage from home allows her to juggle the responsibilities of mother and household manager, while generating some extra income for her children and herself on the side.

From the time I was eighteen, I have been taking care of other peoples' babies until they were old enough to go to school. I'm a real *débrouil-lard*. That's how I was raised. I learned how to work, to not be lazy. Taking care of other people's children is a big job.

Patricia's use of *débrouillard* clearly refers to the French understanding of being resourceful and hardworking. Her various income-earning projects indicate that she is ambitious and a hard worker. Yet her income from these efforts is modest, in part because with her home-based side work, she remains invisible to potential clients. Patricia did express interest in having more clients, yet her sense of pride compels her to depend only on herself to locate them. Meanwhile, the parents and teachers who might help her locate new clients and increase her revenue from child care or sewing activities remain untapped. "I never ask for people to bring me clients. I find them myself. I don't need to ask for help."

In contrast, Patricia's husband, Eric, uses his formal sector work at the post office to seek out clients for a variety of informal activities. These informal activities include teaching swimming lessons and hiring unde-clared workers to do repairs on the house or the car. As I found was often the case for men, Eric's workplace colleagues regularly discuss their needs for home improvements and car repairs. They share information about how to get things done and whom to call upon to do them. This kind of personal network, reinforced through knowledge and contacts associ-ated with undeclared earnings, provides the men of Eric's circle a source of reputation. It is also through his workplace contacts that he recruits most of his new swimming clients. Because Eric uses his contacts at work to access a wholly different set of associations, his effective social network is both broad based and economically useful. By tapping his networks to reach new clients for his undeclared side activity, Eric simultaneously sig-nals his competence in another domain and his valued reputation in his own circle.

MIDDLE-INCOME HOUSEHOLDS

At the middle income level of households, members have access to more resources, larger social networks, better educations, and better jobs than do lower-income individuals. Working women who live in middle-income households are more likely to be employed in the formal sector (88 percent) than moderate- or low-income women (69 and 33 percent, respectively). Among working men at this level, 80 percent have formal sector work compared to 72 percent at the moderate income level and 44 percent at the low income level.

Many men and women of middle-income households, like their moderate-income counterparts, pursue undeclared income on the side of their formal employment (37 and 21 percent, respectively). Because they have the time and networks in place to do so, men create wholly separate income-producing schemes away from their formal employment. Among women, those with domestic obligations do not have the time to create businesses on the side of their work. Those who hire domestic help and do have the time and interest do not create distinct businesses, as men do. Instead they generally pursue undeclared work as an extension of their formal work. Thus, despite the higher levels of skills and education that women at this level typically possess, their patterns of informal work organization resemble those employed by women of lesser means.

Like women of more modest means, middle-income women are unlikely to act as buyers of informal goods and services. As many men demonstrate, the economic benefit of acting as a buyer of goods off the books is that one is able to multiply the opportunities to create profit because one's own time is not required to produce it. Even in selling informal goods or services, many men have found ways to decrease their personal investment of time in order to generate more income at less cost to themselves.

Women of middle-income households remain tied to the home and to the time they can themselves invest in a side earning activity. Because they commonly work at respectable functionary or mid-level management jobs, the social networks available to them in the workplace are large. Yet here, too, women remain reluctant to use their networks in the way men do. Almost all of the middle-income women I interviewed indicated that while they may indeed "know" people who could help them earn more money from their side activity, they simply do not feel comfortable calling on these people for such help. The following case study illustrates distinctions typical of male and female ways of organizing side work at this socioeconomic level.

MIDDLE-INCOME PROFILE: CLARICE AND BENJAMIN   Clarice is a sixty-year-old high school teacher of natural science. She has a college education and lives with her husband, Benjamin, who is sixty, and their handicapped son, aged twenty-seven, in a comfortable home in a middle-income, upwardly mobile neighborhood. Benjamin is a mid-level government functionary who works at the customs office.

In addition to her teaching job, Clarice works at home to earn extra income by making cakes and pastries to sell and by hosting Tupperware parties. Her clients for the pastries are mostly contacts from school who want her cakes to take to events like family reunions and communions. For her Tupperware parties, Clarice is comfortable "inviting" her colleagues from school to her home, but she is not comfortable asking them to give her names of their friends in order to extend her reach. Thus, although her personal network is as large as her husband's, she does not use it similarly to access new potential clients. Nor does she impose any requests for concrete help from any of them. She explains that she is not much of a *débrouillard*, even though she believes that being one is a good thing. The context of her usage reveals that she is talking about creole-style *débrouillardism*.

> I don't really consider myself a *débrouillard*. But my husband, he certainly is. He has a property in the country, family land, where he grows bananas, avocados, mangos, everything. He gives some to friends, but he also sells a lot to the kitchen at the hospital.

Benjamin, who has four fewer years of schooling than his college-degreed wife, works on the side of his customs job to manage the cultivation and harvesting of his crops. Without investing much of his own time, he coordinates the labor of others he has recruited to cultivate his fruit trees and vegetables. Part of what is cultivated is consumed by the family and given as small gifts to friends and relatives. However, the surplus is sold to the local hospital kitchen, where a relative works.

In contrast to Clarice, then, Benjamin earns undeclared money without doing most of the work himself. This entrepreneurial orientation is in part possible because he makes use of his network of contacts at work, sometimes as end-clients for his products but also as conduits for information about available workers and markets for his gardening venture. By occasionally giving some of these contacts sacks of fresh fruits or vegetables, he builds on a relationship of reciprocity and gains favors for the future. In addition, by hiring undeclared workers to cultivate the garden and by tapping the goodwill of a distant relative who ensures the purchase of any surplus for the hospital, Benjamin organizes his work to multiply his income and his potential for future entrepreneurial success.

Women, Men, and Economic Practice

Despite the fact that both Clarice and Benjamin earn extra income out-side their formal jobs, the organization of their individual work follows from their distinctly gendered goals for autonomy and status. In turn, these distinct goals carry different implications for economic growth. Clarice's extra work is labor intensive and strictly home based. Thus, while her husband (with less education) has organized his economic activities to grow beyond the time he is required to personally invest, Clarice's ability to generate extra income is entirely dependent on how much time she herself gives these additional tasks.

HIGH-INCOME HOUSEHOLDS

High-income Afro-Creole households commonly mirror standards of European respectability. They are dominated by married couples without children or with nuclear family structures (85 percent). There are many women in high-income households who do not work, a reflection of the European ideal in which women tend the home and children. But this situation is changing as more and more young women choose to pursue professional careers to express their own competence and to establish the financial independence they have come to desire. To afford high-status material goods for themselves, their children, and their households, many of these professional women also supplement their formal income with undeclared side income. Men are also drawn to exhibit their high status through material goods such as cars and clothes. But, unlike most women I interviewed, high-income men are likely to invest some of their money in PRACTICES ways that feed their own economic growth.

HIGH-INCOME PROFILE: MARGUERITE AND JACQUES Marguerite is a thirty-five-year-old licensed child psychologist who works at the local mental hospital. She supplements her income by working some evenings giving lessons in child psychology to private school teachers. She also generates extra, undeclared income serving as an expert witness in evaluating the mental state of legal defendants and crime victims.

Marguerite has done well professionally and, in terms of formal income, earns as much as her husband, Jacques, who is a bank accountant. Her personal networks are wide, since her work at the state hospital is well known and connects her to officials at the local tribunal. Marguerite's networks contribute to her professional exposure and to her credibility as an expert witness and a teacher of her discipline. Since Marguerite has a live-in housekeeper and a full-time nanny for her daughter, she has, in theory, the time she needs to realize her professional ambitions and build her economic base. However, she states that

> I used to do more things on the side, but now I don't do so many classes. Having a young daughter has changed my whole view of life. I am less ambitious about these side activities, even though they do make money and help me buy extra things like a new washing machine. Now, I'm more interested in devoting my extra time to my daughter.

Marguerite points to a common finding in my research: that, for women, the appeal and feasibility of side activities depends partly on one's status in the life course. In my sample, mothers with young children are the least likely to pursue side work of all working-age women. But, while women like Marguerite display their pleasure with their roles as primary childrearing parent, she does this in the context of a robust career that also includes some side work. It is noteworthy that the kind of consumption that Marguerite's extra work affords—a new washing machine—is destined for the good of the household.

By contrast, her husband, Jacques, is constantly engaged in informal work on the side of his banking job. He does not have an advanced college degree, like Marguerite, but by pursuing the reputation he gains from such clever economic strategies, he has nonetheless created more economic mobility for himself than she has. By using his financial contacts and clout, he was able to secure a loan to build a commercial office property. The rental income is undeclared and the property costs him little in personal time to manage. As a result, the investment he made at one moment ten years ago now returns large profits. While Jacques is likely to exercise discretion in discussing his undeclared activities with metropolitans at the bank, Marguerite indicated that both of their families are oriented to *débrouillardism* and that they have a large circle of *débrouillard* friends.

WOMEN WHO PRACTICE CREOLE ECONOMICS LIKE MEN

I have indicated that most women do not practice creole economics, and among those who do, most follow expected codes of respectability for women. I did, however, meet a handful of women who relate to the satisfaction so many men describe of working for themselves off the books. These women, who call themselves *débrouillards* in the creole sense, share an interesting set of profiles: most grew up without a father or key male influence at home and learned from a significant female figure the importance of *débrouillardism* in making it through life. And although these women often began their adult lives with a modest standard of living, many have since achieved middle-income standing. The following profile will demonstrate how the small but defiantly independent group of local women relate to creole economics like men do.

CHARLOTTE, THE SEAMSTRESS

Charlotte is a thirty-two-year-old single mother who alone supports her five-year-old daughter. In this sense, her situation hardly resembles that of a local man's. No man I ever met supported his children without help from a female companion. Some unattached men live alone; many live with their mothers, but only in rare cases do men raise children as single parents. Beyond this difference, however, a striking similarity exists: Charlotte strives to model her economic life as a complete *débrouillard* in the creole sense, as someone who operates outside the law, who is cunning and clever. It is this clear identity that leads her to make the choices she does for keeping her work undeclared and for pursuing the many other strategies she does to enhance her economic position under the radar of the French state.

PRACTICES   Charlotte's unusual story of creole economics by design reveals how a single mother can advance her financial standing in ways that a formal sector job alone might not. As far as the state knows, Charlotte remains unemployed and in need of the extra allocations it provides, including unemployment insurance and housing aid, neither of which she would be eligible to receive if she reported her actual income from dressmaking. She claimed that she was a *débrouillard*, and in her explanation of this term, it was apparent that she was talking about creole-style *débrouillards*.

> Life goes to the most clever, you know. Even if what you do is not within the norms or the law.

Charlotte makes beautiful clothes as her full-time, undeclared work. Keeping her economic life informal permits her to hide the income she

earns as an enterprising seamstress in order to collect the maximum possible number of subsidies each month from an unaware French state. Charlotte and her daughter live in a modest, high-rise complex in an apartment that is clean but spare. On my first visit, there was only one sewing machine in view, perched on a small table where Charlotte had been working when I rang the doorbell. A long cut of fabric patterned in bright tropical flowers draped off the edge of the table, held in place by the teeth of the machine.

At the time of our interview, nearly five years since she had worked as a declared secretary, she was still receiving unemployment benefits. Though this was the last year she would be compensated and the payments had fallen steadily each year, she was still receiving 1,000F/month ($200US) in income. She also said that she had filed an application for RMI aid, a government subsidy to insure a minimum income to all adults without any source of revenue. If her application is accepted, she will be receiving a third unlawfully procured source of government aid for which she feels no guilt in receiving.

Charlotte's daughter has never known her father, just as Charlotte never knew hers. As Charlotte was growing up, her mother insisted she complete her *baccalauréate*, known as *"le* BAC*"* (comparable to a rigorous high school degree in the US). After earning her BAC, she found a declared job as a secretary in a private accounting firm, but was fired five years later when her employer learned she had become pregnant. So, at the age of twenty-seven, without a job and with a child on the way, Charlotte decided to make clothes for a living. "It was a struggle to work for someone else. I always wanted the independence of self-employment."

She got some financial help from her modestly employed mother to make a down payment on a sewing machine. In addition, because she had been fired, she also had unemployment benefits coming in. The highly protective French labor laws mean that she was assured of earning exactly the same income as though she were still employed for at least a year after being fired.

This safety net helped subsidize the difficult first year of her self-employment. To promote her outfits, she recruited fashion models to display her work in local nightclubs. Customers came also from her friends and family. Four years after she began her dressmaking business, she no longer has time to dress models. Her customer base is strong and she keeps very busy. In fact, at the first interview, she indicated that what she PRACTICES most needed was someone else to do the routine stitching to free her up to do more specialized work. By the time of my follow-up interview with her, there was another woman working with her in her home, on a second sewing machine. Charlotte claimed the woman was not really an employee, just someone "helping out" a little. Even if the arrangement was not a permanent or long-term one, Charlotte had clearly made progress toward her plan of finding an extra pair of hands. At our second interview, she said she was regularly earning about 5,000F/month ($1,000US), up from 3,500F/month ($700US). She offered no indication of how much she paid the other woman or how long she worked.

Charlotte is a fighter, willing to work hard as well as exploit certain aspects of the law to be successful. She longs to be the head of a business enterprise, to manage and own it. On both of my visits, she was working and, though gracious to me, pressed to get back to work to meet the deadlines of each day.

CONCLUSION

The lessons inherited from slavery were not the same for black men and women. Compared to women, who might be able to curry favor from the master through their sexuality, slave men were more likely to secure advantages for themselves through deceit, trickery, and theft.[47] For male slaves with no direct means to mitigate the authority of white men, a different basis for prestige therefore emerged. Yet distinct male and female ideas about success, autonomy, and economic independence cannot neatly be dichotomized into value systems characterizing men as creole-inspired "reputation" seekers and women as seekers of European "respectability."[48]

In Martinique, women of color have not simply swallowed whole the European rules for respectability. Rather, I believe, they have adapted to the specific creole realities they experience as wives and mothers. Martiniquaise women learned to empower themselves to compensate economically for unreliable male producers who nevertheless exert French-sanctioned authority in their lives. Economic independence lightens the yoke of submission. For women, this double-barreled economic and psychological tool of financial independence seems to have maintained the strength built during two centuries of hard slave labor. Today, some women are creating businesses of their own, enabling them to translate their interests in family and in economic independence into a model of business that stresses protections for employees, a family-oriented, cooperative environment, and, ultimately, a distinctly female, but also creole, version of success. Clearly, these are goals and practices tethered to a woman's experience in creole society.

Therefore, although most women do not attempt to model *débrouillardism* in the ways that men do through creole economics, the tug of women's creole identities remains apparent in the ways that women negotiate the terms of respectability to embrace their own lived, creole realities. It is in this sense, striving for economic independence to avoid one's vulnerability to unreliable men, that creole realities condition the terms of respectability for women in Martinique.

Women, Men, and Economic Practice

Unlike women, many men of color seek to display their own autonomy and intelligence in an illicit economic realm. The informal economy offers them the ideal opportunity to show their creole prowess and gain reputation through *débrouillardism*—by competing to be more clever, more cunning, and more successful in a space of activity that is hidden from French law but on display to other men. Through creole economics, many men who may have good jobs, but as someone else's employee, are able to enjoy being their own boss, making things happen to earn themselves more income, being the one sought out by their own clients. This creole version of *débrouillardism* confers reputation because by observing the qualities of economic cunning and operating outside the law as a good *débrouillard*, a man is able to assert his authority, his autonomy, and his freedom to guide his own economic life: to a point.

Not all men gain reputation equally. At higher income levels, where men are positioned to take advantage of respectability and the advantages this status offers, they exercise greater discretion, trading some benefits of reputation for French respectability. For this reason, the bravado and reputation associated with creole economics is less complicated for moderate-income practitioners than it is for men of means, who attempt to run before the wind of both worlds.

Epilogue

IMAGING THE FUTURE
OF CREOLE ECONOMICS

PLUS ÇA CHANGE, PLUS C'EST LA MÊME CHOSE.
(THE MORE THINGS CHANGE, THE MORE THEY
STAY THE SAME)

French maxim

Everything that weighs on the contemporary moment of widespread, cross-class earning off the books suggests this phenomenon cannot be reduced to economics alone. The Patricks, Michels, Edouards, and the occasional Charlottes who earn undeclared income are also intent on asserting their autonomy and cleverness as they stiff the French state. Their schemes and their pride tell the more complex story about how economic life in Martinique is conditioned by creole values and identities.

Part of this story, as we have seen, is tied to Caribbean histories of slavery, in which creole adaptations for cunning and individualism enhanced survival and a sense of dignity. These adaptations have been stoked with fuel from another part of the story that is specific to Martinique and its close relationship to France. For despite the island's integration and assimilation to France, metropolitan French continue to withhold their acceptance of Martiniquais as truly French. In this gap, in which tropical people descended from slaves are limited in their ability to claim Frenchness, creole identities offer both a refuge from rejection and an assertion of difference.

Creole economics thrives on such assertions of creoleness as it animates the social world of men in Martinique. It is here, among men, where the creole *débrouillard* lives and where the exercise of personal autonomy and freedom from a boss carry the most meaning. Just as courting other women on the side is assumed as a right by many men, so the pursuit of undeclared income is seen as reflecting masculine liberty and entitlement. Coloring the stories of individual men are differences that distinguish a man's skills, his social networks, his resources, and the particular types of opportunities that are within his reach and ability to exploit. By operating in the cracks, out of sight, and on home ground, men in Martinique practice creole economics unimpeded. Below the radar of the French state, they are able to elude its authority and display local styles of cunning without appearing to compromise their Frenchness.

But the tensions that have sustained creole economics amidst Martinique's Frenchness may now be shifting. By the late 1990s, the longstanding denigration of creole language and culture in middle- and upper-income households in Martinique had begun giving way to a surge of popular interest in creole history and identity. This interest is apparent in the revival of storytelling traditions in urban areas; in an explosion of arts and cultural events celebrating creole dance, theatre, and music; in new museums dedicated to island history; in new emphases on creole preparations at fine restaurants; and in high-end, custom-tailored clothing incorporating traditional patterns. Even in Martinique's spectator-oriented Carnaval, I witnessed a new dress craze for parade participants and spectators alike: the ubiquitous display of madras, long associated with traditional Sunday dress.

In urban areas of the island, the use of the Creole language is in stronger evidence than it was ten years ago, during my early fieldwork on the island. At that time, one heard Creole spoken primarily in low-income households and neighborhoods, in market areas of town, around bus terminals, and in large public gatherings such as Carnaval or open-air concerts. Today, it remains true that the language one typically hears on the streets and in the shops, businesses, and government offices of downtown Fort-de-France is

French rather than Creole. But there are important signals that Creole is commanding new respect. Two major radio stations are now broadcasting entirely in Creole. Many radio channels inject Creole banter into their French-dominated programming, and Sunday talk shows or interviews usually feature at least one program in Creole. On major network TV, Creole is heard increasingly from those people interviewed by news reporters. Special television programs now air exclusively in Creole, and there is a new presence of Creole in TV advertising. Driving around town, I am no longer surprised to see billboards with Creole-only messages, or retail marquees with Creole invitations to shop. Increasingly, local festivals, concerts, and art exhibitions are presented and promoted entirely or partly in Creole.

Another indication of the surging popular interest in creole culture is signaled by growing interest among many in traveling for pleasure to other islands in the Caribbean, rather than to other parts of France. With the rise of the standard of living, more people are traveling as tourists or combining business and pleasure trips to neighboring islands.

The appearance of a more public longing to connect with creole identities may reflect the increasing concern among locals of an outside invasion that is beginning to alter the commercial and even residential landscape of the island. As a part of France, Martinique was automatically drawn into the European Union that was formalized in 1992. In the years since protective tariffs and entry visas have been eliminated across borders of EU member states, Martinique has seen dramatic changes. Some of these changes have brought welcome new pots of money to help fund local initiatives of individuals and businesses. But more of the changes are perceived to be detrimental to island life. Waves of real estate prospectors and corporate giants from other European countries, for example, have swept into the tiny island society, accenting the inability of France to protect its overseas departments. And, while France has helped ensure high living standards in Martinique, it cannot prevent the kind of high-stakes competition that open borders allow. Neither can it prevent the acquisition of local land by non-French buyers. The result has been skyrocketing prices of residential real estate and record numbers of local business closures by residents whose small shops cannot compete with the megastore discount alternatives that have cropped up in recent years.

The protectionism and subsidized economy that the French government has pursued in its parental relation to Martinique has acted to insulate islanders from the world of product innovation and merchandising strategies outside France. The false sense of economic security engendered by state welfare programs has instead encouraged Martiniquais to become habituated to unrealistic assumptions of what is required for business survival. In effect, the family romance has allowed mother France to keep her overseas children from growing up. Now, it appears that the longstanding French strategy of "benevolence" to its former colony has fallen in on itself, leaving Martinique unprepared and helpless, like an abandoned adolescent. Islanders have little training in the arts of fending off the competitive advantages of outsiders, outsiders who have no qualms about undermining the island's identity and control of its own economic future.

Considering that Martinique's economic dependency on the French state implies a future that remains politically bound to France, what do the new expressions of creole identity mean? Do they signal finally an adolescent's restlessness with its stunted role in the family romance? Do they foreshadow a political future that severs the umbilical cord to France and exchanges dependency and humiliation for a painful but necessary transition to independence and adulthood? Few Martiniquais seem to think so. Many scholars in fact view the expanding venues for celebrating creole language and culture as superficial, folklorish attempts to promote a sense of the island's history through a sanitized view of its past.[1] With rare references to the deep insults of plantation slavery, these celebrations gloss or dismiss entirely the longest and most wrenching segment of Martinique's history. The lack of widespread interest in a fuller reconnection to the island's past is also apparent when only small followings support public performances that treat slavery explicitly.[2] Instead, the innocuous content of new expressions of creole culture suggest that they pose no challenge to French authority and constitute no sort of prelude to independence from France. The economic devastation most people imagine as the inevitable outcome precludes such a possibility. Year after year, election results confirm that only small minorities of people support sovereignty for Martinique.

Precisely because the political landscape of Martinique appears unlikely to change in the foreseeable future, leaving the family romance unchallenged, local assertions of cultural difference can be safely expressed. For the first time, these assertions of difference are moving to the foreground from a space that has always remained in the background, hidden in the shadow of a more desirable European status and respectability. These days, creole is marketable. Creole is cool.

The question remains, however, whether the movement to publicly celebrate creole identities will help offset islanders' unfulfilled claims of Frenchness. Josephine's statue in the Parc Savane presents a useful symbol for thinking about this question. Although authorities have tried to reattach her missing head, vandals have had the last word: the head remains severed from her body and is regularly resplattered with blood red paint to emphasize the continuing freshness of the wound. Josephine's decapitation and bloody touch-ups underscore an energy that remains intent on resisting numbness to the past and apathy about the present.

While this energy dare not challenge outright Mother France, the hand that feeds it, it remains a vital reminder of the tensions that lie just below the surface of things. It is for this reason that creole economics will likely remain a potent force for managing the strains of plural identities. Unlike the glossy new venerations of local culture, or the gritty dramas that draw too much attention to an uncomfortable past, creole economics offers a quiet, insider way to subvert French authority. So long as Martiniquais feel unresolved in their relation to France, creole economics will likely continue to confer status. And as long as earning off the books is not impeded by new legislation, as long as it fulfills a sense of entitlement and enhances creole reputation, why not carry on? *Débouya pa péché.*

For however disagreeable many find these unlawful acts of self-interest, creole economics is an undeniably effective strategy of cultural resistance. Not a resistance to outside forces or to a cultural enemy, but resistance to the parent France, to the parent's assumption of sameness and treatment as lesser. For a people oppressed by a cultural, political, and economic reality that offers too many benefits to discard, creole economics provides a way to express personal autonomy from the parent's rules without leaving home. In this complex form of opposition within complicity, Martiniquais are able to assert their creole difference, oppose French power, and all the while, remain proudly French.

NOTES

PREFACE

1. As a first-year graduate student in 1987, I had the good fortune to accompany my advisor, Victoria Lockwood, to Tubuai in the Australs archipelago of French Polynesia. My work involved helping her collect household census data, archival data, and longer, in-depth interviews. The Australs chain lies approximately 400 miles south of the Society Islands, which include Tahiti and Bora Bora, among others. The combined populations of French Polynesia number approximately 220,000 (Aldrich & Connell 1998:258).

2. France has ten overseas departments and territories, known as the DOM-TOMS (Aldrich & Connell 1998:27, 3).

3. These represent three of France's four overseas departments (DOMS). The other is Réunion, an island off the east coast of Madagascar in the Indian Ocean.

4. My exploratory research investigations occurred in a period of about three weeks spanning two summers, in 1988 and in 1989.

5. Professor Fred Celimene, for example, suggested that a micro-level study of informal activity could prove useful to the larger, macro-level economic trends that he and his center analyze. Celimene heads the university's center for macro-economic research, modeling, and applied management studies, Centre d'Etudes et de Recherches en Economie, Gestion, Modelisation, Informatique Appliqué (CEREGMIA). See also Crusol 1986.

6. Letchimy was elected mayor of Fort-de-France in May 2001 following the more than fifty-year tenure of poet-politican Aimé Césaire. Letchimy was Césaire's choice to replace him.

CHAPTER 1

1. Although France was more assimilation oriented than Britain or other colonizers, it is not the only former colonizer nation to have maintained political ties to many of its former colonies. Britain, Denmark, the Netherlands, Portugal, Spain, the United States, Australia, and New Zealand all retain distant territories as political dependencies to some degree. Britain has more overseas territories than other ex-colonizers, but the combined populations of these areas is far less (about 400,000) than the combined populations of the French DOM-TOMS (about 2 million) or of the US (more than 4 million, primarily residents of Puerto Rico) (Aldrich & Connell 1998:1, 19–20).

2. Mintz 1985.

3. See O'Shaughnessy's *An Empire Divided* (2000) for discussion of variations in colonizing strategies, particularly those of the British in North America versus the Caribbean.

4. Francophonie summits are worldwide conferences that occur every two years and engage more than twenty-three countries in a celebration of French language and culture. Since 1997, a permanent council has served as an administrative advisory board headed by a General Administrator of Francophonie (Irene Assiba d'Almeida, author of *Francophone African Women Writers*, 1994, personal communication, 1999).

5. Aisha Khan's article "Journey to the Center of the Earth: The Caribbean as Master Symbol" discusses how the Caribbean area has become the "master symbol" for the world, especially because of the creole languages and cultures, which reflect heterogeneous influences, making the area a "site of all that flows" and positioning it to be "heralded as the writ-small of the writ-large that is thought to characterize us all today" (2001:273).

6. Some scholars have extended the idea of "creolization" to serve as the metaphor for the types of culture collision occurring elsewhere (Hannerz 1997). These ideas are explored more fully in Chapter 4.

7. For a full treatment of the overseas territories of France and other former colonizer nations, see Aldrich and Connell's *The Last Colonies* (1998).

8. Price 1998:173.

9. Gilroy 1993; Bongie 2001.

10. Sahlins 1999.

11. Friedman 1994; Hannerz 1997.

12. Ashcroft et al. 1995:3.

13. Price 1998:161.

CHAPTER 2

1. *Béké* refers to the group of French white slaveowners in Martinique. The term also applies to all descendents of these original slaveowners.

2. Josephine was first decapitated in 1991. Although officials have tried to replace the head, the "vandals" have continued to make their point. See photos, p. XXX.

3. Lowenthal 1972:ix.

4. Hansis 1997:39.

5. Several events led French, British, and Dutch colonies to become the sugar bowl of Europe. By the early 1600s, Dutch Jews who had been expelled from Brazil ventured north to the islands, where they introduced techniques for large-scale production of sugar. French settlers, who had arrived in Martinique and Guadeloupe in 1635, had recruited or brought with them European indentured servants to clear land and produce crops. However, by the second half of the seventeenth century, a growing commitment to sugarcane cultivation gradually displaced white indentureship and homestead societies. Producing sugar offered much greater financial rewards and required a much larger and better-adapted workforce (Moitt

2001:7).

6. The first leg of what became known as the "trade triangle" took Europeans with manufactured goods (including French brandy, Dutch linen, Spanish iron, and German muskets) to the west coast of Africa, where African chiefs were seduced with such goods in return for slaves that their followers helped locate and capture. The second leg of the trade triangle, known as the "middle passage," involved the several-week journey across the Atlantic to the West Indies on European slave ships crammed full with captured slaves from West Africa. The export of raw materials, including sugar, molasses, and rum (made from crushed cane stalks), completed the third leg (Rodney 2000; Mintz 1985).

7. For many reasons, the West Indian islands were ideally suited for the cultivation of sugar. The wet, humid climate made it possible to grow sugar year round; the soil was good and there were adequate expanses of flat land. The new techniques for large-scale production of sugar promised rich rewards for planters, who could count on large metropolitan markets in Europe, markets assured by peoples' cravings for the sweet taste.

8. Kovats-Beaudoux 1969; Lewis 1968:51.

9. Higman 1984:379.

10. The French colonial Code Noir of 1685 included no provisions limiting the number of hours a slave could be forced to work. The only limitation was that slaveowners were required to give slaves Sundays off, as well as a few religious holidays (Moitt 2001:38).

11. Lirus 1979:19.

12. This was true in both French and British colonies (Moitt 2001:40).

13. Moitt 2001:46. See also Brereton 1999:78–79; Lirus 1979:20.

14. Moitt 2001:80. On the other hand, conjugal relations were commonplace and "illegitimacy carried no shame" (Moitt 2001:84, 87).

15. It is not surprising that although there was a legal framework to promote slave marriages in the French colonies, the option interested very few slaves (Moitt 2001:87).

16. Moitt 2001:97. Abolition of the slave trade (not slavery) occurred in 1808 in the British colonies and in 1818 in the French colonies (Rogozinski 1999:180).

17. Burton 1997; Moitt 2001:93–97.

18. In the French colonies, the most common reason for freeing slaves was conjugal relations with slaveowners, though most of these manumissions were *libres de fait* (unofficially freed; this meant partial freedom in that these were not officially recognized by the French state and thus carried no official documentation). These *libres de fait* manumissions were considered illicit according to the laws established in 1685 with the French Code Noir (Moitt 2001:151).

19. Geggus 1989:1297. Still, as Moitt points out, the freeing of a slave concubine did not necessarily result in the freedom of her children, just as freeing slave children might not accompany the freeing of their mother. In fact, according to Gautier, planters regularly freed their mixed-race male sons without also freeing their concubines, the slave mothers of these male children (cited in Moitt 2001:159–160).

20. Hoetink 1985:69; Lowenthal 1972:48; Clarke 1957:21.

21. Rogozinski 1999:125.

22. By 1810, 258,000 slaves had been imported to the island, and by 1848, the year of abolition in France, a total of 365,000 slaves had been brought to Martinique. (Blackburn 1988:163,12).

23. Parry et al. 1987:88.

24. According to my informants, the term "mulatto" no longer implies a specific biological heritage. Today, the term connotes a socioeconomic status as well, suggesting that even if someone were technically mulatto, the term would not usually be applied without the presence of correspondingly high social status.

25. Tomich 1990:14.

26. Lowenthal 1972:27.

27. The small islands in the eastern Caribbean are known as the Lesser Antilles, in contrast to the larger islands of the northern Caribbean, called the Greater Antilles.

28. Williams 1970:156. Because these islands produced great wealth, they were the basis of intense warfare and political maneuvering between European nations competing for sovereignty and claims to such wealth. At one point, following the defeat of Napoleon, control of the West Indies fell to Britain. In 1763, France was forced to cede to England all of Canada, the Ohio and Mississippi Valleys, and Grenada just to keep Martinique and Guadeloupe, considered the jewels of the Caribbean (Wagley & Harris 1958:93).

29. Rodney 2000.

30. Van Kley 1994:129.

31. Rodney 2000.

32. Aldrich & Connell 1992:22. As Tomich (1990:18) points out, however, most of the sugar exported to France was not consumed in France. Even working-class British, by contrast, had incorporated sugar into their daily diets.

33. Aldrich 1996:14.

34. Lewis 1968:17.

35. The Moorish occupation of Spain lasted 700 years, until the late fifteenth century.

36. Sociologist Chris Smaje notes that the constitutional basis of French and Spanish colonization in the Americas was a "monarchical absolutism" as compared with the more "confederate" basis for English colonization (2000:149).

37. Smedley 1999:134–135.

38. These fundamental differences in Spanish colonizing strategies had many implications. First, unlike island colonies of the French or British, Spanish island colonies were demographically established as Hispanic settlements with Indians and small proportions of black Africans. Eric Williams points out that in those New World areas dominated by sugar cultivation, three times the number of slaves were needed than in areas where other crops were grown. In Puerto Rico, for example, where as late as 1827 the primary crop was coffee, the plantations were small farms, and compared to the 162,000 whites, there were only 32,000 slaves (1970:109, 122).

39. This situation helps explain why Spanish Creole languages never developed in these areas. In Cuba, especially high numbers of late slave imports strongly impacted the demographic mix, so that by 1827 more than 56 percent of islanders were African descended (Rogozinski 1999:201). These differences are visible today in the higher proportions of Afro-Cubans in Cuba than African-descended peoples in either Puerto Rico or the Dominican Republic.

40. Reflecting my own difficulties in locating material focused on differences with regard to treatment toward Caribbean colonies, David Geggus (1989:1290) states that "historians have been less interested in French attitudes toward the colonies during the revolutionary period than in the colonies themselves." He goes on to say that this absence is especially surprising considering the vital economic role these sugar colonies held for France.

41. Aldrich & Connell 1992:20.

42. Lowenthal 1972:267.

43. Mary Turner notes, for example, that the British planters in Jamaica did not "in any systematic way [attempt] to substitute Christian beliefs for the slaves' religion" (1999:33). The British colonizing pattern has also been described as "aloof" (Lewis 1968:115). See also Mitchell 1963.

44. Many debate the classic thesis proposed by Frank Tannenbaum: that the Latin colonizers treated their New World slaves better than the Anglo Saxons did (Smedley 1999:115). On the other hand, ample evidence suggests that North American slavery was less harsh than the slavery of the Caribbean. Part of this relates to the fact that the plantations were smaller and more diversified, and that the slave to white ratios were less dramatic (O'Shaughnessy 2000).

45. Rosenblum 1988; Mitchell 1963:27.

46. Williams 1970:184.

47. Dayan 2000:193.

48. Singham 1994:129; Van Kley 1994:129; Lowenthal 1972:37. As historian Bernard Moitt indicates, manumission in the French West Indies occurred more often through the informal status known as *libres de fait* (unofficially freed), since the French state attempted to limit the incidence of manumission (Moitt 2001: 153).

49. At the time of the Revolution of 1789, for example, in Saint Domingue, France's most important sugar colony, there were 30,000 whites, 28,000 free coloreds, and 465,000 black slaves (Van Kley 1994:129). See also Blackburn 1988:19.

50. Geggus 1989:1296.

51. Lowenthal 1972:267.

52. Nine general categories of local color terms are commonly cited in local discourse, each incorporating distinctions in skin color, hair texture, cheekbones, and lips. These include *blanc, mulatre, clair, chabin, chappe cool, capre, brun, rouge/marron, noir.*

53. O'Shaughnessy 2000:61.

54. The British planter societies "bequeathed shamefully little toward developing an infrastructure in the islands, such as schools, colleges, roads, and missions,"

which is "reflected in the paucity of architectural remains . . . despite the opulence of its planters" (O'Shaughnessy 2000:5). For example, compared to nine colleges in Britain's North American colonies at the end of the colonial period, there were no universities in the British West Indies. This underdevelopment also contrasts with universities established in Spanish Caribbean areas (O'Shaughnessy 2000:21).

55. According to Andrew Jackson O'Shaughnessy (2000:57), many preferred to avoid the inconveniences of tropical life, operating their plantations with surrogates while they maintained their homes in Britain. In fact, at the time of the American Revolution, it is estimated that at least 2,000 owners of plantations in the British West Indies actually resided in Britain. This estimate comes from the Jamaican planter-historian Edward Long, cited in O'Shaughnessy (2000:4). The author further explains that British plantations in North America were quite different since colonists here were "settler" oriented. North American plantation economies depended on smaller plantations of tobacco or cotton, where slaves were smaller in number relative to the elite white population. These demographic realities help explain the much higher incidence of slave revolts in Caribbean than in North American slave societies.

56. In the French West Indies, there was no post-abolition "apprenticeship" required for former slaves, a system imposed on freed slaves in both the British- and Dutch-controlled areas. The practice was intended to preempt the danger that colonial officials anticipated from the "idleness" they expected freed slaves to exhibit (Williams 1970:300, 329).

57. Aldrich & Connell 1998:19. It is worth remembering that the British withheld the "rights of Englishmen" even to American colonists, and this denial led to the American Revolution.

58. Even the Catholic Church was a major slaveowning entity, though these slaves were frequently manumitted so they could enter the clergy (Smedley 1999: 125).

59. Smedley 1999:127.

60. Smedley cites Tannenbaum's historical work indicating these patterns. She further notes that even Aristotle and Plato believed that some people were "natural slaves" because they had no power of reason, but this designation could apply to anyone, and was not associated with whole categories of geographically or culturally identified people (1999:127).

61. Smaje 2000:157.

62. Lewis (1968:57), referring to the ideas of John Locke. Historian Kenneth Manning explains that the "subjugation of one race to another was put forth as part of a preordained, hierarchical framework" that was unquestioned in its adherence to Christian principles (1993:319).

63. Drescher 2001:427.

64. Beginning with a law in 1664, French slaveowners were required to baptize new slaves and to baptize their children as well (Moitt 2001:80–81). Moitt points out that this law became folded into the Code Noir, which was enacted about

twenty years later. These provisions made all the more clear that the French colonial administration wished to promote "religious conformity" as well as marriage among slaves. However, slaves were not inclined to marry, and the laws promoting it were more an effort to prevent sex and marriage between slaves and whites than anything else (Moitt 2001:82).

65. Sociologist Chris Smaje discusses these varying perspectives about the nature of justifications that led to slavery in his book *Natural Hierarchies: The Historical Sociology of Race and Caste*. He notes that, at the very least, the slave trade was predicated on "the perception of African difference in the context of a self-absorbed and essentializing European Christendom" (2000:139). Moreover, he cites research from Dunn (1972) and Vaughan (1995) in supporting the view that in the early American colonies, "Africans were from the outset always debased in relation to even the rudest among indentured servants" (139).

66. For example, see Winthrop Jordan, *White over Black: American Attitudes toward the Negro 1550–1812* (1968). See also Barbara Fields 1990, cited in Smaje 2000:137.

67. Smaje 2000:151, also citing Canny & Pagden 1987.

68. Moitt 2001:34, referencing Medieval Arab scholars and later Europeans, who also used the biblical account of Canaan's curse to explain the black skin of African peoples. The views of Père Jean-Baptiste Du Tertre are referenced in his four-volume history of the French Antilles, *Histoire générale des Antilles habitées par les Français*, published originally in 1671 and reprinted in 1973. Material presented by Moitt is drawn from 1973 (2):488.

69. David Brion Davis (1984:42), cited in Moitt 2001:34.

70. Père Labat wrote a six-volume treatise on the French Caribbean islands in 1722, *Nouveau voyage aux iles de l'Amérique*. His reflections are cited in Moitt 2001:35.

71. O'Shaughnessy (2000:34, 262), citing Philip Morgan 1991.

72. O'Shaughnessy 2000:34.

73. Moitt 2001:9.

74. Cuvier and Agassiz both cited in Manning 1993:320.

75. Cited in Smedley 1999:234. Nott and George Gliddon's 1854 treatise *Types of Mankind* espoused these ideas. This book became the most popular scientific account of race types and the inherent inequality of races in Britain during the second half of the nineteenth century.

76. Benedict Morel first articulated the concept of degeneration, but it was Arthur de Gobineau's classic essay, "Essais sur l'Inegalité des Races," published in 1853, that discussed how métissage contributed to degeneration (cited in Vergès 1999:96).

77. Smedley 1999; Manning 1993.

78. Lewis 1968:57.

79. Buffon cited in Singham 1994:130.

80. Singham 1994:130.

81. Many claim that the uprising in Saint Domingue was inspired by the French

Revolution in 1789, but others contend that the timing of the revolt precludes this possibility (Trouillot 1995:90–95).

82. Aldrich 1996:21; Williams 1970:283; Mitchell 1963:170.

83. Williams 1970:176, 215.

84. Beet sugar developed in both France and England during the Napoleonic Wars, when Atlantic sea routes became battle sites and sugar exports from the West Indies were disrupted (Aldrich 1996:21). Other new sugar production centers emerged in the Indian Ocean, the South Pacific, Asia, and Africa, all contributing to the erosion of the vital historic link between the production of sugar and the use of slave labor (Tomich 1990:3).

85. Brereton 1999, 1989:85; Williams 1970:151.

86. Aldrich 1996:212,215. Although the inhabitants of France's "old colonies," including Martinique, Guadeloupe, French Guiana, and Réunion, were given status as French citizens and men were allowed to vote in local and national elections, indigenous peoples in other areas of the French Empire were generally not made French citizens unless they became married to one. Exceptions include certain areas of Senegal and the Tahitian islands. Women in France were granted suffrage in 1945.

87. Aldrich & Connell 1992:171. Echoing the sentiments of Frantz Fanon, geographer David Lowenthal singled out the French Caribbean in his historical survey of islands, saying that "prejudice about language is strongest in the French Antilles" because there, "the Negro is proportionately white in direct ratio to his mastery of the French language" (Lowenthal 1972:272).

88. Aldrich & Connell 1992:171.

89. Chamoiseau's novel won the Prix Goncourt in 1992, the most prestigious literary prize awarded in France. Chamoiseau is a contemporary Martiniquais author who has published numerous novels and plays.

90. N'Zengou-Tayo 2000:183.

91. At the time of the Revolution, because of losses to rival England, only a few scattered trading posts remained in French control (in India, Senegal, and the North Atlantic islands of Saint-Pierre and Miquelon). France had not yet established colonies in the Pacific, Indochina, or Africa.

92. Kadish 2000:3–4.

93. Aldrich & Connell 1998:19.

94. For the emerging class of mulattos in the French West Indies, the Revolution of 1789 inspired hope and the confidence that local efforts to dismantle an aristocratic plantation system based on slavery would be bolstered by support from the new Republican government. Meanwhile, the lure of Frenchness was fed by radical politicians and intellectuals in the metropole who invoked the Revolution of 1789 to lobby for abolition in the French National Assembly (Daniel 1993:316).

95. Although abolition was decreed at the central government, it was never enacted in Martinique (Hintjens 1992:66). Since colonial planters and authorities wanted more, not less, local autonomy, they tried to leverage the new idea of

equality to win more control over the islands, to reduce the state's meddling in local affairs, and to ensure representation of their colonies in metropolitan France (Kadish 2000:3; Hintjens 1992:66).

96. Tomich 1990:34–37.

97. The collective sense of French identity has long been tied by scholars to the egalitarian norms and practices of the Jacobin Revolution in 1789. More recently, some have argued that it was not until the 1880s, with the centralization of the educational system, that France became distinctively "French" in the modern ways it is recognized for today. With all schools in the French Empire devoted to teaching the same material in the same sequence, key values promoting the ideals of liberty, equality, and fraternity could be inculcated across cultural and geographic spans. Still others suggest that by the 1860s, extensive road networks and rail lines had been built, creating the means for millions of people to venture out to new areas of their home country. Cheap, widely circulated newspapers coincided with improved literacy so that the nation's news could be shared by households all over France. In this view, by the 1870s, a gradual consensus had emerged among ordinary French citizens in linking the meaning of the Revolution of 1789 to the nation's most prized values of liberty, equality, and fraternity (Hazareesingh 1998: 118, 21, 25).

98. Ezra 2000:6.

99. Aldrich 1996:92. Historians suggest that most ordinary French in fact remained indifferent to the foreign affairs of their government long after colonizing missions had begun. Arguments in opposition to expansion were varied and included the idea that French power would be diluted by efforts to control so many people so far away, that French revenue would be squandered in trying to retain long-distance control of the colonies, that the so-called humanitarian efforts of the colonizing mission were in fact counterproductive, and that the need for a restored source of national pride and energy was misplaced by a focus on colonial expansion. Aldrich further explains that even the pro-colonialist interests representing business, the church, and colonists were often in conflict (1996:89). On the point that no colonizing nation acted according to a single theory or practice of empire building, see Stoler & Cooper 1997:17 and Noiriel 1996:272.

100. Aldrich 1996:92.

101. Aldrich clarifies the point that the colonial lobby consisted of geographers, lawyers, journalists, public servants, and numerous commercial interests including colonists, businessmen, port cities. These varied interests—academic, business, political, and social—may account for the lobby's effectiveness (1996:100–103).

102. Aldrich 1996:110.

103. Hintjens 1992:64. Logistical realities such as the distances of colonies from France and their small European populations made implementation of assimilationist policies throughout the far-flung French Empire difficult and sometimes impossible.

104. In a sense, this kind of post-slavery integration might seem analogous to a hostage deciding after freedom to join up with her captor. The "Stockholm Syn-

drome" is a psychological disorder which involves the affective attachment of prisoners to their captors. Patty Hearst used this disorder as her defense in pleading not guilty to having committed the same crimes as her kidnappers. In effect, she claimed, she had come to psychologically identify with her captors because of their attention to her.

105. Hintjens 1992:66.

106. Kovats-Beaudoux 1969:244.

107. Aldrich & Connell 1992:171.

108. Burton 1994; Suvélor 1981.

109. Negritude involves the idea that African-descended peoples in the Americas should embrace their blackness rather than attempt to deny it, by locating their psychological homeland in Africa. These ideas are discussed in Chapter 4.

110. Despite islanders' campaign to become a part of France and the feverish efforts among upwardly aspiring Afro-Creole people to act and sound fully French, the tug of a different, non-French identity persisted. However, considering the context, in which duplicity and contradiction were a way of life, it posed little concern for Martiniquais to, on the one hand, pledge allegiance to France and seek the benefits of this status, while, on the other hand, quietly embrace their own creole values and practices. It is worth remembering how many apparent contradictions Afro-Creole populations had already embraced. For example, slaves had shown compliance to the master, but they had also subverted the plantation's efficient rhythms. Similarly, Creoles had shown acceptance of Catholicism, but they continued their practices of sorcery.

111. Naipaul 1963.

112. Cabort-Masson 1987.

113. de Miras 1989:371.

114. de Miras 1989:371.

115. The fundamental changes in the economic base of Martinique may be described as "welfare state colonialism." Two Pacific island researchers developed
this concept while studying the economic viability of small island microstates with low internal productivity. According to their findings, welfare state colonialism occurs when an island economy is effectively controlled by a large government sector charged to ensure a decent standard of living and responsible levels of health, education, and communications (Bertram & Watters 1985:508).

116. de Miras 1989.

117. INSEE 2000:61.

118. de Miras 1989:372.

CHAPTER 3

1. A telling contrast with dominant groups in the society includes some migrant groups to the US who specialize in routine, undeclared economic activities such as informal street vending. Anthropologist Paul Stoller, for example, writes about

West African migrants in New York City who represent a significant group of street vendors, selling informally (2002).

2. In a fascinating approach to researching the unregulated economy of the US, economist James Alm attempts to explain why there is such a high degree of tax compliance in the US. He cites a number of factors that likely contribute, including perceptions of the possibilities of detection and punishment. But the primary reason for high compliance, he argues, is the role of social norms. "There is overwhelming evidence that many countries with roughly the same fiscal system also have far different compliance experiences. The only possible explanation . . . is that these countries have different notions of what is socially acceptable behavior" (1996:108).

3. Neoclassical economics began with the ideas of Adam Smith (1723–90), who argued that individuals naturally pursue their own self-interests and that these would benefit the society's interests as well. These ideas echo related assumptions in western thought about human nature and the interrelated notions of rationality and progress. This tradition of western thought, tied to Enlightenment thinking, is perhaps best reflected in Auguste Comte's "positivist" theory that the path of social progress is one defined by reason, a path clearly expressed "in the whole range of scientific studies. . ." (1880:94).

4. Escobar 1995:64.

5. These debates are discussed in Wilk 1996 and Herzfeld 2001.

6. Malinowski 1922.

7. Polanyi's ideas about the embeddedness of local economies in social institutions as well as his understandings of forms of exchange in different kinds of societies (reciprocity, redistribution, and market) remain foundational for economic anthropology. His most commonly cited essay, "The Economy as Instituted Process," was published in 1957 in *Trade and Market in the Early Empires*. For a thorough consideration of the contributions of Polanyi to economic anthropology, see Halperin 1994.

8. Herzfeld 2001:96.

9. Wilk 1996:83; see also Escobar 1995:69.

10. Wilk 1996:104.

11. In *Capitalism: An Ethnographic Approach* (1997:39–54), Daniel Miller makes this point eloquently by distinguishing the ideas of "pure capitalism" as promoted by the abstract, ideal models of lending institutions, and "organic capitalism," as the lived experience of real societies, like Trinidad, located on the periphery of First World nations.

12. Wilk makes this argument in *Economies and Cultures* (1996:13).

13. Sahlins, *Culture and Practical Reason* (1976); Gudeman, *Economics as Culture* (1986); Gudeman & Rivera, *Conversations in Colombia* (1990); Halperin, *The Livelihood of Kin* (1990); Escobar, *Encountering Development* (1995).

14. Escobar 1995:59.

15. Wilk 1996:127, summarizing Sahlins (1976:213–214).

16. A classic example of the social limits on economic gains is Carol Stack's

(1974) *All Our Kin,* an ethnography of a low-income African American community in which expectations of reciprocity effectively preclude the possibility of an individual's upward economic mobility.

17. In her ethnographic study *Russia's Economy of Favours,* Alena Ledeneva (1998: 1) credits this phrase to Martin Walker, a journalist for the British newspaper the *Guardian.*

18. Ledeneva 1998.

19. Werner 2000. According to Werner, some people manage the cultural mandates of gift-giving in strategic ways that enhance their own social networks and thus material self-interest.

20. Verdery 1996.

21. Ong 1999; Rofel 1999; and Zhang 2001.

22. In fact, the usage of these terms reflects a shifting assortment of disciplinary, regional, and theoretical biases, and reflects as well the variations spawned by casual usage among those unfamiliar with these biases. Many economists, as an example, consider the term "second economy" to refer specifically to the undeclared activities of people living in socialist states with command economies (see Pérez-López 1995; Grossman 1989). For a comprehensive review of the variations in meaning and usage of these terms, see Lubell 1991.

23. This definition was established in the seminal work of sociologists Manuel Castells and Alejandro Portes (1989:12–13).

24. Castells and Portes distinguish activities which are "inherently" illegal at the site of their production, such as drug dealing, and those that are made illegal in the process of an undeclared exchange, such as tailoring. The former category of activities is referred to as comprising the "criminal" or "underground" economy (1989:13). See also Portes 1996:156.

25. Because most scholars who focus on informal economies regard Castells and Portes' work to be the best framework for these issues, I am adopting their usage. However, because not all social scientists use the term "informal economy" to mean the same thing, cross-cultural comparisons can be difficult at best. For example, Stoller uses "informal" in the broadest sense, to refer to all activity, criminal and otherwise, among the West African immigrant traders in New York City (2002).

26. As Portes says, "Underground operations are of a nature and size different from those of microentrepreneurs and artisans in the informal sector proper" (1996:157–158).

27. The International Labour Organization, the development agency recognized for its leadership in work on the informal economy, also uses Castells and Portes' operational definition to distinguish informal from criminal activity. As stated in a 2002 ILO document, informal activities "should be distinguished from criminal and illegal activities, such as production and smuggling of illegal drugs, as they are the subject of criminal law, and are not appropriate for regulation or protection under labour or commercial law" (2002a:54). This document contained resolutions concerning the informal economy as produced by the Committee on

the Informal Economy, which met during the ILO's 2002 international conference in Geneva.

28. Gerry 1987:109.

29. Planners reasoned that if informal operators actually practiced a kind of incipient entrepreneurship, then once aid, credit, and training programs were made available, they could make the transition to full-fledged entrepreneurship. Such intervention efforts, targeted at the micro level, would allow poor producers to grow and, eventually, employ others.

30. Through the late 1970s and much of the 1980s, it was the International Labour Organization, headquartered in Geneva, that spearheaded efforts to target for growth those actors who were situated in the "informal sectors" of developing economies. Other international development agencies, including USAID and World Bank, have since joined the effort and also committed significant resources to the micro level of informal economies.

31. In terms of the workforce located in the informal economy, the statistical consultant to the Office of the UN Secretariat reports that in Latin America, the numbers represent about 55 percent; in Asia, between 45 and 85 percent, and in Africa, as much as 80 percent (Charmes 1998; see also United Nations 2000). The World Bank estimates the proportion of informal economic activity in total economic output to range between 25 and 40 percent in Asia and Sub-Saharan Africa (2001:25).

32. ILO 2002a:53.

33. Castells & Portes 1989:16; ILO 2002a:54.

34. Feige 1989; Castells & Portes 1989.

35. Moser 1978; Peattie 1980; Portes 1983.

36. For example, studies have focused on the following groups: women who do "homework" in a Mexican shantytown (Arizpe 1977); street traders in Cali, Colombia (Peattie 1980); flea market vendors in northern California (Lozano 1983); marketers in Huaraz, Peru (Babb 1985, 1988); street traders in Transkei, South Africa (Nattrass 1987); street hawkers in Hong Kong (Smart 1988); wholesale and retail marketers in Madras, India (Lessinger 1988); Cuban and Haitian enclaves in Miami (Stepick 1990); West African street traders in New York City (Stoller 1996); Jamaican women traders (Ulysse 1999); Puerto Rican women in Philadelphia (Mulero-Diaz 2000); Mexican immigrants in Chicago (Raijman 2001).

37. Portes & Walton 1981:91–94.

38. Analyses of such concerns are present in many anthropological studies including, most recently, Stoller's study of West African street traders in New York City (2002). For an edited volume devoted entirely to the study of these problems, see Gracia Clark's *Traders versus the State* (1988).

39. Clark 1988:2; Castells & Portes 1989; McKeever 1998.

40. For exceptions, see Kerner 1988; Grossman 1989; and Browne 1996. For work describing how informal economic activity can lead to upward social mobility for some but not others, see Stepick's comparative research on Cubans and Haitians in Miami (1990) and Browne's research comparing women and men in the informal economy in Martinique (2000).

41. The ILO has long maintained that "most people enter the informal economy not by choice but out of a need to survive," that, "the informal economy absorbs workers who would otherwise be without work or income," and that the informal economy is characterized by "relative ease of entry and low requirements for education, skills, technology and capital" (2002a:54). Recent World Bank publications make clear that ILO conceptualizations have been adopted by this institution as well. A 2001 World Bank publication, for example, similarly portrays informal operators as "subsistence earners" whose households "typically lack both income and social security." The document also echoes ideas held by the ILO in characterizing informal operators and their work: "Workers tend to be low-skilled and wages are generally low in both relative and absolute terms. Capital investments and technological inputs are minimal. Skills and credit are usually acquired through non-institutional sources" (2001:25).

42. In a recent document, the ILO states that "workers and economic units in the informal economy can have a large entrepreneurial potential." Implications of this point are further elaborated as the document concludes that people working in the informal economy "have real business acumen, creativity, dynamism, and innovation, and such potential could flourish if certain obstacles could be removed." By thus removing obstacles in the path to entrepreneurship, the informal economy could "serve as an incubator for business potential and . . . a transitional base for accessibility and graduation to the formal economy" (2002a:54). Because it is assumed that most informal earners made no choice to earn off the books, it is a natural assumption that they would prefer to operate in the formal economy, where social protections and benefits are guaranteed.

43. Exceptions include work by economists such as Peruvian Hernando de Soto. Funded in part by the US Agency for International Development, de Soto dispatched a large team of researchers to document what Lima's "unemployed" were doing to survive and how they circumvented government regulations. According to him, at least 60 percent of urban residents were doing things off the books, contributing to the thriving informal sector. The solution, he argued, was to "informalize" the formal economy, in order to bring these informal operators within the law. See de Soto's *The Other Path* (1989). Development agencies commonly cite de Soto's work and consider his recommendations among the field of policy options.

44. Escobar is referring to the conventional notions of what it took to be economically successful which shaped the post–World War II sense of optimism about transforming poor, underdeveloped economies into prosperous capitalist economies. The optimism was expressed in the founding of the United Nations, a number of international development agencies, and a new field of applied economics known as "development economics." It was during the early post-WWII years that the present conception of poverty was born. The new "institutions of planning" such as the World Bank, the International Labor Organization, and the US Agency for International Development were conceived to rid the world of poverty by creating the conditions for economic growth. Escobar goes on to say that the

inattention given to local context is a product of both the macro-level tools economists use to inform their insights and the positivist bent of their science. He notes, "Most economists . . . believe their knowledge is taken to be a neutral representation of the world and a truth about it" (1995:58).

45. Cernea reported that in his analysis of thirty-five projects designed and implemented by the Bank, only thirteen were considered successful (1991a). See also *Putting People First* (1991b). In this vein, see also work by Robert Chambers (1997).

46. In a recent World Bank newsletter, for example, Bank economist Milan Vodopivec indicates that developing policy options for the unemployed in the Philippines is a complex process that cannot succeed by "transplanting policies that work elsewhere." The key, he said, is to respond to the particular situation, so that the solutions are made to "fit into existing informal, as well as formal, market-based mechanisms" as well as "prevailing norms and culture" (2001:29).

47. The Grameen Bank offers the best documented example of a success story revolving around tiny loans made to individual women for purposes of enhancing their gardening efforts. In 1996, the World Bank made a concrete move to replicate the success of micro-scale lending based on the Grameen Bank model. The Bank created a new experimental mission, Consultative Group to Assist the Poor (CGAP), to develop policy and programs oriented to micro-scale interventions.

48. SEWA, founded in 1972, has helped working women organize who are self-employed, who do home-based work, act as street vendors, and perform other casual work. The ILO reports that SEWA is "the oldest trade union of women who work in the informal economy" and today encompasses more than 250,000 women (2002b:18). Since the 1980s, SEWA has also promoted an international movement to help other women in the informal economy organize. Other women's unions have been formed in other parts of India, in Durban, South Africa, in Australia, and in Canada. In 1997, a global coalition of grassroots organizations, research institutions, and international development agencies was formed called Women in Informal Employment: Globalizing and Organizing (WIEGO) (ILO 2002b:19).

49. Miller 1997:42. Miller also references George & Sabelli (1994:58–72), who discuss these same concerns.

50. In a 1995 book, *Cuba's Second Economy*, economist Jorge F. Pérez-López offers a comprehensive introduction to the various forms of unregulated economic activity that in Cuba occur alongside the country's "first economy." However, descriptions for these activities are based on the limited archival sources available (scant academic literature and official reports from the Cuban press), and on interviews with emigrés. Because there was no fieldwork involved in this study, there is understandably no discussion of how cultural attitudes and values may have shaped the contours of this substantial unregulated economy. Another study of a Caribbean informal economy provides a view of sidewalk vending and foreign exchange black market activities in the context of Jamaica (Witter & Kirton 1990).

This study attempts to evaluate different measures for estimating the size of an informal economy, though in this case, criminal activities are included. Arlene Dávila focused on Puerto Rican informal artisans (1999) and how the marketing of their "folk art" is tied to ideas about national identity and cultural "authenticity."

51. Lowenthal 1972:9.

52. Richardson 1983:7.

53. See, for example, Freeman 2000; Richardson 1983; Sampath 1997; Wirthlin 2000.

54. N'Zengou-Tayo 2000:182. See also Chapter 4 for further discussion of Chamoiseau's novel.

55. Carnegie (1987) argues that Comitas' idea of "occupational multiplicity" is better conceived as "strategic flexibility" since multiple occupations represent only one dimension of a larger Caribbean pattern that includes, for example, flexibly constituted households and relations between women and men.

56. Comitas 1973:171.

57. Wilson 1995.

58. Freeman 2001:1023.

59. Freeman 2001:1027. As I discuss in Chapter 5, because slaves were permitted to sell surplus produce from the side provision plots they gardened for their own subsistence, the habits and value of side work may well be traced to this long-running labor arrangement.

60. Traditional street "higglering" is well documented among Afro-Caribbean women generally. A study of food vendors in Kingston, Jamaica, for example, demonstrates how this female-dominated pattern of street marketing derives from the tradition of trade and marketing brought there by African female slaves. (Powell et al. 1990). For a recent analysis of changing higgler strategies in Jamaica, see Ulysse (1999). Numerous other Caribbean-focused studies have addressed the high proportion of women in the formal work force, a phenomenon associated with the historically strong economic role of women in slave societies. (Momsen 1993; Browne 2000).

61. Sociologist Mary Waters discusses her findings about West Indian migrants in *Black Identities: West Indian Immigration Dreams and American Realities* (1999:112).

62. Lisa Douglass' work with Jamaican upper-class men and women is an important exception to this pattern (1992), though her focus on analyzing family and gender relations does not deal explicitly with economic values related to the discussion here. Daniel Miller has also studied middle- and upper-income people in Trinidad in relation to their consumption practices (1994b).

63. The concept of "cognitive orientation" as employed by Mintz & Price (1992) is explained in Chapter 4. I am using the term to connote a kind of mental map about what practices and beliefs are familiar historically and make sense in the current context.

64. As I discuss in Chapter 7, the implication of affluent involvement in unde-

clared income earning appears to contradict the goals of European-style respectability many scholars have associated with middle and upper class Caribbean people. To distinguish reputation and respectability simply on the basis of class or gender is too constraining to fit the realities in Martinique.

65. In industrialized countries like France, with strong labor laws and heavy social security burdens on employers, the informal economy thrives, despite the fact that most people are not poor as in say, Peru. In the US, where there is a lighter tax burden on employers and self-employed, the informal economy is a less significant phenomenon. Estimates of the size of informal economies are difficult, in part because the tools of tax auditing vary across states, in part because what is being measured also varies. Still, estimates suggest that France's informal economy may represent as much as 23 percent of GNP, while the informal economy of the US is more typically estimated at 6 to 8 percent of GNP (Leonard 1998:15–16).

66. The interest of anthropologists in unearthing cultural histories is perhaps stronger today than ever before, precisely because it is through the excavation of thick layers of historical experience that the ethnic conflicts and identity struggles so many people face today can be made intelligible. Among New World societies, for example, distinct patterns of colonization contribute to distinct economic attitudes and practices visible today. Spanish colonizers forced indigenous peoples to mine gold and silver. For a fee, the Spanish king rewarded colonists with titles and entitlements to labor and land. In contrast, the French and British exercised different strategies of colonization, depending on African-descended slaves and a monocrop system of sugar cane cultivation. As a result, economic practices in Spanish-colonized areas, while certainly variable, still bear a stronger resemblance to each other than they do to economic practices in French- and British-colonized areas of the New World. In Mexico, for example, the legacies of patronage and bribery inherited from Spanish colonization and reproduced over generations continue to characterize everyday life as well as institutional arrangements. Specifically, the favor-based exchanges surrounding political office are strongly apparent in Mexico's informal economy (Lomnitz 1988). These Mexican patterns are notably distinct from those in Martinique where bribery exists but does not represent a common ethic of exchange.

67. James Alm discusses the American norms that act to discourage work off the books (1996).

68. By assuming that informal economies are bounded by the poor, development agencies disregard the undeclared activities of those who are not poor, seeing them as qualitatively different phenomena. (ILO 2002a; 2002b.)

69. Bourdieu (1977) identified four kinds of capital to distinguish the many sources of status people may access: economic (material assets such as property and investments, and income); social (personal networks, group memberships); cultural (meaningful accomplishments such as education, artistry, athleticism, and possessions such as writings, art, musical instruments); and symbolic (prestige of family name, recognition of leadership, heirloom valuables, and luxury goods).

70. The example of functionary salaries shows how increased standards of living can reverberate throughout society and stir unprecedented levels of con-

sumerism. In the 1950s, following a long teachers' strike, France extended the 40 percent *prime de vie chère* (compensation for the high cost of living) to Martiniquais in government functionary jobs. Prior to this time, only metropolitans serving in functionary posts in Martinique were eligible for these benefits. With at least 20,000 official "functionaries" in Martinique, representing nearly 21 percent of the actively employed population, the discretionary income made available to this sector fueled a boom in consumer buying (Tranap 1988:26–27; Gautier 1988:7). Not surprisingly, many of my lower-, moderate-, and even middle-income informants considered the ideal employment to be a functionary post.

71. Domenach 1981:13.

72. Miller 1997:339. Miller wrote two books on his ethnographic work in Trinidad. The first was *Modernity: An Ethnographic Approach* (1994a). The "organic capitalism" he stresses in his second book about Trinidad, *Capitalism: An Ethnographic Approach*, shows that despite their newfound poverty since the late 1980s, local people still assume the rights to consume as though they were a First World population. In fact, he claims, the consumer economy, which demands "shiny peanuts" and "red sweet drink," is the most powerful expression of local culture (1997:328–334).

73. RMI, or Revenue Minimum d'Insertion, is a state allocation instituted in 1988 to provide a guaranteed minimum income to people with few resources.

74. Emphasis on clothing, accessories, hair, and possessions others can see have been cited as Caribbean-specific patterns by numerous authors. See Miller 1994a: 223 and 1994b:73; Freeman 2000:227.

75. Mintz & Price first spoke of "the cock of the hat" as sartorial flair expressed by Caribbean peoples (1992). Richard Burton also describes how during slavery in Jamaica, for example, although slave huts were spare and most slaves had no beds, the emphasis on clothes allowed slaves to restore a sense of their own personalities, their individual humanity. On weekends when there were dances, and on special holidays, extravagant clothes were considered to "restore personalities" and greatly enhance one's reputation (1997:41).

76. See a full examination of this idea in the Caribbean context by Miller (1994b) in an article entitled "Style and Ontology."

77. Friedman's (1994) fieldwork in the French-colonized area of Congo documents how a marginalized man in Congolese society can enhance his local status as someone who is a savvy person, "la sape," through travel to metropolitan France, purchase there of elite label clothing, and display of this clothing back home. James Ferguson (1999) elaborates on the performance of style in Zambian identity, noting how those urban dwellers who invent themselves as "cosmopolitans" contrast with "localists" by wearing international rather than locally affiliated dress styles, by drinking in bars rather than in homes, and by using more elite language.

78. Wilson 1969. Because concern with fashion is a hallmark of French society, the extent to which European standards have shaped the sensibilities of personal style in Martinique is not clear. My own observation of clothing styles in similarly urban areas of Barbados, Antigua, Jamaica, and Puerto Rico suggests that the style

of dress in Martinique reflects many "fashion-conscious" European influences that are less apparent in other Caribbean societies, including concern for quality fabrics and fitted styles. Puerto Rican professional women do wear colorful fitted dresses, but the patterns of chic styles and slender bodies are much less consistent there than in Martinique.

79. All names of local officials have been changed to respect the privacy of these informants.

80. Armet 1990:29; personal interview with staff economist at Central Bank, June 1999.

81. M. Arnaud further pointed out that the practice of not declaring labor in the construction industry became far worse with the enactment of a 1986 law freeing certain activities and purchases from taxation called *le loi de défiscalisation*. This law provides home buyers a five-year tax break on their investment in the construction of a new home. It also provides businesses with large tax breaks for their investments in new facilities, or in the purchase of productive equipment. The law acted as an explosive stimulant to the building industry and the market for informal labor.

82. Others have made clear the "costs" of this form of cheating. One economist noted that "underreporting has a variety of harmful effects: it reduces the tax revenues of the government, it affects public provision of goods and services, it creates misallocations in resource use, it alters the distribution of income in unpredictable ways, it increases feelings of unfair treatment by government, and it generates disrespect for the law" (Alm 1996:103).

83. This phrase, like *le travail au noir*, is a common French reference for the informal economy.

84. In the late 1990s, the French government reduced the cost of declaring household labor.

85. Patterson 1982.

86. See, for example, Freeman 2000; Gmelch 1997.

87. E.g., Wilson 1995; Burton 1997.

88. Sampath 1997:49.

89. Ong 1987.

90. Escobar 1995:218.

CHAPTER 4

1. I never saw Patrick again. It seemed clear to both of us that, in Martinique, it is not realistic for a woman and a man to maintain a nonsexual friendship.

2. A "hybrid identity" is an amorphous but increasingly popular term generally used to suggest the fragmentation of identities by two or more cultural influences (Brah & Coombes 2000; Werbner 2001). However, because the term "hybrid" implies taking stock from separate origins in order to generate a new, synthesized outcome, the association is less appropriate in Martinique, where people main- 233

tain distinct associations of creole and French practices, ideas, and beliefs. Such metaphors of biological reproduction and new genetic synthesis are also criticized by Maurer (1997). The term "métis" or "métissage" similarly conveys mixed parentage, and carries the same problematic implications of "fused" outcomes that hybridity does (Vergès 1999:9). Martiniquais authors Chamoiseau, Confiant, and Bernabé propose the term *créolité* (creoleness) to suggest the multiplicity of identities that are not a synthesis. Their ideas are discussed later in this chapter.

3. Linguist M. C. Alleyne calls Martinique's language situation "diglossic," meaning French and French Creole coexist, but the usage of each is generally separate, not blended, as was more typically observed in British-colonized islands (1985:166). I am not suggesting that the usage of Creole language is necessarily a fitting analogy for other creole practices. In urban Martinique, however, explicitly creole practices and speech occur more often out of sight than the public display of French speech and practice. One important exception to this pattern includes public expressive performances (theatre, dance, storytelling) that are deliberately staged to generate pride in Martinique's local cultural heritage. See also Burton 1997:28.

4. See Khan 2001. Some scholars are in fact using the term "creolization" as a gloss for any type of cultural mixing (Hannerz 1987:551; 1997:126–127). Although this usage appears to be gaining currency, linguists and historians argue that creolization is a term that should be reserved for the profoundly specific circumstances associated with the emergence of new Creole languages. In the Americas, long periods of plantation slavery and forced transplantation of Africans who spoke different native languages constitute an irreducible part of the constituent elements of creolization (see Arends 1995; Price 2001; Trouillot 2002). As Trouillot notes, "The repeated announcement that the world is now in or moving toward a state of hybridity and creolization . . . reinforces the tendency to treat creolization as a totality" rather than recognizing its specificity (1998:194).

5. Michel-Rolph Trouillot (1998) first referred to the mysteries of Creole language development as "the miracle of creolization." Richard Price then incorporated this phrase into the title of a subsequent article as a way to stress the continuing unknown, perhaps unknowable history of Creole genesis and evolution in the many plantation areas where it developed (2001).

6. Valdman 2000.

7. Herskovits (1941/1990) attempted to prove his idea that African cultures remained present in Caribbean societies by itemizing various traits in different societies that he ranked according to their degree of "Africanness." One example he used was the high proportion of matrifocal households, which he claimed demonstrated a consistency with polygamous traditions in West African societies. Frazier used this same example to argue that instead, it was the harshness of slavery that had separated adult males from mother/child units of existence. Thus, he said, there was no need to summon Africa to explain matrifocal patterns.

8. Mintz & Price 1992.

9. It is a widespread, accepted idea among historians of slavery as well as

anthropologists and linguists that in the Americas, African-descended peoples display African continuities in the form of "cognitive orientation," as Mintz & Price argued (see also Berlin 1998; Morgan 1997). However, a minority of "Africa-centric" scholars (e.g., Thornton 1998; Gomez 1998, cited by Price 2001) claim that African ethnicities were kept intact in many New World areas, thus arguing against Mintz & Price's emphasis on the process of creolization.

10. Price 2001:41.

11. This is cited from Mintz' foreword to Peter Wilson's book, *Crab Antics* (1973/1995:ix).

12. For a review of recent research efforts along this line and a more general call to emphasize the need for recognizing different contexts and different patterns of creolization, see Trouillot 2002. For an overview of the anthropology of scholarship about the Caribbean, see Yelvington 2001.

13. Such local factors of slave demography, plantation structure, and attitudes of individual European planters would have shaped the relative weight of contributions from African and European influence (Trouillot 2002).

14. Arends 1995:4.

15. Some linguists believe this process took only one generation, beginning with the children born into slavery on the plantation to parents who were bozals, speaking a native West African language (see Bickerton 1999). Others argue it was a more gradual process (Singler 1995) though still remarkably rapid compared to other languages.

16. Pidgin languages do not usually develop into Creole languages for the simple reason that the circumstances that lead to the development of a pidgin generally involve temporary contact between groups of people with different native languages. Thus, in situations such as trade, ceremony, or security, the reduced communication system provided by a pidgin allows speakers of different native languages to communicate adequately. However, in New Guinea, trade-based pidgins did evolve into full Creole languages among people whose livelihoods depended on commercial exchanges with outsiders.

17. Arends 1995:21.

18. Linguistic understanding of these patterns has been debated. The most common view is that African patterns of syntax form the hidden "substrate" of Creole languages in the Caribbean, while more apparent influences of European languages constitute the "superstrate" vocabulary (Alleyne 1985; Arends 1995). Others, however, maintain that Creole languages in the Caribbean represent an "approximation of approximations" of European languages with relatively little contribution from African languages (see Chaudenson 2001).

19. See, for example, studies in Latin America by June Nash (1979) and John Burdick (1993).

20. Abrahams 1983.

21. These dances are cited in the *Historial Antillais* 1980:492–494, noted in Chaudenson 2001:201.

22. Dramé 1996:235; Roberts 1989:28, 34.

23. Anancy tales involving the trickster Spider are common in the British-colonized areas of the Caribbean (Dance 1985; Burton 1997:63) and are remarkably similar to trickster tales of the Rabbit, which are most common in French-colonized areas like Martinique.

24. As Chris Smaje notes about the New World transformation of Anancy tales, "In Ashanti cosmology Anancy represents a mocking, 'liminal' figure who subverts normal worldly categories like sky and earth, male and female, and so on. In Jamaican versions, he loses this cosmic role and emerges as a cunning underdog who turns the adverse circumstances of everyday life to his advantage" (2000:215).

25. Martiniquais children's folktales are full of stories of Compère Lapin (Brer Rabbit), who represents the same cunning, successful-despite-the-odds qualities one talks about in a *débrouillard*. See, for example, Catalan & Combelles 1981 and Rapon 1991.

26. Gilroy 1993: 29.

27. Glissant 1981:277.

28. Lowenthal 1972:3.

29. DuBois 1903/1989:17.

30. Garvey later helped inspire the Rastafarian movement in Jamaica, including the repatriation principle that held prominence in the early decades of Rasta belief.

31. To fulfill his campaign, Garvey chartered a steamship liner, called Black Star Line, which was set to ship tens of thousands of African-descended peoples back "home." Although Garvey's plan was thwarted due to financial and legal troubles, he had by 1920 built an allegiance of more than 100,000 followers from the US and Caribbean.

32. Cited in Rosenblum 1988:9.

33. In a sophisticated treatment of French assimilationist policies toward its colonies, Elizabeth Ezra argues that, despite France's public assertions promoting such assimilation, the "colonial unconscious" can be exposed for its fundamental
reservations about assimilating colonial subjects. She notes that between the world wars, "time after time, cultural texts showed that the desire to preserve cultural distance—the essence of the colonial unconscious—underlay expressions of exoticism that seemed to promote contact between cultures . . . Colonial culture's manifest content, the discourse of assimilation, concealed a latent but powerful desire for cultural separation" (Ezra 2000:152–153).

34. Today, Césaire's poem *Cahier d'un Retour au Pays Natal* (Return to My Native Home) stands as the defining lyric call to Negritude. It was published originally in 1939 and reprinted in 1988.

35. Cited in Collins 1972:xvii.

36. Davis 1997.

37. Dash 1995.

38. Although the intellectual movement had run its course by the late 1970s, as mayor of Fort-de-France since 1945, Césaire found the resources and personnel to institutionalize his commitment to link Martiniquais to their underexplored Afri-

can identities in everyday life. In 1981, Césaire founded a sprawling cultural center for the community as a space to put the principles of Negritude into practice. SERMAC (Service Municipal d'Action Culturelle) houses workshop facilities for contemporary dance, traditional dance, painting, printing, basket weaving, music, woodwork, theater, and costume design. The center remains funded by the Regional Council and the municipal government of Fort-de-France and is managed by Jean-Paul Césaire, Aimé Césaire's son.

39. After completing his studies in philosophy in Paris, Glissant did not return to his homeland Martinique until twenty years later, in 1965, when at the age of thirty-seven he accepted a local post as a high school teacher. Already a prolific author of poetry and novels, Glissant was inspired by the changes he witnessed in his homeland and devoted years to writing essays and developing his ideas on the crisis of identity faced by Martiniquais. Today, Glissant lives and teaches in the US.

40. In 1981, Glissant published a collection of essays titled *Le Discours Antillais* (Caribbean Discourse). This book is recognized today as having led the way out of Negritude.

41. Dash 1995. Stuart Hall discusses how the relational nature of identity helps explain the predicament of Jamaicans and other British West Indians who migrate to Britain (2000).

42. The authors describe *créolité* as "the interactional or transactional aggregate of Caribbean, European, African, Asian, and Levantine cultural elements, united on the same soil by the yoke of history" (Bernabé et al. 1990:94).

43. Bernabé et al. 1990:89.

44. Condé 1998; Price and Price 1999.

45. Providencia is located due east of Nicaragua, near the larger island of San Andreas.

46. The coexistence of both a creole and a European status system effectively disputed "structuralist" claims by R. T. Smith and his followers. For structuralists, Caribbean peoples all shared the same set of European-derived, normative structures. The unusual forms of family life (such as female-headed households without male providers) and kinship networks common to many Caribbean peoples were explained as a product of stratification—resource constraints simply prevented some people from achieving the European ideals that they had internalized. Alternate interpretations of these same family forms came from M. G. Smith, who claimed instead that not one but multiple normative structures coexisted in Caribbean societies, creating inherently "pluralist" populations (cited in Lewis 1968:36).

47. These ideas of reputation and respectability are applied to the context of gender and creole economics in Chapter 7.

48. Wilson 1973/1995; Burton 1997.

49. In *Wretched of the Earth* (1965), Frantz Fanon also emphasized the importance of shedding the artifacts of colonial influence.

50. Hintjens 1992; Burton 1993; Vergès 1999.

51. Hall 2000:147.

52. Price 1998:182.

53. Beriss 1993. See also Burac 1995.

54. Interestingly, my research indicated that for wealthy mulattos or others with strongly Caucasian facial features, these kinds of encounters with racism were less often reported. It may be that racism declines in proportion to one's perceived "whiteness," which may be achieved through wealth, phenotype, and respectable behavior.

55. Suvélor 2001 (personal communication); Confiant 1991 (personal communication).

56. Glissant echoes Fanon, who three decades earlier (1952, translated in 1967) warned of the dispossession of Martiniquais, who make the dangerous mistake of locating their psychic selves with France, to which they can never assimilate.

57. See Bhabha's (1990) "The Third Space."

58. de Certeau (1984:29–42). Britton (1999:28) elaborates this idea for the slave context of the French Caribbean, noting that "unable to overturn the relations of oppression, [the tactic] aims to destabilize them and to turn the master-slave opposition into an unbalanced situation, never static, always in the process of being redefined." Richard Burton (1997:50–51) also applies de Certeau's ideas in the slave context.

59. Wylie 1957:335.

60. Larousse 1987:283–284.

61. Harrap 1997:143.

62. Ludwig et al. 1990:99.

63. Roberts 1989; Burton 1993.

64. An example of how attempts to express opposition within complicity do not necessarily work can be seen in a study by David Beriss (1993), who interviewed Antillean stage performers in a theatrical troupe in Paris. He found that their strategic effort to express West Indian difference and at the same time win the blessing of French "high art" presented real conundrums. Put simply, aiming to express difference on French terms (high culture versus folklore) and in metropolitan sites seemed to reproduce the folk stereotypes of Antillean peoples as "exotic representatives of Frenchness" rather than to compel consideration of the work as art. When such performance is exposed to the views of critics and the wider public, "the gaze of the Other" may present serious difficulties for finding a satisfying way to express difference. Perhaps creole economics thrives because it lives in the shadows and far from the "family home."

65. See Aiwha Ong's (1999) discussion of similar predicaments among Chinese immigrants to the US. She notes that, despite Bourdieu's contention that economic and symbolic capital can be interchanged, the wealthy Chinese cannot buy the acceptance of white Anglo society because they lack the required physical (symbolic) attributes of whiteness.

66. Martinique has been called the "isle of intellectuals" by scholars (e.g., Lucien Taylor, cited in Price 1998).

CHAPTER 5

1. Patterson, *Slavery and Social Death* (1982).

2. In 1789, for example, 150 years after the first slaves had arrived in Martinique, the local population included 83,000 slaves, 10,600 whites, and 5,000 free people of color (Blackburn 1988:19–20).

3. Blackburn 1988:30; Burton 1997:48.

4. Lazarus-Black 1994:253; Roberts 1989:32. The tactics correspond to the ideas articulated by Michel de Certeau (1984) and discussed in the previous chapter.

5. Craton 1997:190; Burton 1997:50.

6. Craton 1997:189.

7. See Scott, *Domination and the Arts of Resistance* (1990).

8. Scott 1990:18.

9. Scott 1990:18–19.

10. Burton 1997:49.

11. Moitt 2001:54; Tomich 1990:265.

12. Tomich 1993:234.

13. Tomich 1990:260.

14. Diman-Antenor 1995:5; Tomich 1990:266.

15. Tomich 1990:266.

16. Moitt (2001:56) notes that although slave women performed most of the market vending, slave men profited more because of their ability to dominate women. See also Tomich 1990:274–276.

17. Curtin 1969:19.

18. Bastide 1971; Craton 1997:190.

19. Cited in Mintz & Price 1992:39.

20. Patterson 1982:222.

21. Chamoiseau 1997:39.

22. Burton 1997:41.

23. Wilson 1995:193.

24. Mintz & Price 1992:30.

25. Abraham 1983:xvi.

26. Chamoiseau 1994:xii.

27. Condé cited in Arnold 1996:257.

28. Chamoiseau 1994:xii.

29. Craton 1997:190.

30. Laurent & Césaire 1976:13; Joyner 1986; Arnold 1996:262.

31. Goldenberg 1970:3.

32. Arnold 1996:257.

33. Dramé 1996:235; Roberts 1989:28, 34; Glissant 1981.

34. Chamoiseau 1994:xiii.

35. Dramé 1996:249.

36. Weiss 1985:45–47.

37. Burton 1993:468.

38. Scott 1990:19, 199.

39. Confiant 1995:13.

40. Roberts 1989:36.

41. Chamoiseau 1994:xii.

42. Césaire 1978; Confiant 1995; Suvélor 1981.

43. Fanon 1967:174.

44. Burton 1993:468.

45. Vergès 1999:62.

46. Tomich 1993:241.

47. Serge Letchimy received his PhD from Paris University in 1985. Before being elected mayor of Fort-de-France in 2001, Letchimy headed the local firm of SEMAFF (Société d'Equipement et Mènagement à Fort-de-France), which he founded to study urban problems and develop programs to address them, particularly in the area of housing.

48. Based on personal interviews with Serge Letchimy, Raphaël Confiant, and Roland Suvélor.

49. The origin of the Creole version, *débouya*, is not known.

50. Roberts 1989; Burton 1993.

51. I have already cited many of these authors in the discussion of local consumption patterns in Chapter 3. These authors include Mintz & Price (1992); Burton (1997); Miller (1994); and Freeman (2000).

52. The phrase is spelled according to the most recent *Dictionnaire Créole Français* (Ludwig et al. 1990:99).

53. Raphaël Confiant has written numerous novels, poems, and essays in French Creole and in French. His best-known works include the critically acclaimed novel *Le Nègre et L'Amiral* (1988) and his co-authored book-length essay on Martiniquais self-identity, *Eloge de la Créolité* (Bernabé et al. 1990).

54. Roland Suvélor is the elder statesman of Martinique's history and has contributed significantly, both as editor and author, to a six-volume work called *Historial Antillais*. These volumes present a thorough and incisive history of the Antilles and were published in successive years in the 1970s and 1980s. Suvélor is widely published in scholarly journals as well, writing most often about the cultural and historic influences which have shaped Martiniquais self-identity and behavior.

CHAPTER 6

1. I am defining "productive" in line with economists who distinguish undeclared "productive" work from undeclared "rent" income: undeclared "productive" work is activity in which a good or service is created and exchanged but is simply not taxed according to law; this kind of economic activity contributes to economic productivity. By contrast, income generated from tax evasion, fraud, or transfer payments constitutes "rent" income that makes no contribution to the productive base of the economy (see Osterfeld 1992).

2. Using cluster analysis, I analyzed data from numerous variables to determine broad-level variations in socioeconomic status. The variables analyzed included income, number of earners, household debt, and household amenities including dishwasher, air-conditioning, and domestic help.

3. In 1990, the minimum monthly wage in Martinique was 4,408F ($882US, based on exchange rates of 5F to $1US) (Madras Plus 1991:353). By 1998, the minimum wage had increased to 6,797F ($1,132 based on the higher rates of exchange, 6F to $1US) (INSEE 2000:81). As part of the European Union, Martinique's currency converted to the Euro in 2002.

4. Browne 2000.

5. The law, designed to boost employment and help stimulate investment and growth locally, permitted individuals to deduct 25 percent of the cost of building a new home from their taxable income over a five-year period. Non-retail or tertiary businesses were allowed to deduct 37 percent of the cost of their investment in capital equipment or facilities from their profits in order to reduce their tax burden. But there was ample latitude for abuse, since the actual use of an investment for business growth is very difficult to monitor. According to officials from the state tax collection office, there were many perverse and unintended effects of this law (Monrose 1991 [personal communication]).

CHAPTER 7

1. The idea that both women and men in Caribbean societies pursue a kind of individual autonomy is discussed in Mintz & Price 1992.

2. Barrow 1998:xiii.

3. Moitt 2001:40.

4. Moitt 2001:59; 62. According to Moitt, male slaves sometimes served as cooks, too.

5. In addition, women domestic slaves managed to use their sexual leverage with their master to "ensure the continuity of personnel and personal relationships" that they favored (Moitt 2001:72–73, 98).

6. Geggus 1989:1287. For a discussion of the inconsistencies with regard to slave manumission in the French areas, see Moitt (2001:159–160).

7. Moitt 2001:77.

8. The Code Noir explicitly forbade the breakup of slave families, but this was among the many provisions of the Code that were regularly ignored by slaveowners (Moitt 2001:163).

9. Moitt 2001:79, 83. If married, a male slave could legally claim authority over his wife and rights of paternity to his children.

10. Mintz & Price 1992:72. Nineteenth-century French scholar André Lachariere wrote that "polygamy reigns in the colonies . . . where unions among slaves are tenuous" (cited in Moitt 2001:84).

11. Moitt 2001:163.

12. Suvélor 2001 (personal interview).

13. Powell et al. 1990.

14. For a discussion of Martiniquais versus Puerto Rican types of patriarchal control, see Browne 2001. See also Safa 1995; Gautier 1995.

15. Safa 1995:47.

16. In addition, as discussed earlier, the constraining influences of Catholicism on women in French areas were somewhat offset by the fact that these women had experienced the profound influence of long-term slavery and thus had become accustomed to the primacy of their labor in the economic sphere.

17. Poirier & Dagenais 1986.

18. See Browne 2001. The British-installed Anglican Church imposed fewer faith-based restrictions on women than did Catholicism. After abolition, the religious beliefs of colonists in places like Barbados similarly did less to suppress the economic independence of women that had been established during slavery than in either the French or Spanish areas.

19. Hall 1995:54.

20. Brereton 1999:102.

21. Brereton 1999:103, citing missionaries J. M Phillippo and William Knibb, and Governor Light of British Guiana, in 1838.

22. Smaje (2000:195). Sociologist Chris Smaje goes on to note the "historical irony" of this situation; in contrast to the female slaves, who sought freedom from the impositions of plantation work, feminists have typically struggled to pry open the world of work to women.

23. Brereton 1999:106.

24. As discussed in Chapter 4, these distinct tugs of a desire for assimilation and a desire to exhibit one's cultural difference continue to plague the identities of Martiniquais people.

25. As discussed in Chapter 4, W. E. B. DuBois identified these dual influences on creolized peoples as a "double consciousness" (1903/1989).

26. Mosse 1985, cited in Olwig 1990:95.

27. Wilson 1995.

28. Mintz & Price 1992:79.

29. Tomich 1990:274–276.

30. Connie Sutton (1974) led the critical treatment of Wilson's work, followed by others, including Olwig 1990; Douglass 1992; Besson 1993; Yelvington 1995; Burton 1997; and Freeman 2000. Besson has shown, for example, that because lower-class women in the British Caribbean are active in the outside, "public," space of men, they too may compete for reputation. Freeman has demonstrated how Barbadian infomatics workers dress and handle their work in ways that reveal the interpenetration of European and creole systems of status. Douglass has argued against Wilson's notion that European values represent an imposition, stating that creole values are no more "authentic" than European ones (1992:254).

31. Burton 1997:167.

32. See, for example, studies by Bolles 1996; Freeman 2000; Olwig 1990; and Safa 1995.

33. Audric 1991:19–22; INSEE 1995:43.

34. INSEE 1995:55, 44.

35. The political realm shows an even more exaggerated imbalance in the representation of women. At the municipal level, women in Martinique represent 15 percent of elected officials; at the highest levels of government, they hold less than 2 percent of the elected positions. (Gautier 1995:133). Since 2001, a new French gender parity law requires that 50% of those on election ballots will be women.

36. Thanks to Jane Albritton, guitarist and writer, who gave me this idea in explaining how strings require an "essential tension" to produce sound.

37. Carla Freeman identifies a similar pattern in Barbados, saying that "respectability as it is understood today in Barbados reflects, not a superimposition of nineteenth-century European values of feminine domesticity, but rather a femininity imbued with the ideals of marriage, nuclear family, propriety, as well as those of wage/professional work and independence. The tension between or simultaneity of these ideals is itself a creation of creolization, and a particular Caribbean reality" (2000:110).

38. Roland Suvélor 2001 (personal communication).

39. As Wilson J. Moses argues, the notion of "twoness" is problematic because black women and men are dealing with multiple tugs on their identity in addition to European and African-American cultural values, such as ideologies of gender, sexuality, and class (1993:274–290). While I agree that all people experience multiple tugs on their identity, I treat the influences of gender and class as aspects of identity that cannot be separated from race. My use of DuBois' idea of "twoness" does not preclude differentiating the experiences of Afro-Caribbean women from men or rich from poor; it simply asserts that the profoundly race-based oppression that characterizes Afro-Creole histories compels us to look first at race, and second at gender, class, and other sources of difference within race. My ethnographic experience strongly confirms the overwhelming significance of race in relation to other aspects of local identity.

40. I am using the term "significant" here to reflect actual statistical chi-square tests of gender patterns which proved significant. For further discussion of these patterns, see Browne 2001.

41. Niels Sampath links freedom and autonomy to reputation in Trinidad when he states that "a strong reputation which emphasizes personal 'freedom' is deemed important in the post-slavery, post-plantation, post-colonial environment" (Sampath 1997:49).

42. The emphasis on fulfilling expectations in the domestic realm is also apparent in the way women build their social networks. In my comparative study of male and female social networks in 1996, I found that women across socioeconomic classes tend to build networks of kin relations, whereas men across classes develop networks of people who are not generally kin (Browne 2000).

43. This is not to say that creole economics by default does not carry cultural meaning, as I discussed in Chapter 6. When women and men have regular declared jobs, however, their choice to pursue side work offers a more compelling basis to examine the differing ideals for males and females in the realm of economics.

44. For a description of the cluster analysis that yielded the four income levels of low, moderate, middle, and upper, please see Chapter 6, note 2.

45. "Rounding out the end of the month" is a common euphemistic way of referring to extra side income.

46. See Browne 2000 for a discussion of social network research across class and by gender in Martinique.

47. These strategies are discussed in Chapter 5.

48. Karen Fog Olwig argues that, to the extent that reputation and respectability are gendered phenomena, it is less because each sex is instinctively drawn to one system of values versus the other, than because of "different access to public institutions that men and women have experienced as a result of the colonial gender structures which were imposed on them in the post-emancipation era" (1990:96).

EPILOGUE

1. These ideas are shared by authors such as Richard Price, Edouard Glissant, and Maryse Condé, and are discussed more fully in Chapter 4.

2. For example, Patrick Chamoiseau's play *L'Esclave Vieil Homme et la Molosse* (The Old Slave and the Big Dog) drew reasonable attendance for the several-night performance at L'Atrium, a small stage theatre, but the play had a short run. No one I knew was interested in seeing it with me. Another event commemorating the anniversary of abolition took place in Diamant and was videotaped for rebroadcast to island audiences. No one I knew cared about watching it or had videotaped it to watch later.

Afro-Creole (or Afro-Caribbean)—refers to people who are descended from African slaves and who have grown up in a creole society. An Afro-Creole person carries a mixed biological heritage, part African and part European, as well as ancestry that may include East Indian, Asian, Syrian, Lebanese, or other elements.

béké—refers to the island's white Creoles, who are descendants of French white slaveowners in Martinique. *Békés* remain economically dominant despite the fact that they represent only about 1 percent of the island's population. They are also generally endogamous, though marrying other whites is increasingly acceptable.

Creole—refers to people who were born and raised in the Caribbean region, or to a specific language (French Creole, English Creole, Dutch Creole) that emerged in the context of plantation slavery. Because descendants of slaves and slaveowners alike are considered part of the early mix of people who formed creole societies, these groups are today distinguished as Afro-Creoles or white Creoles. For a fuller explanation of the historical circumstances associated with Creole peoples and languages, see Chapter 4. When the term is used in a more generic sense, I use lowercase (creole cuisine, creole cultures, creole economics, or creole music).

creole economics—refers to the cultural economy of Martinique characterized by creole values related to autonomy and cunning, which many people demonstrate by earning money as their own bosses, off the books.

(by design)—refers to the undeclared economic activities people pursue for extra income, on the side of their regular jobs.

(by default)—refers to work off the books when no other income alternatives are available.

débouya pa péché—Creole proverb meaning "it is not a sin to be a *débrouillard.*"

débrouillard—French term that has distinctly exaggerated meaning in Creole usage.

(French)—a person who is resourceful or has initiative.

(Creole)—a person who is resourceful in a clever or cunning way that often transgresses the law. Commonly used to describe someone who pursues economic activity "off the books." As Frantz Fanon observed, the *débrouillard* in Martinique is the human embodiment of the trickster Rabbit in creole folktales.

débrouillardism/débrouillardise—an act typical of a *débrouillard.*

défiscalisation (le loi de)—A law put in place in Martinique in 1986 in order to boost employment and help stimulate investment and growth locally.

DOM *(département d'outre mer)*—an overseas department of France, a legal status equivalent to any other French department, irrespective of its geographic location. France has four DOMs—Martinique, Guadeloupe, French Guiana, and Réunion, an island off the east coast of Madagascar.

functionary—a civil servant or professional public service employee (e.g., teacher, firefighter, doctor, administrator). In Martinique, functionaries earn 40 percent more than their counterparts in continental France, though this "cost of living" accommodation is now under threat.

hexagon—refers to the shape of the French state on the European continent.

INSEE—Institut National de la Statistique et des Etudes Economiques (Institute for National Statistics and Economic Studies). This office performs the French census and research on a broad variety of economic and demographic patterns. INSEE maintains a research center and archive library in Fort-de-France, Martinique.

Josephine (Empress)—Josephine was a *béké* from Martinique, born in 1763. In 1796, she married General Napoleon Bonaparte. Thirteen years later, after he had become emperor of France and she had given him no heirs, they were divorced. She died in 1814. In Martinique, the monument to her was built in 1859 in the Parc Savane, where it stands today. In 1991, vandals decapitated the statue to express their discontent with continuing control by *békés* and metropolitan French in the island. Although authorities have attempted to replace Josephine's head, vandals continue to sever it and regularly paint blood marks on the neck wound to emphasize the continuing freshness of their discontent.

metropole—refers to the geographic nation-state of France in Europe.

metropolitan—refers to white French who were born and raised in continental France and to continental France, generally. Often used in distinction to people or products of DOM-TOM origin.

mulatre (mulatto)—literally, a person born of a parent of African descent and a parent of European or Euro-American descent. In actual usage, however, "mulatto" typically refers to those light-colored individuals who possess high social standing.

se débrouiller—refers to the act of taking initiative, being resourceful and self-reliant.

TOM *(territoire d'outre mer)*—an overseas territory of France, a less integrated status than DOM, but one which assures a political connection to France as well as certain economic benefits and immigration rights. French TOMs include, for example, New Caledonia and the Pacific islands of French Polynesia.

Abrahams, Roger. 1983. *African Folktales*. New York: Pantheon Books.

Aldrich, Robert. 1996. *Greater France: A History of French Overseas Expansion*. New York: St. Martin's Press.

Aldrich, Robert, and John Connell. 1992. *France's Overseas Frontier: Départements et Territoires D'Outre-Mer*. Cambridge: Cambridge University Press.

————. 1998. *The Last Colonies*. Cambridge: Cambridge University Press.

Alleyne, M. C. 1985. "A Linguistic Perspective on the Caribbean." In *Caribbean Contours*, ed. Sidney Mintz and Sally Price, 155–179. Baltimore: Johns Hopkins University Press.

Alm, James. 1996. "Explaining Tax Compliance." In *Exploring the Underground Economy: Studies of Illegal and Unreported Activity*, ed. Susan Pozo, 103–128. Kalamazoo, Mich.: W. E. Upjohn Institute for Employment Research.

Andrews, William L., and Henry Louis Gates Jr., eds. 1999. *The Civitas Anthology of African American Slave Narratives*. Washington, D.C.: Civitas Counterpoint.

Arends, Jacques, ed. 1995. *The Early Stages of Creolization*. Amsterdam: John Benjamins Publishing Company.

Arizpe, Lourdes. 1977. "Women in the Informal Labor Sector: The Case of Mexico City." In *Women and National Development*, ed. Wellesley Editorial Committee, 25–37. Chicago: University of Chicago Press.

Armet, Auguste. 1990. *Société et Santé a la Martinique: Le Système et le Masque*. Paris: Présence Africaine.

Arnold, A. James. 1996. "Animal Tales, Historic Dispossession, and Creole Identity in the French West Indies." In *Monsters, Tricksters and Sacred Cows: Animal Tales and American Identities*, ed. James A. Arnold, 255–268. Charlottesville: University Press of Virginia.

Ashcroft, Bill, Gareth Griffiths, and Helen Tiffin, eds. 1995. *The Post-Colonial Studies Reader*. London and New York: Routledge.

Audric, G. 1991. "Les Contrastes de l'Emploi." *Antiane Eco: La Revue Economique des Antilles et de la Guyane* 14:19–22.

Babb, Florence E. 1985. "Middlemen and 'Marginal' Women: Marketers and Dependency in Peru's Informal Sector." In *Markets and Marketing*, ed. Stuart Plattner. Monographs in Economic Anthropology No. 4. New York: University Press of America.

————. 1988. "From the Field to the Cooking Pot: Economic Crisis and the Threat to Marketers in Peru." In *Traders versus the State: Anthropological Approaches to Unofficial Economies*, ed. Gracia Clark, 17–40. Boulder: Westview Press.

Barrow, Christine, ed. 1998. *Caribbean Portraits: Essays on Gender Ideologies and Identities*. Kingston: Ian Randle Publishers.

Bastide, Roger. 1971. *African Civilizations in the New World*. New York: Harper and Row.

Beriss, David. 1993. "High Folklore: Challenges to the French Cultural World Order." *Social Analysis* 33:105–129.

Berlin, Ira. 1998. *Many Thousand Gone: The First Two Centuries of Slavery in North America.* Cambridge, Mass.: The Belknap Press of Harvard University Press.

Bernabé, Jean, Patrick Chamoiseau, and Raphaël Confiant. 1990. *Eloge de la Créolité: In Praise of Creoleness.* Paris: Gallimard.

Bertram, I. G., and R. F. Watters. 1985. "The MIRAB Economy in South Pacific Microstates." *Pacific Viewpoint* 26:497–519.

Besson, Jean. 1993. "Reputation and Respectability Reconsidered: A New Perspective on Afro-Caribbean Peasant Women." In *Women and Change in the Caribbean: A Pan-Caribbean Perspective,* ed. Janet H. Momsen, 15–37. Kingston, Jamaica: Ian Randle.

Bhabha, Homi K. 1990. "The Third Space." In *Identity: Community, Culture, Difference,* ed. Jonathan Rutherford, 207–221. London: Lawrence and Wishart.

Bickerton, Derek. 1999. "Perspectives on Creole Language History." *New West Indian Guide* 73:97–102.

Blackburn, Robin. 1988. *The Overthrow of Colonial Slavery, 1776–1848.* London: Verso.

Bolles, A. Lynn. 1996. *Sister Jamaica: A Study of Women, Work, and Households in Kingston.* Lanham, Md.: University Press of America.

Bongie, Chris. 2001. "A Street Named Bisette: Nostalgia, Memory, and the Cent-Cinquantenaire of the Abolition of Slavery in Martinique (1848–1998)." *The South Atlantic Quarterly* 100(1):215–257.

Bourdieu, Pierre. 1977. *Outline of a Theory of Practice.* Cambridge: Cambridge University Press.

Brah, Avtar, and Annie E. Coombes. 2000. "Introduction: The Conundrum of 'Mixing.'" In *Hybridity and Its Discontents: Politics, Science, Culture,* ed. A. Brah and A. Coombes, 1–16. London and New York: Routledge.

Brereton, Bridget. 1989. "Society and Culture in the Caribbean: The British and French West Indies, 1870–1980." In *The Modern Caribbean,* ed. Franklin W. Knight and Colin A. Palmer, 85–110. Chapel Hill: University of North Carolina Press.

———. 1999. "Family Strategies, Gender and the Shift to Wage Labour in the British Caribbean." In *The Colonial Caribbean in Transition: Essays on Postemancipation Social and Cultural History,* ed. Bridget Brereton and Kevin Yelvington, 77–107. Barbados: The Press University of the West Indies.

Britton, Celia. 1999. *Edouard Glissant and Postcolonial Theory.* Charlottesville: University Press of Virginia.

Browne, Katherine E. 1996. "The Informal Economy in Martinique: Insights from the Field, Implications for Development Policy." *Human Organization* 55(2):225–234.

———. 2000. "Work Style and Network Management: Gendered Patterns and Economic Consequences in Martinique." *Gender & Society* 14(3):435–456.

———. 2001. "Female Entrepreneurship in the Caribbean: A Multisite Pilot Investigation of Gender and Work." *Human Organization* 60(4):326–343.

Burac, Maurice. 1995. "The French Antilles and the Wider Caribbean." In *French and West Indian: Martinique, Guadeloupe, and French Guiana Today*, ed. Richard D. E. Burton and Fred Reno. Charlottesville: University Press of Virginia.

Burdick, John. 1993. *Looking for God in Brazil: The Progressive Catholic Church in Urban Brazil's Religious Arena*. Berkeley: University of California Press.

Burton, Richard D. E. 1993. "Débrouya pas Peché, or Il y a Toujours Moyen de Moyenner: Patterns of Opposition in the Fiction of Patrick Chamoiseau." *Callaloo* 16(2):466–481.

———. 1994. *La Famille Coloniale: La Martinique et la Mère-Patrie, 1789–1992*. Paris: Harmattan.

———. 1997. *Afro-Creole: Power, Opposition, and Play in the Caribbean*. Ithaca: Cornell University Press.

Cabort-Masson, Guy. 1987. *Les Puissances d'Argent en Martinique: La Caste Béké*. Martinique: Laboratoire de Recherches de L'Association Martiniquaise d'Education Populaire (AMEP).

Carnegie, Charles V. 1987. "A Social Psychology of Caribbean Migrations: Strategic Flexibility in the West Indies." In *The Caribbean Exodus*, ed. Barry B. Levine, 32–43. New York: Praeger.

Castells, Manuel, and Alejandro Portes. 1989. "World Underneath: The Origins, Dynamics, and Effects of the Informal Economy." In *The Informal Economy*, ed. Alejandro Portes et al., 11–37. Baltimore: Johns Hopkins University Press.

Catalan, Sonia, and Henri Combelles. 1981. *Tim Tim? Bois Sec! Contes Créoles*. Paris: Les Editions Didier.

Cernea, Michael, ed. 1991a. *Using Knowledge from Social Science in Development Projects*. World Bank Discussion Papers No. 114. Washington, D.C.: The World Bank.

———. 1991b. *Putting People First: Sociological Variables in Rural Development*. New York: Published for the World Bank by Oxford University Press.

Césaire, Aimé. 1988. *Cahier d'un Retour au Pays Natal*. Paris: Présence Africaine.

Césaire, Ina. 1978. *L'Idéologie de la Débrouillardise dans les Contes Antillais*. Espaces Créoles 3. Fort-de-France: Centre Universitaire des Antilles-Guyane.

Chambers, Robert. 1997. *Whose Reality Counts? Putting the First Last*. London: Intermediate Technology.

Chamoiseau, Patrick. 1994. *Creole Folktales*. Trans. Linda Coverdale. New York: The New Press.

———. 1997. *Texaco*. New York: Pantheon Books.

Charmes, Jacques. 1998. *Informal Sector, Poverty, and Gender: A Review of Empirical Evidence*. Washington, D.C.: The World Bank.

Chaudenson, Robert. 2001. *Creolization of Language and Culture*. London and New York: Routledge.

Clark, Gracia, ed. 1988. *Traders versus the State: Anthropological Approaches to Unofficial Economies*. Boulder: Westview Press.

Clarke, Edith. 1957. *My Mother Who Fathered Me*. London: George Allen and Unwin.

Collins, Marie. 1972. *Black Poets in French*. New York: Scribner's Sons.

Collins, Merle. 1998. "Sometimes You Have to Drink Vinegar and Pretend You Think Is Honey: Race, Gender and Man-Woman Talk." In *Caribbean Portraits: Essays on Gender Ideologies and Identities*, ed. Christine Barrow, 377–390. Kingston: Ian Randle Publishers.

Comitas, Lambros. 1973. "Occupational Multiplicity in Rural Jamaica." In *Work and Family Life: West Indian Perspectives*, ed. Lambros Comitas and David Lowenthal, 157–173. Garden City, N.Y.: Anchor Press.

Comte, Auguste. 1880. *A General View of Positivism*. Trans. J. H. Bridges. London: Reeves and Turner.

Condé, Maryse. 1998. "Créolité without Creole Language?" In *Caribbean Creolization*, ed. Kathleen M. Balutansky and Marie-Agnès Sourieau, 101–109. Gainesville: University Press of Florida.

Confiant, Raphaël. 1988. *Le Nègre et l'Amiral*. Paris: Editions Grasset.

———. 1995. *Contes Créoles des Amériques*. Paris: Editions Stock.

Constant, Fred. 1990. "Decolonisation Revisited: The Case of the Non-Sovereign West Indies." *Caribbean Affairs* 3:151–163.

Craton, Michael. 1997. *Empire, Enslavement, and Freedom in the Caribbean*. Kingston, Jamaica: Ian Randle.

Crusol, Jean. 1986. *Changer la Martinique: Initiation à l'Economie des Antilles*. Paris: Editions Caribéennes.

Curtin, Philip D. 1969. *The Atlantic Slave Trade: A Census*. Madison: University of Wisconsin Press.

Dance, Daryl C. 1985. *Folklore from Contemporary Jamaicans*. Knoxville: University of Tennessee Press.

Daniel, Justin. 1993. "Political Constraints of Economic Dependency: The Case of Guadeloupe and Martinique." *Caribbean Studies* 26(3–4):311–334.

Dash, J. Michael. 1995. *Edouard Glissant*. New York: Cambridge University Press.

Dávila, Arlene. 1999. "Crafting Culture: Selling and Contesting Authenticity in Puerto Rico's Informal Economy." *Studies in Latin American Popular Culture* 18:159–170.

Davis, David Brion. 1984. *Slavery and Human Progress*. New York: Oxford University Press.

Davis, Gregson. 1997. *Aimé Césaire*. London: Cambridge University Press.

Dayan, Joan. 2000. "From the Plantation to the Penitentiary: Chain, Classification, and Codes of Deterrence." In *Slavery in the Caribbean Francophone World*, ed. Doris Y. Kadish, 191–210. Athens: University of Georgia Press.

de Certeau, Michel. 1984. *The Practice of Everyday Life*. Berkeley: University of California Press.

de Miras, Claude. 1989. *L'Economie Martiniquaise: Développement sans Croissance*. Martinique: ORSTOM.

de Soto, Hernando. 1989. *The Other Path: The Invisible Revolution in the Third World*. Trans. June Abbott. New York: Harper and Row.

Diman-Antenor, Delile. 1995. "Ainsi Naquit le Chômage, puis il se Développa." *Antiane Eco: La Revue Economique des Antilles et de la Guyane* 28:3–6.

Domenach, Hervé. 1981. "Chomage et Sous-Emploi dans les DOM." *Revue Econo-mie et Statistiques* 137:3–23.

Douglass, Lisa. 1992. *The Power of Sentiment: Love, Hierarchy, and the Jamaican Family Elite*. Boulder: Westview Press.

Dramé, Kandiovra. 1996. "The Trickster as Triptych." In *Monsters, Tricksters, and Sacred Cows: Animal Tales and American Identities*, ed. James A. Arnold, 230–254. Charlottesville: University Press of Virginia.

Drescher, Seymour. 2001. "Capitalism and Antislavery." In *Slavery*, ed. S. Enger-man, S. Drescher, and R. Paquette, 426–432. Oxford: Oxford University Press.

DuBois, W. E. B. 1903. *The Souls of Black Folk*. Reprinted 1989. New York: Bantam.

Escobar, Arturo. 1995. *Encountering Development: The Making and Unmaking of the Third World*. Princeton: Princeton University Press.

Ezra, Elizabeth. 2000. *The Colonial Unconscious: Race and Culture in Interwar France*. Ithaca: Cornell University Press.

Fanon, Frantz. 1967. *Black Skin, White Masks* (Originally published in 1952 as *Peau Noire, Masques Blancs*). New York: Grove Press.

———. 1965. *The Wretched of the Earth*. New York: Grove Press.

Feige, Edgar L., ed. 1989. *The Underground Economics*. New York: Cambridge University Press.

Ferguson, James. 1999. *Expectations of Modernity: Myths and Meanings of Urban Life in the Zambian Copperbelt*. Berkeley: University of California Press.

Fields, Barbara. 1990. "Slavery, Race, and Ideology in the United States of America." *New Left Review* 181:95–118.

Frazier, E. Franklin. 1942. "The Negro Family in Bahia, Brazil: A Problem in Method." *American Sociological Review* 7:465–478.

Freeman, Carla. 2000. *High-Tech and High Heels in the Global Economy: Women, Work, and Pink Collar Identities in the Caribbean*. Durham: Duke University Press.

———. 2001. "Is Local: Global as Feminine: Masculine? Rethinking the Gender of Globalization." *Signs* 26(4):1007–1037.

Friedman, Jonathan. 1994. *Cultural Identity and Global Process*. London: Sage.

Gautier, Arlette. 1995. "Women from Guadeloupe and Martinique." In *French and West Indian: Martinique, Guadeloupe, and French Guiana Today*, ed. Richard D. E. Burton and Fred Reno, 119–136. Charlottesville: University Press of Virginia.

Gautier, Gérard. 1988. *Enquete sur l'Emploi de 1986*. Fort-de-France: INSEE.

Geggus, David. 1989. "The Haitian Revolution." In *The Modern Caribbean*, ed. Franklin W. Knight and Colin A. Palmer, 21–50. Chapel Hill: University of North Carolina Press.

Gerry, Chris. 1987. "Developing Economies and the Informal Sector in Histori-cal Perspective." In *The Informal Economy*, ed. L. A. Ferman, S. Henry, and M. Hoyman, 100–119. The Annals of the American Academy of Political and Social Science. Newbury Park, Calif.: Sage.

References Cited

Gilroy, Paul. 1993. *The Black Atlantic: Modernity and Double Consciousness.* Cambridge: Cambridge University Press.

Glissant, Edouard. 1981. *Le Discours Antillais.* Paris: Gallimard.

Gmelch, George. 1997. *The Parish behind God's Back: The Changing Culture of Rural Barbados.* Prospect Heights, Ill.: Waveland Press.

Goldenberg, Marcel. 1970. *Nature et Culture dans les Contes Populaires du Compère Lapin en Martinique.* Fort-de-France: CERAG.

Grossman, Gregory. 1989. "Informal Personal Incomes and Outlays of the Soviet Urban Population." In *The Informal Economy: Studies in Advanced and Less-Developed Countries,* ed. Alejandro Portes et al., 150–170. Baltimore: Johns Hopkins University Press.

Gudeman, Stephen. 1986. *Economics as Culture: Models and Metaphors of Livelihood.* London: Routledge Kegan Paul.

Gudeman, Stephen, and Alberto Rivera. 1990. *Conversations in Colombia.* Cambridge: Cambridge University Press.

Hall, Catherine. 1995. "Gender Politics and Imperial Politics: Rethinking the Histories of Empire." In *Engendering History: Caribbean Women in Historical Perspective,* ed. Verene Shepherd, Bridget Brereton, and Barbara Bailey, 48–59. New York: St. Martin's Press.

Hall, Stuart. 2000. "Old and New Identities, Old and New Ethnicities." In *Theories of Race and Racism,* ed. Les Back and John Solomos, 144–153. London: Routledge.

Halperin, Rhoda. 1990. *The Livelihood of Kin: Making Ends Meet "The Kentucky Way."* Austin: University of Texas Press.

———. 1994. *Cultural Economies, Past and Present.* Austin: University of Texas Press.

Hannerz, Ulf. 1997. "Scenarios for Peripheral Cultures." In *Culture, Globalization, and the World System,* ed. Anthony King, 107–128. Minneapolis: University of Minnesota Press.

———. 2002. "Notes on the Global Ecumene." In *The Anthropology of Globalization: A Reader,* ed. Jonathan Xavier Inda and Renato Rosaldo, 37–45. Malden, Mass.: Blackwell Publishers.

Hansis, Randall. 1997. *The Latin Americans: Understanding Their Legacy.* New York: McGraw-Hill.

Harrap. 1997. *Harrap's Dictionnaire: Anglais-Français/Français-Anglais.* Edinburgh: Chambers Harrap Publishers.

Hart, Keith. 1973. "Informal Income Opportunities and Urban Employment in Ghana." *The Journal of Modern African Studies* 11(1):61–89.

Hazareesingh, Sudhir. 1998. *From Subject to Citizen: The Second Empire and the Emergence of Modern French Democracy.* Princeton: Princeton University Press.

Herskovits, Melville J. 1990. *The Myth of the Negro Past.* Boston: Beacon Press. Originally published 1941.

Herzfeld, Michael. 2001. *Anthropology: Theoretical Practice in Culture and Society.* Malden, Mass.: Blackwell Publishers.

Higman, B. W. 1984. *Slave Populations of the British Caribbean*. Baltimore: Johns Hopkins University Press.

Hintjens, Helen M. 1992. "France's Love Children? The French Overseas Departments." In *The Political Economy of Small Tropical Islands: The Importance of Being Small*, ed. Helen Hintjens and Malyn Newitt, 64–75. Exeter, U.K.: University of Exeter Press.

Hoetink, H. 1985. "'Race' and Color in the Caribbean." In *Caribbean Contours*, ed. Sidney Mintz and Sally Price, 55–84. Baltimore: Johns Hopkins University Press.

Institut National de la Statistique et des Etudes Economiques [INSEE]. 1983. *Données Sociales*. Les Dossiers, 5. *L'Histoire Demographique*. Paris: INSEE.

———. 1995. *Femmes en Chiffres*. Fort-de-France: INSEE.

———. 2000. *Tableaux Economiques Régionaux: Martinique 2000*. Fort-de-France: INSEE.

International Labour Organization [ILO]. 2002a. "Resolution concerning Decent Work and *The Informal Economy*." Document prepared for the Ninetieth International Conference of the ILO.

———. 2002b. "Globalization and *The Informal Economy*: How Global Trade and Investment Impact on the Working Poor." In *Working Paper on The Informal Economy*, ed. Marilyn Carr and Martha A. Chen. Geneva: ILO.

Jordan, Winthrop. 1968. *White over Black: American Attitudes toward the Negro 1550–1812*. Chapel Hill: University of North Carolina Press.

Joyner, Charles. 1986. "The Trickster and the Fool: Folktales and Identity among Southern Plantation Slaves." *Plantation Society* 2(2):149–156.

Kadish, Doris Y. 2000. "Maryse Condé and Slavery." In *Slavery in the Caribbean Francophone World: Distant Voices, Forgotten Acts, Forged Identities*, ed. Doris Y. Kadish, 211–223. Athens: University of Georgia Press.

Kerner, Donna O. 1988. "'Hard Work' and Informal Sector Trade in Tanzania." In *Traders versus the State: Anthropological Approaches to Unofficial Economies*, ed. Gracia Clark, 41–56. Boulder: Westview Press.

Khan, Aisha. 2001. "Journey to the Center of the Earth: The Caribbean as Master Symbol." *Cultural Anthropology* 16(3):271–302.

Kovats-Beaudoux, Edith. 1969. "Une Minorité Dominante: Les Blancs Créoles de la Martinique." PhD diss. University of Paris.

Larousse. 1987. *Dictionnaire de Français*. Paris: Librarie Larousse.

Laurent, Joëlle, and Ina Césaire, eds. 1976. *Contes de Mort et de Vie aux Antilles*. Paris: Nubia.

Lazarus-Black, Mindie. 1994. "Slaves, Masters, and Magistrates: Law and Politics of Resistance in the British Caribbean, 1736–1834." In *Contested States: Law, Hegemony, and Resistance*, ed. Mindie Lazarus-Black and Susan F. Hirsch, 252–281. New York: Routledge.

Ledeneva, Alena V. 1998. *Russia's Economy of Favours: Blat, Networking, and Informal Exchange*. Cambridge: Cambridge University Press.

Leonard, Madeleine. 1998. *Invisible Work, Invisible Workers: The Informal Economy in Europe and the US*. New York: St. Martin's Press.

Lessinger, Johanna. 1988. "Trader vs. Developer." In *Traders versus the State: Anthropological Approaches to Unofficial Economies*, ed. Gracia Clark, 139–164. Boulder: Westview Press.

Lewis, Gordon K. 1968. *The Growth of the Modern West Indies*. New York: Monthly Review Press.

Lirus, Julie. 1979. *Identité Antillaise*. Paris: Editions Caribéennes.

Lomnitz, Larissa. 1988. "Informal Exchange Networks in Formal Systems: A Theoretical Model." *American Anthropologist* 90:42–55.

Lowenthal, David. 1972. *West Indian Societies*. London: Oxford University Press.

Lozano, Beverly. 1983. "Informal Sector Workers." *International Journal of Urban and Regional Research* 7(3):340–362.

Lubell, Harold. 1991. *The Informal Sector in the 1980s and 1990s*. Paris: Organisation for Economic Co-Operation and Development (OECD).

Ludwig, Ralph, Daniele Montbrand, Hector Poullet, and Sylvaine Telchid. 1990. *Dictionnaire Créole Français*. Paris: Servedit/Editions Jasor.

Madras Plus. 1991. *Guide Annuaire Pratique de la Martinique*. Fort-de-France: Editions Exbrayat.

Malinowski, Bronislav. 1922. *Argonauts of the Western Pacific*. Reprinted 1961. New York: Dutton.

Manning, Kenneth R. 1993. "Race, Science, and Identity." In *Lure and Loathing: Essays on Race, Identity, and the Ambivalence of Assimilation*, ed. Gerald Early, 317–336. New York: Penguin Books.

Maurer, Bill. 1997. *Recharting the Caribbean: Land, Law, and Citizenship in the British Virgin Islands*. Ann Arbor: University of Michigan Press.

Maximin, Daniel. 1998. "Antillean Journey." In *Caribbean Creolization: Reflections on the Cultural Dynamics of Language, Literature, and Identity*, ed. Kathleen M. Balutansky and Marie-Agnès Sourieau, 13–19. Gainesville: University Press of Florida.

McKeever, M. 1998. "Reproduced Inequality: Participation and Success in the South African Informal Economy." *Social Forces* 76(4):1209–1241.

Miller, Daniel. 1994a. *Modernity: An Ethnographic Approach*. Oxford: Berg.

———. 1994b. "Style and Ontology." In *Consumption and Identity*, ed. Jonathan Friedman, 71–96. Chur, Switzerland: Harwood Academic Publishers.

———. 1997. *Capitalism: An Ethnographic Approach*. Oxford: Berg.

Mintz, Sidney W. 1985. *Sweetness and Power: The Place of Sugar in Modern History*. New York: Viking Press.

Mintz, Sidney W., and Richard Price. 1992. *The Birth of African-American Culture: An Anthropological Perspective*. Boston: Beacon Press. Originally published 1976.

Mitchell, Sir Harold. 1963. *Europe in the Caribbean: The Policies of Great Britain, France, and the Netherlands towards Their West Indian Territories in the Twentieth Century*. Stanford: Stanford University Press.

Moitt, Bernard. 2001. *Women and Slavery in the French Antilles 1635–1848*. Bloomington: Indiana University Press.

Momsen, Janet H. 1993. *Women and Change in the Caribbean: A Pan-Caribbean Perspective*. London: James Currey; Kingston, Jamaica: Ian Randle; Bloomington: Indiana University Press.

Morgan, Philip D. 1991. "British Encounters with Africans and African Americans, Circa 1600-1780." In *Strangers within the Realm: Cultural Margins of the First British Empire*, ed. Bernard Bailyn and Philip D. Morgan. Chapel Hill: University of North Carolina Press.

———. 1997. "The Cultural Implications of the Atlantic Slave Trade: African Regional Origins, American Destinations, and New World Developments." *Slavery and Abolition* 18:122–145.

Moser, Caroline. 1978. "Informal Sector or Petty Commodity Production: Dualism or Dependence in Urban Development?" *World Development* 6(9–10): 1041–1064.

Moses, Wilson J. 1993. "Ambivalent Maybe." In *Lure and Loathing: Essays on Race, Identity, and the Ambivalence of Assimilation*, ed. Gerald Early, 274–290. New York: Penguin Books.

Mosse, George L. 1985. *Nationalism and Sexuality: Respectability and Abnormal Sexuality in Modern Europe*. New York: Howard Fertig.

Mulero-Diaz, Maria D. 2000. "Strategies for Survival in a Changing Economic Structure: Puerto Rican Women in the Informal Economy." PhD diss., Temple University.

Munford, Clarence J. 1986. "Slavery in the French Caribbean, 1625–1715." *Journal of Black Studies* 17(1):49–69.

Naipaul, V. S. 1963. *The Middle Passage: Impressions of Five Societies: British, French, and Dutch in the West Indies and South America*. London: Andre Deutsch.

Nash, June. 1979. *We Eat the Mines and the Mines Eat Us: Dependency and Exploitation in Bolivian Tin Mines*. New York: Columbia University Press.

Nattrass, Nicoli. 1987. "Street Trading in Transkei—A Struggle against Poverty, Persecution, and Prosecution." *World Development* 15(7):861–875.

Noiriel, Gérard. 1996. *The French Melting Pot: Immigration, Citizenship, and National Identity*. Trans. Geoffroy de Laforcade. Minneapolis: University of Minnesota Press.

Nott, Josiah, and George Gliddon. 1854. *Types of Mankind*. Philadelphia: J. B. Lippincott.

N'Zengou-Tayo, Marie-José. 2000. "Exorcising Painful Memories: Raphaël Confiant and Patrick Chamoiseau." In *Slavery in the Caribbean Francophone World*, ed. Doris Y. Kadish, 176–187. Bloomington: Indiana University Press.

Olwig, Karen Fog. 1990. "The Struggle for Respectability: Methodism and Afro-Caribbean Culture on Nineteenth-Century Nevis." *Nieuwe West-Indische Gids*. 64(3 & 4):93–114.

Ong, Aihwa. 1987. *Spirits of Resistance and Capitalist Discipline: Factory Women in Malaysia*. Albany: State University of New York Press.

———. 1999. *Flexible Citizenship: The Cultural Logics of Transnationality*. Durham: Duke University Press.

O'Shaughnessy, Andrew Jackson. 2000. *An Empire Divided: The American Revolution and the British Caribbean.* Philadelphia: University of Pennsylvania Press.

Osterfeld, David. 1992. *Prosperity versus Planning: How Government Stifles Economic Growth.* Oxford: Oxford University Press.

Parry, J. H., Philip Sherlock, and Anthony Maingot. 1987. *A Short History of the West Indies.* New York: St. Martin's Press.

Patterson, Orlando. 1982. *Slavery and Social Death.* Cambridge, Mass.: Harvard University Press.

Peattie, Lisa R. 1980. "Anthropological Perspectives on the Concepts of Dualism, the Informal Sector, and Marginality in Developing Urban Economies." *International Regional Science Review* 5(1):1–31.

Pérez-López, Jorge F. 1995. *Cuba's Second Economy.* New Brunswick, N.J.: Transaction Publishers.

Poirier, Jean, and Huguette Dagenais. 1986. "En Marge, la Situation des Femmes dans l'Agriculture en Guadeloupe: Situation Actuelle, Questions Méthodologiques." *Environnement Caraïbe* 2:151–186.

Polanyi, Karl. 1957. "The Economy as Instituted Process." In *Trade and Market in the Early Empires,* ed. K. Polanyi, C. M. Arensberg, and H. W. Pearson, 234–269. New York: The Free Press.

Portes, Alejandro. 1983. "The Informal Sector: Definition, Controversy, and Relation to National Development." *Review* 7(1):151–174.

———. 1996. "The Informal Economy." In *Exploring the Underground Economy: Studies of Illegal and Unreported Activity,* ed. Susan Pozo, 147–162. Kalamazoo, Mich.: W. E. Upjohn Institute for Employment Research.

Portes, Alejandro, and Walton, John. 1981. "Unequal Exchanges and the Urban Informal Sector." In *Labor, Class, and the International System,* ed. Alejandro Portes and John Walton, 67–106. New York: Academic Press.

Powell, Dorian, Eleanor Wint, Erna Brodber, and Versada Campbell. 1990. *Street Foods of Kingston.* Mona, Jamaica: Institute of Social and Economic Research, University of the West Indies.

Price, Richard. 1998. *The Convict and the Colonel.* Boston: Beacon Press.

———. 1999. "Modernity, Memory, Martinique." In *The African Diaspora: African Origins and New World Identities,* ed. Isidore Okpewho et al., 76–88. Bloomington: Indiana University Press.

———. 2001. "The Miracle of Creolization: A Retrospective." *New West Indian Guide* 75(1/2):35–64.

Price, Richard, and Sally Price. 1999. "Shadowboxing in the Mangrove: The Politics of Identity in Postcolonial Martinique." In *Caribbean Romances: The Politics of Regional Representation,* ed. Belinda Edmondson, 123–162. Charlottesville: University Press of Virginia.

Raijman, R. 2001. "Mexican Immigrants and Informal Self-Employment in Chicago." *Human Organization* 60(1):47–55.

Rapon, Alain. 1991. *Ti-Fène et la Rivière Qui Chante.* Martinique: Les Editions de la Caravelle.

Richardson, Bonham C. 1983. *Caribbean Migrants: Environment and Human Survival on St. Kitts and Nevis.* Knoxville: University of Tennessee Press.

Roberts, Bryan R. 1989. "Employment Structure, Life Cycle, and Life Chances: Formal and Informal Sectors in Guadalajara." In *The Informal Economy*, ed. Alejandro Portes et al., 41–59. Baltimore: Johns Hopkins University Press.

Roberts, John. 1989. *From Trickster to Badman: The Black Folk Hero in Slavery and Freedom.* Philadelphia: University of Pennsylvania Press, 1989.

Rodney, Walter. 2000. "How Europe Became the Dominant Section of a World-wide Trading System." In *Caribbean Slavery in the Atlantic World*, ed. Verene Shepherd and Hilary Beckles, 2–10.

Rofel, Lisa. 1999. *Other Modernities: Gendered Yearnings in China after Socialism.* Berkeley: University of California Press.

Rogozinski, Jan. 1999. *A Brief History of the Caribbean.* New York: Facts on File.

Rosenblum, Mort. 1988. *Mission to Civilize: The French Way.* New York: Anchor Press.

Safa, Helen I. 1995. *The Myth of the Male Breadwinner: Women and Industrialization in the Caribbean.* Boulder: Westview Press.

Sahlins, Marshall. 1976. *Culture and Practical Reason.* Chicago: University of Chicago Press.

——. 1999. "What Is Anthropological Enlightenment? Some Lessons of the Twentieth Century." *Annual Review of Anthropology* 28:i–xviii.

Sampath, Niels. 1997. "Crabs in a Bucket: Reforming Male Identities in Trinidad." *Gender and Development* 5(2):42–54.

Scott, James C. 1990. *Domination and the Arts of Resistance: Hidden Transcripts.* New Haven: Yale University Press.

Singham, Shanti Marie. 1994. "Betwixt Cattle and Men: Jews, Blacks, and Women, and the Declaration of the Rights of Man." In *The French Idea of Freedom: The Old Regime and the Declaration of Rights of 1789*, ed. Dale Van Kley, 114–153. Stanford: Stanford University Press.

Singler, John Victor. 1995. "The Demographics of Creole Genesis in the Caribbean: A Comparison of Martinique and Haiti." In *The Early Stages of Creolization*, ed. Jacques Arends, 203–232. Amsterdam: John Benjamins Publishing Company.

Smaje, Chris. 2000. *Natural Hierarchies: The Historical Sociology of Race and Caste.* Malden, Mass.: Blackwell Publishers.

Smart, Josephine. 1988. "How to Survive in Illegal Street Hawking in Hong Kong." In *Traders versus the State: Anthropological Approaches to Unofficial Economies*, ed. Gracia Clark, 99–117. Boulder: Westview Press.

Smedley, Audrey. 1999. *Race in North America: Origin and Evolution of a Worldview.* Boulder: Westview Press.

Smith, M. Estellie. 1989. "The Informal Economy." In *Economic Anthropology*, ed. S. Plattner, 292–317. Stanford: Stanford University Press.

Stack, Carol B. 1974. *All Our Kin: Strategies for Survival in a Black Community.* New York: Harper and Row.

Stepick, Alex. 1990. "Community Growth versus Simply Surviving: The Informal Sectors of Cubans and Haitians in Miami." In *Perspectives on the Informal Economy*. Monographs in Economic Anthropology, No. 8, ed. M. Estellie Smith, 183–206. Lanham, Md.: University Press of America.

Stoler, Ann Laura and Frederick Cooper. 1997. "Between Metropole and Colony: Rethinking a Research Agenda." In *Tensions of Empire: Colonial Cultures in a Bourgeois World*, ed. Ann Laura Stoler and Frederick Cooper, 1–56. Berkeley: University of California Press.

Stoller, Paul. 1996. "Spaces, Places, and Fields: The Politics of West African Trading in New York City's Informal Economy." *American Anthropologist* 98(4):776–89.

———. 2002. *Money Has No Smell: The Africanization of New York City*. Chicago: University of Chicago Press.

Sutton, Constance. 1974. "Cultural Duality in the Caribbean." *Caribbean Studies* 14(2):96–101.

Suvélor, Roland. 1981. "Regard Critique sur la Societé Antillaise." In *Historial Antillais*, 451–460. Fort-de-France: Dajani Editions.

Thornton, John. 1998. *Africa and Africans in the Making of the Atlantic World, 1400–1800*. Cambridge: Cambridge University Press.

Tomich, Dale W. 1990. *Slavery in the Circuit of Sugar: Martinique and the World Economy, 1830–1848*. Baltimore: Johns Hopkins University Press.

———. 1993. "*Une Petite Guinée*: Provision Ground and Plantation in Martinique, 1830–1848." In *Cultivation and Culture: Labor and the Shaping of Slave Life in the Americas*, ed. Ira Berlin and Philip D. Morgan, 221–242. Charlottesville: University Press of Virginia.

Tranap, A. 1988. "Le Poids du Secteur Public." *Antiane Eco: La Revue Economique des Antilles et de la Guyane* 7:25–27.

Trouillot, Michel-Rolph. 1995. *Silencing the Past: Power and the Production of History*. Boston: Beacon Press.

———. 1998. "Culture on the Edges: Creolization in the Plantation Context." *Plantation Society in the Americas* 5:8–28.

———. 2002. "Culture on the Edges: Caribbean Creolization in Historical Context." In *From the Margins: Historical Anthropology and Its Futures*, ed. Brian K. Axel, 189–210. Durham: Duke University Press.

Turner, Mary. 1999. "The Colonial State, Religion, and the Control of Labour: Jamaica 1760–1834. In *The Colonial Caribbean in Transition*, ed. Bridget Brereton and Kevin A. Yelvington, 26–42. Gainesville: University Press of Florida.

Ulysse, Gina. 1999. "Uptown Ladies and Downtown Women: Informal Commercial Importing and the Social/Symbolic Politics of Identities in Jamaica." PhD diss., University of Michigan.

United Nations. 2000. *The World's Women: Trends and Statistics*. New York: United Nations.

Valdman, Albert. 2000. "The Creole Language of Slavery." In *Slavery in the Caribbean Francophone World*, ed. Doris Y. Kadish, 143–163. Athens: University of Georgia Press.

Van Kley, Dale. 1994. "Introduction." In *The French Idea of Freedom: The Old Regime and the Declaration of Rights of 1789*, ed. Dale Van Kley, 5–22. Stanford: Stanford University Press.

Vaughan, Alden. 1995. *Roots of American Racism*. Oxford: Oxford University Press.

Verdery, Katherine. 1996. *What Was Socialism and What Comes Next?* Princeton: Princeton University Press.

Vergès, Françoise. 1999. *Monsters and Revolutionaries: Colonial Family Romance and Métissage*. Durham: Duke University Press.

Wagley, Charles, and Marvin Harris. 1958. *Minorities in the New World*. New York: Columbia University Press.

Waters, Mary C. 1999. *Black Identities: West Indian Immigrant Dreams and American Realities*. Cambridge, Mass.: Harvard University Press.

Weiss, Jaqueline Shachter. 1985. *Young Brer Rabbit and Other Trickster Tales from the Americas*. Owings Mills, Md.: Stemmer House Publishers.

Werbner, Pnina. 2001. "The Limits of Cultural Hybridity: On Ritual Monsters Poetic License and Contested Postcolonial Purifications." *Journal of the Royal Anthropological Institute* 7:133–152.

Werner, Cynthia. 2000. "Gifts, Bribes, and Development in Post-Soviet Kazakstan." *Human Organization* 59(1): 11–22.

Wilk, Richard R. 1996. *Economies and Cultures: Foundations of Economic Anthropology*. Boulder: Westview Press.

Williams, Eric. 1970. *From Columbus to Castro: The History of the Caribbean 1492–1969*. London: Thetford Press Limited.

Wilson, Peter J. 1969. "Reputation and Respectability: A Suggestion for Caribbean Ethnology." *Man* 4(1):170–184.

———. 1995. *Crab Antics: A Caribbean Case Study of the Conflict between Reputation and Respectability* (Originally published 1973). Prospect Heights, Ill.: Waveland Press.

Wirthlin, Karin. 2000. "Tourism and Barbados: An Examination of Local Perspectives." Master's thesis, Colorado State University.

Witter, Michael, and Claremont Kirton. 1990. *The Informal Economy in Jamaica: Some Empirical Exercises*. Kingston, Jamaica: Social and Economic Research, University of the West Indies.

World Bank. 2001. "Appreciating the Informal Economy." In *Spectrum*, no. 23009: 27–28.

Wylie, Laurence. 1957. *Village in the Vaucluse*. Cambridge, Mass.: Harvard University Press.

Yelvington, Kevin. 1995. *Producing Power: Ethnicity, Gender, and Class in a Caribbean Workplace*. Philadelphia: Temple University Press.

———. 2001. "The Anthropology of Afro-Latin America and the Caribbean: Diasporic Dimensions." *Annual Review of Anthropology* 30:227–260.

Zhang, Li. 2001. *Strangers in the City: Reconfigurations of Space, Power, and Social Networks within China's Floating Population*. Stanford: Stanford University Press.

References Cited

creole adaptations of African tales, 90, 126; as *débrouillard*, 120, 236n25; double meanings of, 127; story of Lion and Tiger and, 126–27; as trickster hero, 126
British colonization. *See* colonization
Browne, Katherine E., 227n40, 230n60, 241n4, 242nn14,18, 243nn40,42, 244n46
Burton, Richard, 122, 185, 217n17, 224n108, 232n75, 233n87, 234n3, 236n23, 237n48, 238n58,63, 239nn3,5, 10,22,37, 240nn44,50,52, 242nn30–31

Candomblé, 88
Caribbean identities, 94. *See also* creole identities
Caribbean societies: consumption patterns in, 64–66, 232n72, 74–78, 233n78; informal economies and, 55–56, 229–30n50; as master symbol of polycultural trends, 11, 216n5; particularities of, 5
case study profiles. *See* informants
Castells, Manuel, and Alejandro Portes, 226nn23–26, 227nn33–34,39
Catholic Church: co-existence with sorcery, 88, 224n110; colonization and, 88; French vs. Spanish, 24, 183; *mission civilisatrice* and, 25; as part of European Christendom, 27; as part of Martinique's French identity, 8; restrictiveness on women and, 182–84, 242nn16,18; slavery and, 220n58; South America and, 5
Cernea, Michael, 54, 229n45
Césaire, Aimé, 34, 37, 91–94, 96, 215n6, 236nn34,38, 237n38
Césaire, Ina, 240n42
CGAP (Consultative Group to Assist the Poor), 229n47
Chamoiseau, Patrick, 33, 55, 95, 124–27, 222n89, 230n54, 239nn21,28,34, 240n41, 244n2

Chaudenson, Robert, 235nn18,21
Christianity: colonization and, 88; European gender order and, 183; slavery and, 25–28, 220n62, 221n65
Cluny neighborhood, 165, 168, 171–72
Code Noir: baptism of slaves and, 220n64; paternalism and, 26; slave families and, 241n8; slave land and, 122; slave working hours and, 217nn10,18
code switching, 81, 84, 196, 216, 234n3
cognitive orientations, definition of, 230n63. *See also* creole identities
Collins, Merle, 177
colonization: British, 19–20, 22–24, 216n5, 218nn28,38, 219n43; 220nn55,57, 231n66, 234n3, 236n23; Dutch, 19–20, 23–24, 216n5, 220n56; French, ix–x, xii, 5, 12, 19–24, 39, 88, 120, 183, 218nn28,36,38, 219n40, 220n56, 222nn86,91,95, 223n99, 231n66, 232n77, 236nn23,33; French vs. British, 24–27, 35, 183, 215n1, 218nn32,36; Spanish, 19–20, 24–25, 182–83, 218nn36,38, 219n39, 220n54, 231n66, 242n18; 220nn54,56, 242n18
Comitas, Lambros, 55
Compère Lapin. *See* Brer Rabbit
concubinage, French practice of, 26
Condé, Maryse, 125, 237n44, 239n27, 244n1
Confiant, Raphaël, 95, 149, 238n55, 240nn39,42,48,53
Congo, 232n77
consumption: affluence and, 165, 167–68; class and, 159; debt and, 69; in Fort-de-France, 17–18; French encouragement of, 63; of French goods, 18; gender and, 203; imports/exports/economy and, 75; in Martinique, 16, 64–69, 83, 231–32n70; in Trinidad, 64, 230n62, 232n72. *See also* Caribbean societies, consumption in
Craton, Michael, 239nn5–6,18,29

credit, buying on, 66–67, 69
Creole, definition of, 85. *See also* creole
  culture; creole folktales; creole
  identities; creole language
creole culture: African influences on,
  86, 88–90; and Césaire, 237n38;
  Creole expression of, 9; *créolité* and,
  95; *débrouillardism* and, 131; economic practice and, 15; vs. European
  values, 36–37; formation of, xii, 21,
  86; as gaining public popularity,
  210–12; Glissant and, 94; indicators of, 10, 85–90, 210; as "master
  symbol" of globalization, 11, 216n5;
  music and dance in, 89–90, 103,
  125, 210, 234n3; and public display,
  234n3; resistance and, 14; stigmatization of, 33, 37, 129, 148, 210
creole economics: arguments about,
  layout of, xii, xiii; *békés* and, 15; buyers and sellers, 53, 152–55, 170, 200;
  context of, 130, 151–52; creole adaptations and, 132; Creole language
  and, 234n3; cultural difference and,
  12, 100, 103; *débrouillardism* and,
  120, 210; by default, 159, 244n43;
  definition of, 10, 50; economic and
  non-economic influences on, 14–16,
  63–69, 76–80, 104, 150–53, 175;
  Frenchness and, 19, 84, 213; gender
  and, 161–62, 197, 200, 204, 243n42;
  gender (high-income) and, 202;
  gender (middle-income) and, 199,
  200; gender (moderate-income)
  and, 197–200; high income, 153,
  155, 168–74, 184, 196, 231n64; the
  household and, 153, 158, 162; low-
  income, 153, 155, 157, 161, 184,
  231n64; men and, 161, 193, 210; middle-income, 153, 155, 164–65, 168,
  184, 196, 231n64; moderate-income,
  153, 162–64, 196, 231n64; morality
  of, 11, 132, 141–50, 164, 195, 206; as
  refuge, 14, 100, 119; resistance and,

101, 103, 123, 213; seedbeds of, 122–
  23, 130, 150; social networks and,
  167–68, 172–73, 198–200, 202, 210,
  243n42. *See also* informal economy,
  in Martinique
creole folktales and storytelling, 85–86,
  89–90, 103, 120, 125–27, 131, 149–50,
  184, 192, 234n3, 236nn23–25. *See also*
  Brer Rabbit
creole identities: Afro-Caribbean, 81,
  94; cognitive orientations of, 56, 72,
  209, 230n63, 235n9; *créolité* and, 95;
  cultural validation of, 122; economics and, 15, 60, 84, 101, 119; European and other influences on, 84; as
  having no indigenous past, 91; as insoluble, 10, 100, 104; men and, 193,
  195–96, 208; plantation histories
  shaping, 85–86; as plural identities,
  84, 91, 100, 213, 233–34n2; in postcolonial studies, 11, 95; as refuge,
  14, 210; revival of, 210, 212–13; as
  valorizing illicit economic activity,
  100–04, 152, 210; women and, 188,
  191–93, 204, 207
creole language: absence of in Spanish
  islands, 219n39; African influences
  on, 88; code switching, 84; *créolité*
  ideas about, 95; *débrouillardism*
  and, 131–32, 192; diglossic version of, 234n3; disdain for, 33, 37;
  emergence of, 87–88, 234nn4–5,
  235nn15–16; folktales and, 126; pop
  culture/revival of, 210–12; resilience
  of, 9; slavery and, 21, 87; use among
  men, 82–83; vs. standard French,
  32, 222n87
creole values: class and, 196; *débrouillardism* and, 63, 175; gender and,
  187–88, 193; in relation to European
  values, 66, 188, 224n110, 242n30;
  respectability and, 96, 184; shaping
  economic behavior, xii, xiii, 4, 60,
  63, 77, 175

Dominica, 39, 100, 157
DOM-TOM, 215n2 (preface), 215n1
(ch. 1)
double consciousness: challenges to
idea of, 243n39; Creole/French
code-switching, 196; Du Bois' ideas
of, 91, 242n25; Wilson's ideas of, 96
Douglass, Lisa, 230n62
Drescher, Seymour, 28
dress/style: European influence and,
232–33n78; gaze-orientation, 65;
"good hair," 135; men, 65–66, 185;
race and, 66, 128, 232n75; race,
gender, and status, 66–67, 232n77;
slavery and, 232n75; women and,
66, 185, 233n78
Du Bois, W. E. B., 91, 96, 236n29,
242n25, 243n39
duplicity. See opposition within complicity; slavery
Du Tertre, Père, 29, 221n68

economic development in Martinique,
38
economic theory: formalist and substantivist, 45–46, 48; neoclassical
assumptions, 44–46, 48, 80, 225n3
economies and cultural meaning:
anthropological studies of, 43–49,
79–80, 226nn16,19; in Chinese
guanxi, 48; in creole economics by
default, 244n43; development planning and, 151, 229nn45–47, 230n50;
in Kazakhstan, 47; in Romania,
48; in Russian *blat*, 47, 226n17; in
Trinidad, 232n72
emancipation, 128. See also abolition
engagés, 21
Ermitage neighborhood, 156, 160–65
Escobar, Arturo, 43, 46, 54,
225nn4,9,13–14, 228n44, 233n90
European Union, xiii, 211, 241n3
extended family households, 158

family romance. See France, as Mother
France; Martinique, as "love children"
Fanon, Frantz, 37, 100, 127, 149,
222n87, 237n49, 238n56, 240n43
Ferguson, James, 65, 232n77
Figure 1 (undeclared vs. declared income by class), **62**
Figure 2 (informal buyers and sellers
by class and gender), **154**
fieldwork, 14–15, 132–34, 137–38
folklorization of memory, 12
folktales. See creole folktales
forced migration/slavery, x, 5, 8, 10,
85, 86
Fort-de-France: case studies in, 102,
166; Césaire and, 215n6, 236n38;
consumption patterns in, 17–18, 64;
Creole and French language use
in, 210; fieldwork in, 14, 137; gaze
orientation in, 65; history of, 8, 130;
informal economy in, 155; mayors
of, 215n6; neighborhoods in, 88,
156, 164–65, 172; population of, xii;
social experiences in, 56–57, 81, 83,
134; visual descriptions of, 3–4, 74
France: as Mother France in "family
romance," 97, 99, 212, 213; political
incorporation to, 37, 38, 40, 129. See
also assimilation to France; departmentalization
Frazier, Franklin, 86
Freeman, Carla, 56, 230n53, 232n74,
233n86, 240n51, 242n30, 243nn32,37
French attitudes: toward colonies, 31–
32, 34–35, 219n40, 223n99, 236n33;
toward Martiniquais, 99, 102
French Caribbean, x, 129
French colonization. See colonization
French government: colonial, 26,
222n86; DOM and, 37, 38. See *also*
French law; French welfare and
labor protections
French Guiana, x, 4, 9, 19, 37, 93, 129

French identity: Césaire's ideas and, 93; code switching and, 81, 84; early indications of, 223n97; embraced locally, 38; future of creole economics and, 213; modeled by mulattos, 32, 37; as projected in island infrastructure, 18; tensions with creole identity, 85, 104–05, 210, 224n110, 238n64; women and, 191

French law: CNIL (La Commission National Informatique et Liberté), 73; *le loi de défiscalisation*, 233n81, 241n5; *les droits d'homme*, 74, 174

French Polynesia, ix, 215n1

French Revolution, 31, 33–35, 222nn91,94, 223n97

French welfare and labor protections: defiscalization law and, 233n81; after DOM status, 38, 97, 224n110; high taxes and, xi; as incentive for informal earning, 63, 72, 231n65; laws to stimulate economy and, 241n5; leading to low productivity and unemployment, 38–39; as paternalistic, 26; resulting in material and identity problems, 12, 39, 40; as sheltering influence, 211–12; as used by informal economic operators, 157–59, 204–06; as "welfare state colonialism," 224n115

CREOLE
ECONOMICS

Friedman, Jonathan, 13, 65, 216n11, 232n77

Garvey, Marcus, 91, 93, 96, 236nn30–31

Gates, Henry Lewis Jr., 119

"gaze of the Other," 97. *See also* Martinique, as gaze-oriented

gens de couleur libres (free people of color), 22, 25–26, 33. *See also* mulatto

Ghana, 50

Gilroy, Paul, 13, 81, 90, 216n9, 236n26

Girvan, Norman, xi

Glissant, Edouard, 93–94, 100, 236n27, 237nn39–40, 238n56, 239n33, 244n1

globalization, 5, 13

Gmelch, George, 233n86

Grameen Bank, Bangladesh, 54, 229n47

Greater Antilles, 218n27. *See also* map of Martinique and Caribbean

Griffiths, Gareth, 13

Guadeloupe, x, 4–5, 8–9, 19, 21, 23, 32, 37, 104, 125, 129, 216n5, 218n28, 222n86

Gudeman, Stephen, 46, 225n13

Haiti, 21, 31, 39, 88, 100, 121, 157, 163

Hall, Catherine, 183, 242n19

Hall, Stuart, 97, 237n41

Halperin, Rhoda, 46, 225n13

Hannerz, Ulf, 13, 216nn6,11, 234n4

Hart, Keith, 50–51

Herskovits, Melville, 86, 234n7

hidden transcripts, 121

Hintjens, Helen, 222n95, 223n103, 224n105, 237n50

Hoetink, H., 217n20

hybridity, *créolité* and rejection of, 95. *See also* creole identities; plural and hybrid identities

identities. *See* creole identities; plural and hybrid identities

income, undeclared vs. declared. *See* Figure 1

independence, African, 94

independence, English Caribbean, 94

independent postcolonial states. *See* postcolonial states

informal economic operators, 51–54, 56, 76, 228nn41–43

informal economy, general: in Caribbean societies, 55–56, 227n40, 229n50, 230n60; cross-class studies and, 55–56; cultural meaning of and development planning, 16, 49–53, 227nn38,40, 228nn42,44, 229nn44,46–48, 230n50, 231n68;

development assumptions about, 50–53, 61; economic dependency and, 40; entrepreneurship and, 55, 60, 227n29, 228nn41,42, 231n68; the poor and, 51–53, 225–26n16; social research about, 52, 227n36; as under-studied, xi; U.S. comparison to France, 231n65; visible vs. less-visible segments of, xii; vs. criminal or underground economy, 49, 226n24–27

informal economy, Martinique: compared to metropolitan France, 72, 101, 152; creole adaptations and, 132; creole values and, 10, 132; cross-class studies and, 58, 61–62, 72, 76–78, 152–53, 155, 164, 170–71, 174–75, 196–97, 208; *débrouillards* and, 48, 139; enforcement of laws against, 69–76; entrepreneurship and, 67, 77, 140, 155, 167, 173, 175, 201; gender and, 186; idiomatic phrases of, 133, 136, 138, 145, 198, 233n83, 244n45; poor and, 62, 63, 72, 75, 155, 157; prosecution and, 71, 74–75; relevance to development planning, 76. *See also* Figure 1; Figure 2

informants (selected): Central Bank analyst (M. Bellance), 68–69; female *débrouillard* (Charlotte), 204–07, 209; by gender and income (high, Marguerite and Jacques), 202–03; by gender and income (middle, Clarice and Benjamin), 200–02; by gender and income (moderate, Patricia and Eric), 198–99; by income (high, Edouard), 139, 170, 193, 195, 209; by income (high, Michel), 139, 145, 171–74, 209; by income (low, Marie and Jean-Marc), 159–61, 163, 165, 171; by income (middle, Martin), 165, 167–68, 171; by income (moderate, Julian), 163–65, 171; Patrick, 43,

57–61, 65, 69, 76–79, 81–84, 132, 137, 155, 168, 209, 233n1; state prosecutor (M. Guillaume), 74–75, 100; tax official (M. Monrose), 72–75, 241n5; work inspector (M. Arnaud), 70–74, 233n81

INSEE (Institut National de la Statistique et Etudes Economiques), 14, 224n117, 243nn33–34

International Labour Organization (ILO), 51, 226n27, 227nn30,32, 228nn41–42,44, 229n48, 231n68. *See also* development planning

ISER (Institute for Social and Economic Research), xi

Jamaica, xi, 3, 12, 23, 35, 55, 97, 123, 219n43, 220n55, 229n50, 230nn60,62, 232nn75,78, 236n30, 237n41

Jordan, Winthrop, 221n66

Josephine (Empress), statue of, 18–19, 36, 213, 216n2

Kadish, Doris, 222n92, 223n95
Khan, Aisha, 216n5, 234n4
Kovats-Beaudoux, 36

Lazarus-Black, Mindie, 239n4
Ledeneva, Alena, 226nn17–18
Lesser Antilles, 218n27. *See also* map of Martinique and Caribbean
Letchimy, Serge, xii, 130, 215n6, 240nn47–48
liberté, égalité, fraternité, 10, 33, 35–36, 93–94
libres de fait (unoffically freed), 217n18, 219n48
Lockwood, Victoria, 215n1
Lomnitz, Larissa, 231n66
Lowenthal, David, 19, 55, 216n3, 217n20, 218n26, 219nn42,51, 222n87, 230n51

Malaysia, 79

male authority and "machismo," 182, 183, 184, 207, 241n9, 242nn14,18

Malinowski, Bronislav, 45

Manning, Kenneth, 220n62, 221n77

manumission, 27, 219n48, 241n6

map of Martinique and Caribbean, **6–7**

Martinique: economic dependency and, 39, 40, 97, 99, 211–12; Frenchness of, 17–19, 32, 38, 104, 210; as gaze oriented, 16, 64–66, 68, 134–35, 210, 232–33n78; impact of EU on, 211, 241n3; individualism and, 145, 153; as "love children" in family romance, 97, 212–13; skin colors in, 135, 219n52; social contradictions in, 4–14, 100, 122, 186, 224n110

matrifocal/matricentric, 157–58, 181–82, 188, 234n7

Maurer, Bill, 234n2

Mauritius, 95

Maximin, Daniel, 3

men and creole economics: concern with autonomy, 77, 161, 187–88, 208, 241n1; different goals vs. women, 186–87, 191–93, 199, 202–03, 244n43; reputation and, 96, 185, 187, 193, 199, 207–08, 210; respectability and, 193–96; social world of, 18, 81, 210, 243n42; vs. women, 162. *See also* Figure 2

métissage, 94, 234n2

metropolitan France: as home in "family romance," 97; products consumed from, 18. *See also* France; French government

Miller, Daniel, 54, 64, 225n11, 229n49, 230n62, 232nn72,76, 240n51

minimum guaranteed income. *See* RMI

minimum wage, Martinique, 241n3

Ministry of the Interior, Martinique, 70

Mintz, Sidney, 86–87, 181, 215n2, 217n6

mission civilisatrice, 25

modernization theory, 50

modern vs. traditional sector, 51

Moitt, Bernard, 22, 29, 181, 216n5, 217nn10,12–19, 219n48, 220n64, 221nn64,68,70,73, 239nn11,16, 241nn3–11

Momsen, Janet H., 230n60

morality issues. *See débrouillardism*, morality of; slavery, moral adaptations to

Morgan, Philip , 235n9

mulattos: as color designation, 135, 218n24; freedom from slavery and, 180; as lobbyists for incorporation into France, 36; in population after Revolution, 26, 222n94; in Saint Domingue revolt, 31; social mobility and, 22–23, 32–33, 92, 128–29, 169, 238n54; socioeconomic status and, 218n24

multiple livelihoods. *See* occupational multiplicity

Naipaul, V. S., 38, 224n111

Napoleon, 18, 34, 36, 218n28

narratives of history, 12–13, 212–13, 244n2

Nash, June, 235n19

Negritude, 37, 92–94, 224n109, 236n34, 237n38

neoclassical economics. *See* economic theory

Noiriel, Gérard, 223n99

noncompliance. *See* opposition within complicity

N'Zengou-Tayo, Marie-José, 151, 230n54

occupational multiplicity: after abolition, 55–56, 128, 230n55; as adaptive to urban migrants, 130; the Rabbit and, 149; as survival strategy, 78

off-the-books work (*le travail noir*), 101, 233n83

Olwig, Karen Fog, 242nn26,30, 243n32, 244n48

Ong, Aihwa, 226n21, 233n89, 238n65

opposition within complicity: as assertion of individuality, 14, 61; creole *débrouillard* and, 103, 131–32; creole economics and, 79, 100–01, 213; definition of, 13; *la tactique* and, 101, 238; neoclassical economics and, 80; slavery and, 120–22, 184, 224n110; stakes of, 141, 149

O'Shaughnessy, Andrew Jackson, 215n3, 219nn44,53, 220nn54–55, 221nn71–72

pan-Africanism, 94. *See also* Negritude

parallel economy, 75

Patterson, Orlando, 120

performance of identity, 65–66, 125, 134, 232n77

pidgin language, 87, 235n16. *See also* creole language

plantation economy, 20. *See also* slavery; sugar cane plantations

plural and hybrid identities: Caribbean as master symbol for, 11; Caribbean scholarship of, 5; definition of hybrid identity, 233–34n2; double consciousness and, 91; hybrid vs. plural identities, 84; métissage and, 234n2; tug of, 9. *See also* creole identities; hybridity

Polanyi, Karl, 45, 225n7

Portes, Alejandro, 226nn24,26

postcolonial states: creole identity and, 11–12; *créolité* and, 95; independent states vs. Martinique, 4, 35, 39, 94, 215n1; lack of indigenous past and, 91; opposition within complicity and, 13; plural identities and, 5, 84; tensions of, 81

Powell, Dorian, 230n60

préfet, 34

Price, Richard, 12–14, 86–87, 184, 216nn8,13, 234nn4–5, 235nn8–10, 237n44, 238n52, 244n1

Price, Sally, 237n44

"productive" economic activity, 240n1

Protestants/Protestantism, 5, 24, 183

Provence, ethnography of, 103

Providencia island, 55, 96, 237n45

public transcripts, 121, 234n3

Puerto Rico, 3, 25, 182, 218n38, 219n39, 230n50, 232–33n78, 242n14

racial/color hierarchy: *békés* and, 148; British, 97; in France, 93, 97, 98, 99, 100, 210; in low-income neighborhoods, 160; in Martinique, 99, 148; in metropole, 97–99; mulatto social mobility in, 33, 37, 169, 238n54; range of skin tones, 135, 219n52; and slavery, 30

racism felt by Martiniquais: in Martinique, 99, 148; in metropole, 97–99

Rastafarian/Rasta belief, 236n30

reputation, creole: class and, 196, 231; code switching and, 83–84; cultural difference and, 103; *débrouillardism* and, 61, 63, 78, 146; debt and, 69; dress/style and, 66; gender and, 187–88, 190, 192, 195, 197, 207–08, 237n47, 242n30, 243n41, 244n48; informal entrepreneurship and, 60; slavery and, 123, 184–85; vs. respectability, 95–96, 184–85, 242n30; women and, 188, 191–92

respectability, European: class and, 202, 230–31n64; code switching and, 83–84; dress/style and, 66; gender and, 184, 187, 196–97, 231n64, 237n47, 244n48; men and, 193, 195–96, 208; mulattos and, 36; slave women and, 180; vs. reputation, 95–96, 184–85, 242n30; women and, 188, 191–93, 202, 207

Index